Mercedes-Benz Sport-Light Coupé

THE COMPLETE STORY

TITLES IN THE CROWOOD AUTOCLASSICS SERIES

ALFA ROMEO 105 SERIES SPIDER
ALFA ROMEO 916 GTV AND SPIDER
ASTON MARTIN DB4, DB5 & DB6
ASTON MARTIN DB7
ASTON MARTIN V8
AUDI QUATTRO
AUSTIN HEALEY 100 & 3000 SERIES
BMW CLASSIC COUPÉS 1965–1989
BMW M3
BMW M5
BMW Z3 AND Z4
CITROEN DS SERIES
CLASSIC JAGUAR XK: THE 6-CYLINDER CARS 1948–1970
CLASSIC MINI SPECIALS AND MOKE
FERRARI 308, 328 & 348
FORD CONSUL, ZEPHYR AND ZODIAC
FORD ESCORT RS
FORD TRANSIT: FIFTY YEARS
FROGEYE SPRITE
GINETTA ROAD AND TRACK CARS
JAGUAR E-TYPE
JAGUAR F-TYPE
JAGUAR MKS 1 AND 2, S-TYPE AND 420
JAGUAR XJ-S
JAGUAR XK8
JENSEN V8
JOWETT JAVELIN AND JUPITER
LAMBORGHINI COUNTACH
LAND ROVER DEFENDER
LAND ROVER DISCOVERY: 25 YEARS OF THE FAMILY 4×4
LAND ROVER FREELANDER
LOTUS ELAN
MAZDA MX-5
MERCEDES SL & SLC 107 SERIES 1971–2013
MERCEDES SL SERIES
MERCEDES-BENZ 'FINTAIL' MODELS
MERCEDES-BENZ CARS OF THE 1990S
MERCEDES-BENZ S-CLASS
MERCEDES-BENZ W113
MERCEDES-BENZ W123
MERCEDES-BENZ W124
MERCEDES-BENZ W126 S-CLASS 1979–1991
MERCEDES-BENZ W201
MG T-SERIES
MGA
MGB
MGF AND TF
MORGAN 4/4: THE FIRST 75 YEARS
PORSCHE 924/928/944/968
PORSCHE AIR-COOLED TURBOS 1974–1996
PORSCHE BOXSTER AND CAYMAN
PORSCHE CARRERA: THE AIR-COOLED ERA
PORSCHE CARRERA: THE WATER-COOLED ERA
PORSCHE WATER-COOLED TURBOS 1979–2019
RANGE ROVER: THE FIRST GENERATION
RANGE ROVER: THE SECOND GENERATION
RELIANT THREE-WHEELERS
RILEY: THE LEGENDARY RMS
ROVER 75 AND MG ZT
ROVER P5 & P5B
ROVER SD1
SAAB 99 & 900
SHELBY AND AC COBRA
SUBARU IMPREZA WRX AND WRX STI
SUNBEAM ALPINE & TIGER
TOYOTA MR2
TRIUMPH SPITFIRE & GT6
TRIUMPH TR6
TRIUMPH TR7
TVR 1946-1982
TVR: CARS OF THE PETER WHEELER ERA
VOLVO 1800
VOLVO AMAZON
VW KARMANN GHIAS AND CABRIOLETS

Mercedes-Benz Sport-Light Coupé

THE COMPLETE STORY

NIK GREENE

THE CROWOOD PRESS

First published in 2021 by
The Crowood Press Ltd
Ramsbury, Marlborough
Wiltshire SN8 2HR

enquiries@crowood.com

www.crowood.com

British Library Cataloguing-in-Publication Data
A catalogue record for this book is available from the British Library.

ISBN 978 1 78500 822 1

Typeset and designed by D & N Publishing, Baydon, Wiltshire

Printed and bound in India by Parksons Graphics

Acknowledgements

First and foremost I would like to thank the various people with whom I have spoken in the 'archive' department of Daimler Stuttgart: I cannot express the pleasure I get from delving through the information, and I will never take for granted that opportunity I have had over the last few years. I am never allowed to mention them by name, but rest assured I appreciate every single person there for putting up with my demands.

In particular I would like to thank all at Crowood for turning my work into a real book.

Thank you Gerrit den Hollander for your treasured catalogue and brochure information; also Philip Morgan, for the pictures of your beautiful C107 500 SLC; and a big thank-you, Harry Niemann, for your valued assistance with research and your amazing books.

Finally, my wife Trudy: thanks for all the tea and patience.

CONTENTS

INTRODUCTION

The concept of the 'Coupé' dates back to the days when horsepower literally meant how many animals you harnessed to your carriage, and subsequently, when automotive design was still dominated by body shapes that were very much based on the horse-drawn carriage. First, there were open and closed carriages, and then there were Coupés.

It is thought that the Coupé was developed from the style of carriage known as the Berlin coach, which was designed as a vehicle for individual luxury travel over long distances with not a small amount of prestige. The Coupé came about as a secondary carriage to the Berlin coach, as owners needed something smaller but just as salubrious for days out and 'shopping' trips.

This type of carriage focused exclusively on the passengers, offering an intimate atmosphere, and simply exuding style, elegance and luxury in every way; it did not have space even for luggage, and if this were necessary for an extended trip, it would have been transported in a separate baggage cart.

Although many have misunderstood the Coupé concept to signify 'two-door', that is not strictly true; from the French word 'couper', meaning 'to cut', the body style still looked like a traditional four-seat carriage, but truncated, so that only two people were protected by the body and roof. The driver would often sit up front, enjoying the pleasures of open-air motoring, while his passengers would sit in comfort.

An English four-wheel 'Brougham' Coupé coach.

A two-wheel, single-horse Coupé coach.

There were a multitude of adaptations of four-wheel Coupé carriages, and even a number of two-wheel versions; these were often drawn by a single horse, and sometimes the driver held the reins and steered from inside an enclosed cab area, rather than being seated outside. As a fast yet comfortable city tourer, the Coupé style quickly became synonymous with wealth and speed, and generally the people who chose this mode of travel also liked to demonstrate a sense of style and individuality.

As Daimler-Mercedes and Benz invented the entire notion of the automobile, it was only natural that they would boast a rich history in the Coupé body style. The brand has somewhat pioneered the form, releasing such landmark Coupés both in a 'saloon/sedan' style as well as a sporty version – and every one of these Coupés has marked a pivotal moment in the evolution of the motorcar.

THE IMAGE OF THE SPORTS CAR

In the early years of racing development, Mercedes-Benz designed what became known as the legendary 'Silver Arrow' for motor sport, with ever flatter, narrower, and more streamlined bodies. In doing so they found that there was simply not enough room around the front end for the brand's traditional radiator, so the engineers developed an elliptical radiator grille – this quickly became the model for the current sports-car look at Mercedes-Benz.

Head of design Dr Fritz Nallinger, also a member of the Mercedes Board of Management, explained that, at a time when they were considering production of a road-going sports car, if they were to move forwards with a sports-car design then a new radiator face would have to be designed to reflect both the Daimler-Benz name as well as their sporting heritage. Although initially met with criticism from those who thought the public would not recognize the brand, this two-pronged approach to radiator design, even on its production vehicles, has become not only recognizable, but also a 'badge of honour' for anyone driving one to date.

Since then, these roadster and Coupé versions have had a broad 'face', modelled on the Silver Arrows, and a large Mercedes three-pointed star in the middle, clearly marking it out as part of the brand. Initially designers took the idea from the large, centrally positioned, three-pointed star on the large vertical radiator of all Mercedes-Benz trucks. However, this idea was not one sided; once entrenched into the minds of the public, a similar SL-style grille was used on all their trucks and buses.

THE TRADEMARK RADIATOR GRILLE

Daimler-Benz automobiles have come to be recognized by their radiator grille, whether it be the slightly V-shaped chrome-work or the 'three-pointed star' sitting proudly atop it. However, the pointed or V-shaped radiator was not a feature that adorned all vehicles produced by the world's oldest car maker. In 1926 Daimler and Benz merged to become Daimler-Benz AG, the model range was restructured, and vehicles were offered under the brand name 'Mercedes-Benz'. Initially it was only the large, 6-cylinder, supercharged vehicles that were equipped with the pointed radiator, but the new 'amalgamated' models, the 8/38bhp and 12/55bhp models, as well as the 8-cylinder Nürburg of 1928, were given a flat radiator generally, to characterize the smaller class of car.

At this early stage of motor manufacturing, the Daimler radiator design was copied widely by other manufacturers, mostly due to its engineering efficiency; this was even the case at Benz & Cie before the two companies merged. Very often, the only visible difference between any of the company's automobiles, especially from the front, was the logo. It was Mercedes-Benz, however, who quickly recognized that the radiator shape had become not just an engineering necessity, but was also a recognizable style feature of all Mercedes-Benz models, along with, of course, the Mercedes three-pointed star, which has also become a familiar feature on the front of every Mercedes-Benz model from the merger in the mid-1920s.

Emil Jellinek was maybe the first person to recognize that 'naming' an automobile would define it as a brand when he named his Daimlers after his own daughter 'Mercedes'.

Around the middle of the 1930s, many car manufacturers recognized that the image of their brand could be strongly influenced by the radiator design. They therefore endeavoured to give their vehicles a new, distinctive front in order to emphasize the sense of belonging to the brand. The designers at Mercedes-Benz chose a different path. They retained the traditional shape but adapted it almost imperceptibly and with great care to any changes to the vehicle's overall shape. This adherence to the traditional visual symbol proved a significant competitive advantage for the brand.

The V-shaped radiator grille of the bigger supercharged engines versus the flat front of the non-supercharged engine.

The typical Mercedes front underwent many changes over the years, but has remained an unmistakable and characteristic feature. The first Mercedes radiators stood up tall and straight against the oncoming wind, then in 1937, the radiator grille on the Mercedes-Benz Type 170V, although retaining the basic high, streamlined form, was tilted backwards slightly, giving a clear visual reflection of the vehicle's exceptional dynamics.

This basic stylistic configuration continued well into the 1960s until when, to meet advancements in aerodynamics, the Mercedes-Benz radiator became wider and lower in accordance with the trend of making the bonnet flatter.

The already beautiful radiator design in 1901.

The W136 170V Cabriolet showing off its raked radiator grille to emphasize movement.

ABOVE: **The Uhlenhaut Coupé showing its open-mouth grille.**

LEFT: **1935 W25 and 1937 W125 showing the evolution of the radiator mouth in racing.**

BELOW: **The L319 small truck adopted the SL-style grille in 1954 (left), and the original truck three-pointed star (right).**

TIMELINE

The Blitzen (lightning) Benz record car	1909–1911
W29 540K Streamliner	1938
SLS AMG GT3/4	since 2013
W194 300SL	1952
W194/11 300SL Prototype	1953
Mercedes-Benz racing-car transporter	1954–1967
W196 300SLR (Uhlenhaut Coupé)	1955
W198 300SL (Gullwing)	1954–1963
SLX Coupé design study	1965
C111/1	1969
C111/2	1970
C111/2Diesel	1976
C107 SLC	1971–1981
C126 Series-1 S-Class	1981–1985
C126 Series-2 S-Class	1981–1985
C112 Experimental Coupé	1991
C140 S-Class Series-1	1992–1996
F200 'Imagination Coupé'	1996
C140 S-Class Series-2 CL-Class	1996–1998
C215 series CL-Class Coupés	1999–2006
C216 series-1 CL-Class Coupés	2006–2010
C216 series-2 CL-Class Coupés	2010–2014
C217 series CL-Class Coupés	2014–2018
C199 SLR McLaren	2004–2009
C197 SLS AMG	2010–2015

CHAPTER ONE

EARLY RACING HISTORY

The earliest motor races were contested over the ruler-straight *routes nationales* of France, and for good reason. First, the French received the emergence of the horseless carriage as a practical means of transport with more understanding and far fewer restrictions than those that plagued it elsewhere, particularly in England. Second, these early French pioneers were faced with the task of proving that carriages drawn by mechanical means could, in fact, represent an effective replacement to those behind horses or other suitable animals.

The automobile's rise to ascendancy on the roads proved a slow and arduous process in which social, economic and political factors all played a role, and the primary intention of these early races was more about proving that these new-fangled vehicles could run with a modicum of reliability and safety. The general public at the time was already sceptical of what these auto cars – or automobiles, or motor cars, as they were variously called – were capable of achieving, so it was vital to prove that they were able to cover a reasonable amount of ground faster and more efficiently than animal-propelled carts and carriages.

Engineers and constructors alike also knew that this was an ideal way of pushing their technical abilities, and many improvements in the design and construction of the motor car itself were made in a very short time – but importantly too, these races became very well supported by those who saw a big commercial and financially beneficial future for the motor car. The connection between Daimler and Jellinek was made initially to build a car for one of these races. Daimler also supplied engines to Peugeot via Panhard-Levassor.

This Panhard-Levassor, with an engine power output of 3.5HP (2.6kW), came fourth out of twenty-one vehicles that started; fifteen finished, nine with Daimler engines.

The first automotive competition was held just eight years after the invention of the automobile by Gottlieb Daimler and Carl Benz. A reliability trial was organized for 'horseless carriages' on 22 July 1894 by the Parisian newspaper *Le Petit Journal*. A total of 102 vehicles applied to take part, including cars with petrol engines, steam and electric vehicles, hydro-mobiles, and vehicles with compressed air, gas or electro-pneumatic drive systems. The event organizers allowed twenty of these to take part.

After a distance of 126km (78 miles), the first to cross the finishing line was a De-Dion-Bouton steam-powered car, closely followed by two vehicles by Panhard-Levassor and the Peugeot brothers, both powered by engines built under the Daimler licence. These were eventually declared joint victors, since the steam car did not comply with the rules of the competition and was instead awarded second place. They were followed by five more cars equipped with petrol engines, including a Roger-Benz, a French automobile manufacturer called Emile Roger who sold Benz cars and used a Benz engine. Therefore Daimler's lighter 'universal petrol engine' and the Benz petrol engine had proved themselves in public as drive systems that must now be taken seriously.

The world's first 'proper' automobile race took place a year later in 1895 on a route from Paris–Bordeaux–Paris. Once again, after 1,192km (740 miles) of racing, the winner's name was Panhard-Levassor. Further proof of the reliability of the petrol engine was the fact that six of the first eight finishers were cars equipped with Panhard-Levassor engines built under the Daimler licence, and two Benz vehicles. Then in 1896 three cars with Daimler engines achieved a triple victory at the Paris–Marseille–Paris event, completing the 1,728km (1,074 miles) at an average speed of 25.2km/h (15.7mph).

What Daimler and Maybach soon realized was that these Panhard-Levassor vehicles were so reliable because instead of placing the engine at the rear, like they had done, Panhard had placed the engine and radiator system at the front but with a rear-wheel-drive system. Maybach and Daimler responded almost immediately with the 'Daimler Vis-à-Vis'. The 6HP, 2-cylinder Phoenix engine was transposed to the front for the first time along with Maybach's newly patented radiator design. It consisted of many small tubes exposed to the air flow, which were continually flushed by coolant.

Compared with the earlier coiled-tube radiators and fly-wheel cooling, much more air was able to flow through the radiator area, which in turn permitted the water reservoir to be substantially reduced in size, thus reducing weight. This innovative design, without which development of the

The Nice–Magagnon–Nice race on 21 March 1899. Hermann Braun wins the touring race in a 24HP two-seater Daimler Phoenix racing car.

Vis-à-Vis 1897 6HP.

BELOW: **The honeycomb radiator was launched on 20 September 1900 (patent no. DRP 122766). The 'three-pointed star' can be clearly seen.**

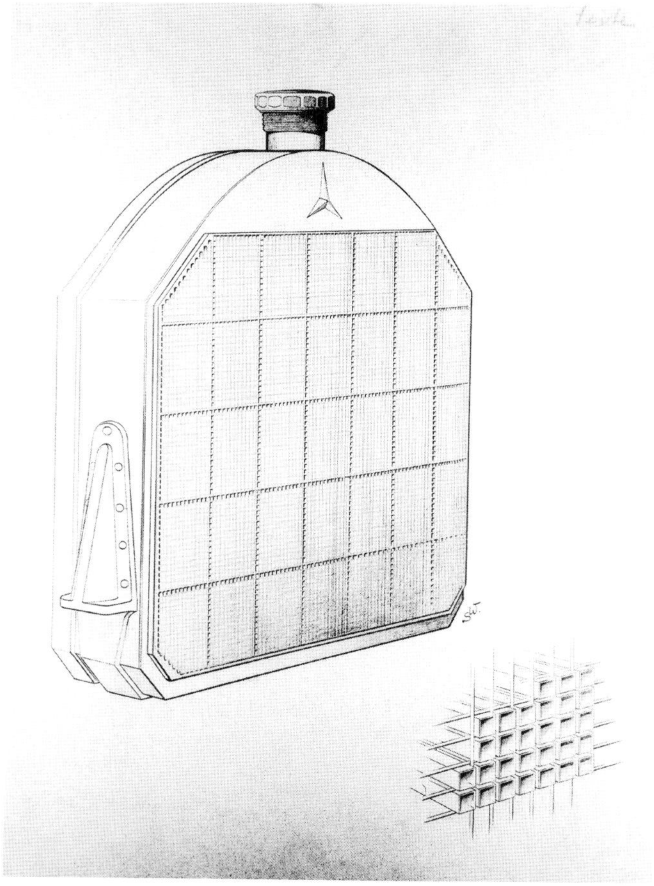

high-performance automobile would have been inconceivable, represented an important milestone in automobile development. However, Maybach never rested on his laurels, and on 8 August 1901 he filed for the protection of the so-called 'honeycomb radiator' – patent number 'DRP 122 766'. This new type of radiator was described as a 'cooling and condensation device based on the cross-flow principle'; although based on the original tubular radiator it had a much improved cooling capacity, and was space adaptable.

It was the 24HP Cannstatt-Daimler racer of 1901 that first used this radiator, and more importantly, it was organically integrated into the front body style; in this it was the final break away from the design concept of the first automobiles, which had been modelled on the coach design. This innovative design constituted a significant milestone in automotive development, in that at the time it fulfilled an important cooling capability requirement for vehicle engine design with increasingly higher power outputs.

Almost every car from that moment forward featured a similar radiator design, but never for one second did anyone see anything other than the ability to keep the engine at a bearable working temperature. It was certainly not seen by car manufacturers as a way of personalizing their brand, at least until DMG introduced the V-shaped grille. As engines got bigger and more powerful they needed bigger radiators, but with this came the realization that smaller, smoother, more integrated, rounded

The Daimler Rennwagen began to define automobile shape, including the placement of the radiator.

The V shape to the grille served better aerodynamics as well as a more efficient cooling surface area.

bodies were more aerodynamic. Technically the 'V' shape was purely intended to add around 30 per cent more surface area to the movement of air around the radiator.

Both Daimler and Benz engineers, independently of one another, found with their experiments that air flow was not the 'be all and end all' of cooling efficiency. When air is moving too fast, you get into boundary layer issues where heat doesn't get carried away because air isn't actually touching fins and tubes; it was necessary to actually restrict the air flow sufficiently so it would 'touch the sides' as it flowed through.

Maybach answered this by fitting a decorative grille in front of the actual core of the radiator for all racing cars with the V grille. This extended into production road automobiles too.

BENZ & CIE

Carl Benz could work up little enthusiasm for motorsports events; however, he could see that DMG's market success was undoubtedly the result of their successful participation in races, and eventually this made the Mannheim Company seriously consider designing a competitive racing car. In 1903 they took on the young French designer Marius Barbarou, and put him in charge of the design department with a team of selected colleagues. He developed a few cars and finally landed the 'big hit' with the Benz Parsifal in 1903.

Marius Barbarou with a 1903 Benz Parsifal.

Marius Barbarou Paris–Madrid (in Bordeaux), 24 May 1903.

Targa Florio, April 1907. Fritz Erle with mechanic Georg Gass with the Targa–Florio–Rennwagen.

In 1908 Benz and his engineers introduced a shell-style cowling as an extension to the bodywork, as can be seen from this Prince Heinrich automobile.

The style progressed over the next two years, and was used in what was to become the fastest car in the world.

It was Barbarou's forward thinking that started to change the body profile from functionally square to a smoother, more rounded appearance, while also integrating the radiator grille into the body shape.

THE BLITZEN (LIGHTNING) BENZ: THE 200BHP RECORD CAR

At the beginning of 1909, Julius Ganss, working for Benz, was given permission to design a car that could reach a speed of over 200km/h (124.28mph). This car was based on the 150bhp Benz Grand Prix car.

In its first version, this gigantic 4-cylinder engine had an output of 184bhp at 1,500rpm, which could be increased to 200bhp at 1,600rpm by precision tuning. The engine weight was 407kg (897lb). The car was first raced by Fritz Erle in the kilometre race at Frankfurt/Main in August 1909. With a flying start, Erle covered a measured kilometre in 22.6sec – that is, at an average speed of 159.3km/h (99mph), winning the Grand Duchess of Hesse Prize for cars over 36 fiscal (taxable) HP.

At that time the car was still fitted with the body of the Benz Grand Prix car, and entered competitions under that name. In the same year, Ganss raced the Benz for the first time: he participated in a sprint race at Brussels, and clearly outclassed his competitors. Shortly after that, Ganss would significantly improve Erle's best result at Brooklands, England, when he covered a measured kilometre with a flying start at an average speed of 202.7km/h (126mph). That was the first time the 200km/h (124.28mph) barrier was broken in Europe. The Benz record car established even more records: for instance, it covered a measured kilometre with a standing start at a speed of 31.326sec, and a measured mile at a speed of 41.268sec, breaking the existing records held by Darracq.

During this time designers and engineers in Mannheim had set to work on a new body for the record car, which was to give the vehicle its typical look. The tests revealed, however, that the old racing tracks in Europe were no longer adequate for these speeds, and ultimately the Benz Company began to concentrate all its activities in America.

The large 21.5-litre 4-cylinder engine put out 200bhp/147kW. The record-breaking car with the trendsetting streamlined bodywork achieved spectacular success on its first trials, and went down in history as the 'Blitzen Benz' ('Lightning Benz'). It was not only the first car in Europe to exceed the magical 200km/h (124.28mph) mark – it also held the record as the fastest car in the world, with Bob Burman at the Daytona Beach, when it achieved a top speed of 228.1km/h (141.74mph). It kept this record until 1919.

The bore was increased to 185mm; this engine had the largest displacement (at 21,500cc) ever to be used in a racing or record car by Benz & Cie or DMG.

Original 150bhp Benz Grand Prix race cars (pre-Lightning body shape).

The original Benz record car (with a basic Lightning body).

The Benz record car was faster than any aircraft in its time; similar speeds were only reached in aviation ten years later.

For the first time the 'Blitzen Benz' ('Lightning Benz') design adhered to the principles of aerodynamics while simultaneously exuding vitality.

DMG also experimented with radiator cowling and body shape in the 16/45bhp Knight record car.

The Lightning Benz influenced the aesthetic design of automobiles generally to a considerable extent. The chassis, the engine compartment and front part were no longer separated from the bodywork at the bulkhead, but formed an integral unit. This design feature became standard on all passenger cars from that moment forwards.

AERODYNAMICS: A NEW TOOL IN DESIGN

Aerodynamics was a subject that was heavily preoccupying the automotive industry, and thus also the companies Daimler-Motoren-Gesellschaft and Benz & Cie, during the early part of the twentieth century. Triggered by the fascination for speed records and motor racing, wind resistance had become a serious consideration in normal passenger-car manufacturing as early as the 1920s, and even more so in the 1930s. The pinnacle of this development process was marked by the '540K Streamliner': built in 1938, its aerodynamically tuned aluminium body made it a fitting candidate for high-speed tests by Daimler-Benz, and later for tyre-testing apparatus for the tyre manufacturer Dunlop.

As previously mentioned, Benz & Cie had gained their own purposive experience with aerodynamics over the 1909/1910 period, with the 200bhp racing car that became known from 1911 on as the 'Blitzen Benz', or 'Lightning Benz', which had set several world records. It was followed in the early 1920s by the 'Teardrop' car, so called because of its characteristic design. This was also the world's first mid-engined racing car. In the early 1920s, Daimler-Motoren-Gesellschaft undertook aerodynamic studies of racing cars intended for use in Indianapolis.

The 540K Streamliner was one of the first automobiles to be built using wind-tunnel testing. Although not an original photo, this was the same Untertürkheim-based wind tunnel.

The 'Teardrop' car was originally designed by Edmund Rumpler. The technical concept of the 'Teardrop', with its consequent streamlined shape and mid-engine, was so revolutionary that Benz obtained the reproduction rights for this car immediately.

In 1932 Reinhard von Koenig-Fachsenfeld caused quite a stir with a streamlined body for the Mercedes-Benz SSKL, in which Manfred von Brauchitsch promptly won the Avus race ahead of Rudolf Caracciola.

BELOW: **The Schlörwagen was an effort to create a truly aerodynamic car that would do justice to the new network of high-speed autobahns being constructed across Germany. The sole design brief was to create a car with the lowest drag coefficient possible, yet a car that was still practical.**

This time in automotive evolution became the era of trail-blazing pioneers of aerodynamics such as Edmund Rumpler, Paul Jaray, Wunibald Kamm, Freiherr Reinhard von Koenig-Fachsenfeld and Karl Schlör von Westhofen-Dirmstein, all of whom understood that aerodynamics was not all about racing and so worked to improve the efficiency of passenger cars. Karl Schlör had a streamlined body built based upon a Mercedes-Benz 170H (W28), which attracted a lot of attention at the time. In the wind tunnel the model produced an excellent drag coefficient of 0.113, which would be an impressive figure even by today's standards.

Several vehicles illustrate the efforts undertaken by Daimler-Benz to reduce wind resistance. The design of the rear-engined 130, 150 and 170H models, for example, was influenced by aerodynamic considerations. This can be seen particularly clearly in the lines of the model 150 sports saloon that attracted so much attention and ultimately proved successful in the '2,000km through Germany' long-distance race of July 1934.

When it came to vehicles for long-distance races such as this, or the planned long-distance Berlin–Rome run, originally set for 1938, the idea of the streamlined body played a similarly important role. After all, here, too, the objective was to achieve the highest possible speed and the lowest

The 150 sports saloons ultimately proved successful in the '2,000km through Germany' long-distance race of July 1934, partly due to their aerodynamic design.

possible fuel consumption – in other words, to improve overall efficiency.

A 500K Coupé that took part in the same event bears witness to the efforts to achieve low wind resistance in the luxury car segment as well. With its curved windscreen and gently sloping rear section, this one-off vehicle, produced in the special vehicle production unit at Sindelfingen under Hermann Ahrens, is strongly reminiscent of the 500K 'Autobahn Courier' that had made its debut in March 1934 at the International Motor and Motorcycle Show (IAMA) in Berlin.

The years 1935 and 1936 brought similarly designed four-door versions based on the volume-produced models 200 (W21), 290 (W18) and 320 (W142). A characteristic feature of them all is that from a conventional front-end design the roofline curves back and downwards in a gentle arc to merge seamlessly into the rear section. In addition, the rear wheel arches are fully enclosed.

The rapidly expanding autobahn network brought new challenges for vehicle manufacturers and the associated accessories industry. A particularly important part in solving

The two-door 500K Coupé set an early milestone in terms of progressive and innovative design. Further vehicles derived from it would go on to be created in the special vehicle production unit.

the problem of how to sustain high cruising speeds on the new autobahns was played by the tyre industry. The task was to develop tyres for high-performance vehicles, which by this time might weigh as much as 3 tonnes. And it was for this reason that the tyre industry began increasingly to look around for test vehicles that might be up to this development challenge. In Germany, the Mercedes-Benz 540K was one of the few vehicles that could meet this demand. For this vehicle and its proposed use in high-speed situations, the special vehicle production unit built a streamlined body in sheet aluminium that was designed in accordance with the very latest insights into aerodynamic performance.

Fitted with the streamlined body of 1938, with which the Cd value of 0.57 for a classic Coupé had been drastically reduced to a remarkable 0.36, cruising speeds of 165 to 170km/h (102 to 106mph) could be achieved, and with supercharger, a top speed of 185km/h (115mph) – at that time most extraordinary figures on public roads. However, it was established at a board meeting in April 1938 that not every detail of the proposed streamliner would reach the requisite standard in time to meet the deadline, with the outcome that three conventionally designed 5.4-litre supercharged models should be deployed instead. But then Berlin–Rome was postponed until 1939, and ultimately cancelled completely due to the outbreak of World War II.

In their quest for favourable aerodynamics the engineers also recognized that the brand emblem standing proud on the upright Mercedes-Benz radiator represented something of a challenge. One possible solution was suggested by a 500K streamlined model designed in 1935 for a customer

A streamlined 500K special, built for the Dutch East Indies Co. in 1935. The vehicle offered a possible solution as to how the upright radiator that was so characteristic of the brand could be incorporated into an aerodynamically styled body.

The 'Ponton' passenger car took the aerodynamic lessons learned and became the first production Mercedes-Benz with integrated headlights.

EARLY PROTAGONISTS

As always there are important people who shoulder the responsibility of innovation and change, sometimes dreamers and sometimes visionaries, and sometimes working against the direction of the company – but ultimately these are the people who facilitate the evolution of a company.

Hermann Ahrens.

HERMANN AHRENS

Born 14 March 1904 in Uslar; died 9 November 1995 in Stuttgart.

Hermann Ahrens was one of the outstanding vehicle designers of his era. The basis for this ability was provided by an extremely solid, technical education: following an apprenticeship as a fitter, he trained as an engineering draughtsman, studied mechanical and electrical engineering in the 1920s in Bingen and Varel, and graduated with distinction as an engineer.

After roles at the D-Werke in Berlin-Spandau and the Horch factory in Zwickau, he joined Daimler-Benz AG on 12 September 1932, where he took charge of the special vehicle production unit at the Sindelfingen plant. Ahrens had come to the attention of the Sindelfingen plant manager, Dr Wilhelm Haspel, over the course of the various popular Concours d'Élégance that took place around that time, such as in Nice, Wiesbaden or Baden-Baden, where the mighty Horch cars that he had designed won prizes for their appearance.

During his time in the special vehicle production unit, Ahrens himself designed or oversaw the design of the bodyshells for such outstanding models as the 380 (W22), 500K (W29), 540K (W29 and W24), the Grand Mercedes (W07 and W150), G 4 (W31), 600 (W148 and W157) and the off-road sports models 170 (W15), 200 (W21), 170VS (W136) and 230 (W143 and W153).

Particularly when it came to exclusive models in the special class, one vehicle was seldom the same as the next. Even if they sometimes looked the same, or very similar, from the outside, the interior details would have differed significantly from one to another, as each car was appointed to the individual specification of its purchaser. Among them were a few vehicle bodies that, to look at, did not have what had by then become the expected appearance of a Mercedes-Benz luxury car.

Ahrens worked not only on passenger cars, but also on commercial vehicles. In the early 1940s he designed a bus that, with its flowing lines and angled radiator, differed significantly in shape from what had been conventional up to that point. Due to the war, however, this 4.5-tonne vehicle was never built. It was not until after World War II, in 1949, that a slightly modified version of it came on to the market.

From 1943 on, Ahrens, as head of the special commission on vehicle bodies, became the father of the angular truck cabs built out of wooden planks: known as 'standardized army cabs', these were built without using any steel.

Ahrens' departure from Daimler-Benz AG in 1945 was dictated by legislation imposed by the Allied Control Council. He worked initially in the field of interior architecture before being taken on again on 1 April 1949, at Haspel's urging, as head of development for bus and commercial vehicle bodies and for special assignments. Among these were the larger passenger-car models 300 (W186, later W189) and 300S (W188).

Ahrens' period of responsibility as far as buses were concerned covered the transition to self-supporting vehicles with flush-mounted and rear-mounted engines, and in terms of trucks, the design of the short-nosed and cab-over-engine models through to the concept for the COE generation of trucks that were built from 1973 until 1996. It was Ahrens who introduced a second 'Mercedes face' to the commercial vehicle range, one with more pronounced horizontal styling elements as first seen on the successful O321H model; this added to the familiar front end with the classic Mercedes radiator, so contributing to the widespread familiarity of this new, characteristic feature of Mercedes-Benz vehicles.

in the Dutch East Indies (from 1949 Indonesia) by Hermann Ahrens' special vehicle production unit. The enclosed Mercedes-Benz pointed radiator, as also the substitution of free-standing headlamps with headlamps that were integrated into the wings, were ideas that were consequently implemented on the Dunlop works 540K Streamliner.

The market for used vehicles also saw streamlined bodies gaining in popularity, with the result that work continued until 1942 on bodies of this type based around the proposed successor to the 170V. This work was abandoned due to the war situation. However, in 1953 the 'Ponton unitary body' was released as the W120.

WIND-TUNNEL HISTORY

The emergence of the wind tunnel at the Mercedes-Benz plant in Untertürkheim was closely linked to the aforementioned experiences gleaned from aeronautical engineering, and to the countless aerodynamically optimized prototypes and race cars that had attracted so much public attention during the 1920s and 1930s.

Dr-Ing. Wunibald Kamm, a graduated engineer, worked in vehicle development at Daimler-Motoren-Gesellschaft (DMG) from 1922 to 1925. Following periods at the Schwäbische steelworks (SHW) in Aalen and the Deutsche Experimental Institute for Aviation (DVL) in Berlin-Adlershof, he became Professor and Chair of the Stuttgart Technology University. On 15 July 1930 he founded the 'Research Institute for Automotive Engineering and Aircraft Engines' as a non-profit foundation at the Technical University for the Württemberg Ministry of Culture and Ministry of Economics.

In the period that followed, the names and statutes underwent some changes: FKFS came to stand for Forschungsinstitut für Kraftfahrwesen und Fahrzeugmotoren Stuttgart (Research Institute for Automotive and Vehicle Engines), with the word 'Flugzeugmotoren' (aeroplane engines) being replaced by 'Fahrzeugmotoren' (vehicle engines). The institute still exists today and is an independent foundation under public law, receiving no public funding.

1934: The First Wind Tunnel

When it was founded in 1930, the institute was located in front of the Untertürkheim plant owned by the then Daimler-Benz AG when approached from the direction of Bad Cannstatt. The plant and the institute were separated at the time by a railway embankment, which no longer exists today.

Professor Dr-Ing. E. h. Wunibald I. E. Kamm (1893–1966).

In the tax year 1934, a small wind tunnel with a jet diameter of 70cm (27.6in) was installed to conduct tests on vehicle models. In addition, starting in 1935, aerodynamic resistance tests began to be carried out in the small wind tunnel and with coast-down tests using normal-sized vehicles. In the year that followed, a water-flow tunnel was built for aerodynamic resistance measurements on vehicle models.

Wunibald Kamm's Wind Tunnel

A wind tunnel for full-scale vehicles came into existence between 1939 and 1943. Wunibald Kamm recognized that the full complexity of vehicle aerodynamics could not be measured using only a model version, and that research facilities for full-size vehicles were indispensable. The wind

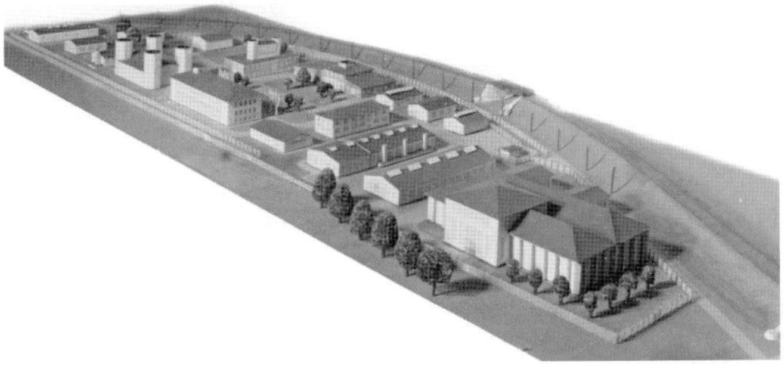

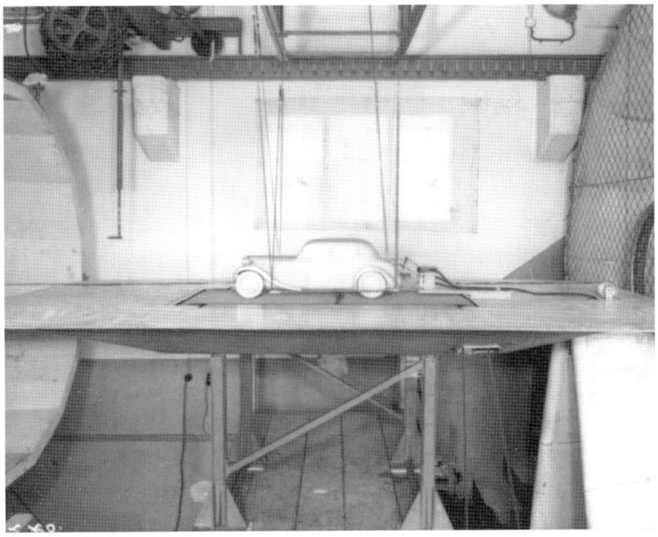

a

Kraftwagenvollprüffeld

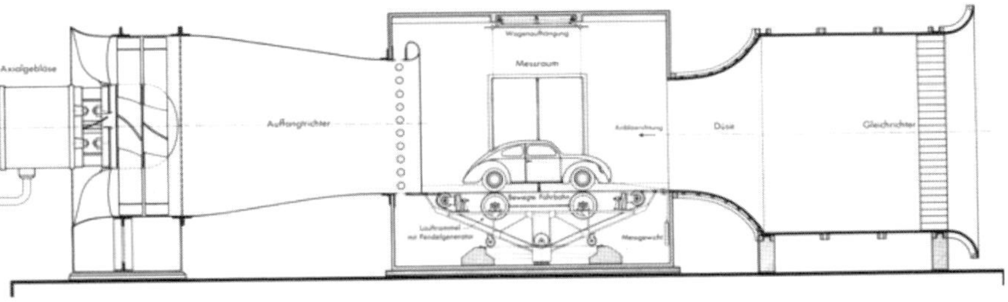

b

ABOVE LEFT: **(*Top*) 1931: the original Professor Baumann's 'Laboratory for scientific and practical work on engines and motor vehicles'. (*Bottom*) 1937: under the FKFS, expansion was fast.**

ABOVE RIGHT: **Early test bed with closed air-resistance measurements on a 1:5 vehicle model (1935).**

LEFT: **A 'full vehicle test field', issued in 1938, with a four-roller dynamometer treadmill and floor turntable.**

tunnel created by Kamm was a system based on the 'Göttingen design', with horizontal air ducting, one closed measurement section and one measurement section three-quarters open; it was 125m (410ft) long.

Although the institute was destroyed in 1944 and 1945 by air raids on the Untertürkheim plant, the main wind tunnel survived, though heavily damaged – immediately following the liberation by the French, it was actually scheduled to be dismantled. However, the institute's new director, Professor Paul Riekert, managed to save the wind tunnel by filling it so full of vehicles and instruments that he was able to present it to the 'Occupation Authority' as an important warehouse for the institute.

By 1950, the test site at the Technical University became a focus of deliberation for Dr Wilhelm Haspel, Managing Director of the then Daimler-Benz AG. During a meeting of the Board of Management on 10 May 1950, he voiced his opinion that if any property purchases were to be made, the test site at the Technical University should be considered first and foremost, since test beds and the wind tunnel were already located there.

The Daimler-Benz Wind Tunnel

In 1954, the company acquired, from the City of Stuttgart, property lots on the other side of the railway embankment, on which Mercedes-Benz commercial vehicle testing is located today, and also where the FKFS wind tunnel is found. At the same time, the FKFS was once again able to take over operations of the wind tunnel after the restrictions of World War II. From 1960 onwards, vehicle development at Mercedes-Benz used more and more of the wind tunnel's capacity; this increased to 40 per cent of capacity in 1970.

The actual wind tunnel and institute were then fully acquired by Daimler-Benz AG in 1970, although the FKFS retained administrative authority until 1974. The company then began a renovation project costing 8 million Deutschmark, and the modernization of the complete installation, which took nearly two years to complete. In April 1976, the Engineering Department at Mercedes-Benz began operating the installation, now with four times more capacity.

As part of the capacity increase, a wind-tunnel weighbridge, a multi-point pressure system and a roller-type performance test rig were installed. Built into a rotating base plate, the wind-tunnel weighbridge replaced the suspended balance used previously, where the vehicle was suspended by four steel cables in an H-shaped frame, and the four steel cables were suspended by the lifting scales in the turntable.

With the under-floor weighbridge now installed, the vehicle was placed on four contact plates that were fitted level in the floor of the rotating measuring plate. The contact plates were located on four individual lift scales, which were used to measure the lift forces. The rotating measuring plate made it possible to simulate and measure the effects of crosswind.

ABOVE LEFT: **The new full-sized wind tunnel as built by Kamm in 1938.**

ABOVE RIGHT: **The horizontal air-jet cross-section was 32.6sq m (350.8sq ft), and the measurement section was 10m (32.8ft) long. A 1:5 scale model of a Messerschmitt.**

DR WILHELM HASPEL

Dr Wilhelm Haspel.

Dr Wilhelm Haspel was born on 29 April 1898 in Stuttgart, and died on 6 January 1952, also in Stuttgart.

Wilhelm Haspel joined the Daimler-Motoren-Gesellschaft in January 1924 as head of the costing department. From 1925 on, this was followed by special assignments in the accounting, manufacturing administration and statistics departments; he also wrote a doctoral thesis on the topic of 'The calculation of overheads and cost accounting in a motor industry production plant'. He took over the administration of the body plant at Sindelfingen in 1927, then in 1932 the overall management of the plant. As part of the reorganization that he instigated in this role, he initiated the establishment of the special vehicle production unit, appointing Hermann Ahrens as its head. He was a deputy board member under Wilhelm Kissel from the beginning of 1936, and was appointed a full board member in late 1941.

Although his wife was Jewish, the company continued to employ him, in contravention of the wishes of the National Socialist regime. Following the death of Wilhelm Kissel, Haspel was appointed Chairman of the Board of Daimler-Benz AG on 19 August 1942. At the end of October 1945 he was dismissed on the instructions of the American occupying forces.

After his rehabilitation he was once again able, on 1 January 1948, to take up his role as Chairman of the Board of Daimler-Benz AG, without restrictions. From that time on he played a significant part in preserving and expanding the company's commercial vehicle operations, was responsible for the transfer of passenger car assembly from Untertürkheim to Sindelfingen, and bolstered the company's export activities. He was also a fervent advocate of a return to motor sport.

The original H-shaped balance frame.

The new under-floor weighbridge to measure 'lift forces'.

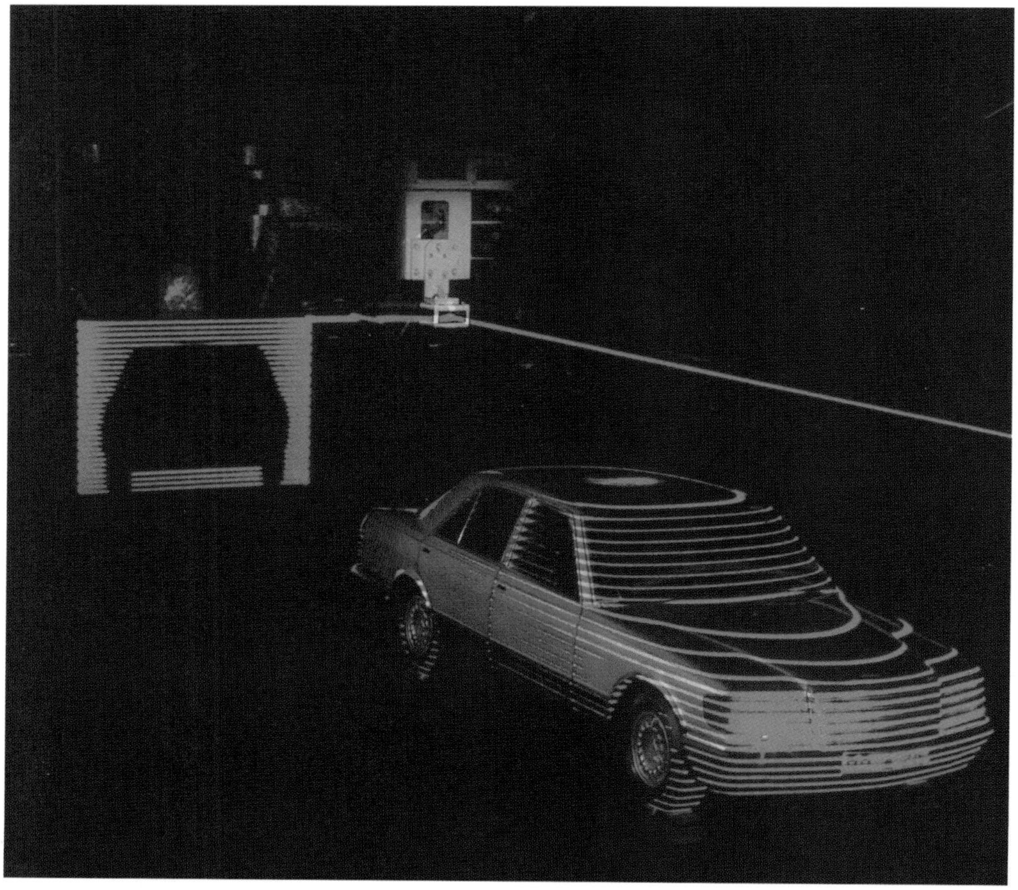

The additional 'optocator' (optical-electronic diode-light laser indicator).

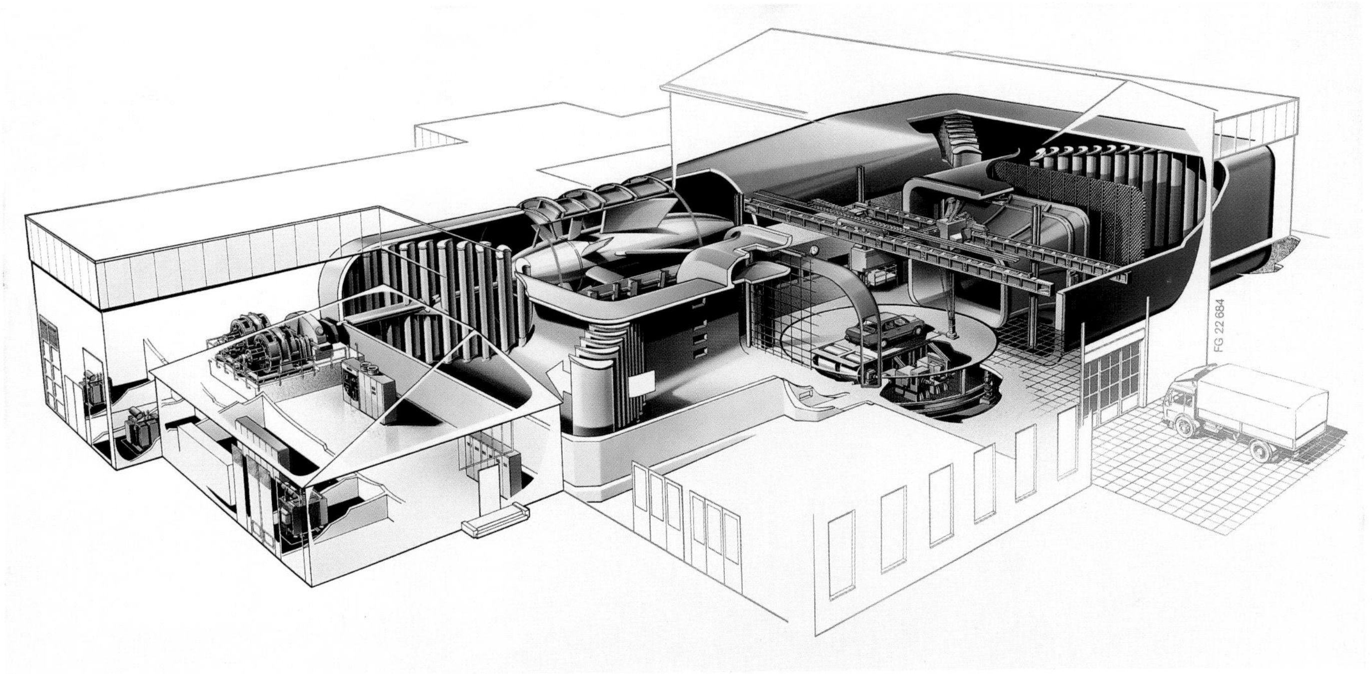

The new, enlarged complex brings systems up to date and able to accommodate commercial vehicles.

In the mid-1980s, the wind tunnel was again modernized with a view to speeding up procedures and attaining more precise measurements. For example, a traversing system was fitted, which enabled quick and precise contour measurement, flow measurement and front surface area measurement. For the contour measurement, which until then had been carried out using templates, photos and measurement with measuring sticks, the contour was now measured for greater precision in coordinates with a so-called 'optocator' (an optical-electronic diode-light laser indicator). And instead of using manually positioned probes, the flow measurement now took place with probes that moved automatically along a measuring point grid. Whereas before the measurement of the front surface area took four hours to complete with a laser procedure, now it only required between half an hour and one hour, thanks to edge tracking.

A further advantage was the capability of measuring full-scale commercial vehicles.

Alongside aerodynamic studies, the wind tunnel could also be used for other jobs, such as contamination measurements, measurements of the wiping precision of windscreen wipers in the high-speed range, temperature measurements at the radiator, and brakes and tests of the passenger-compartment ventilation.

MEASUREMENT INSTALLATIONS AND TECHNICAL DATA

The following are measurement installations and technical data for the wind tunnel at the Mercedes-Benz plant in Untertürkheim:

- Wind-tunnel weighbridge
- Multi-point pressure system
- Roller-type performance test rig
- Traversing system
- Data acquisition system
- Length of the measurement section: 10m (33ft)
- Length of the tunnel axis: 125m (410ft)
- Air jet cross-section: 32.6sq m (350sq ft)
- Maximum flow cross-section: 120sq m (1,290sq ft)
- Maximum blowing speed: 250km/h (155mph)
- Maximum power input: 5,000kW
- Blower diameter: 8.5m (27.9ft)
- Turntable diameter: 12m (39.4ft)
- Swivelling range of the turntable: 180 degrees
- Maximum axle load: 10 tonnes
- Contraction ratio pre-chamber/air jet: 3.6

THE SPECIAL VEHICLE PRODUCTION UNIT

The 1920s and 1930s were a time of upheaval for the automotive industry, especially in Germany due to the financial market crash, and manufacturers were trying not only to distance themselves further from classic body shapes that were often still rooted in the coach and carriage era, but to streamline development and construction in order to become more competitive.

One way to be more competitive was to develop further their strengths, amongst which were their chassis and engines. Numerous body-building companies would often use the Daimler chassis and engine combinations to build their own bodies for customers who could afford to have their own, individual vehicle built, and Daimler began to realize that this form of individualization could be a lucrative business for them, too.

Therefore in 1932 Daimler-Benz AG set up its special vehicle production unit in the Sindelfingen plant, and within a very short space of time the Mercedes-Benz brand had earned itself a reputation for putting wheels under some rather unusual one-off creations and for meeting highly specialized customer requirements. Until the establishment of the special vehicle production unit this service had been met by third-party body-builders.

The plant manager in Sindelfingen at that time, Dr Wilhelm Haspel, was himself a commercially trained engineer, and one of his aims in establishing the special vehicle production unit was that the time-consuming manual craftsmanship involved in producing the special bodies should not disrupt the produc-

The 'Sindelfingen Karosserie' badge, mounted on the left-hand side of the vehicle, became synonymous with unusual vehicle bodies built to the highest standards of quality and craftsmanship.

DR H.C. WILHELM KISSEL

Dr Wilhelm Kissel was born on 22 December 1885 in Hassloch, and died on 18 July 1942 in Überlingen.

Following a commercial apprenticeship and a period of study at the commercial college in Mannheim, Wilhelm Kissel took a job as a clerk for Benz & Cie in 1904. He transferred in 1907 to the purchasing department, and was promoted there to head of department as an authorized company signatory. After his appointment as departmental director, his focus from 1921 lay firmly on the reconstruction of the company in the aftermath of World War I.

From 1924 he played an important role in organizing the pooling of interests with the Daimler-Motoren-Gesellschaft, and in 1926 was appointed to the joint Board of Management established between Benz & Cie and the Daimler-Motoren-Gesellschaft. He chaired the Board meetings of Daimler-Benz AG from 1930 onwards, until the introduction of Germany's new Stock Corporation Law allowed him to adopt the official title of 'Chairman of the Board' on 1 October 1937, a function he held until his death in 1942.

In 1933 he was awarded an honorary doctorate from the technical college in Darmstadt.

Dr h. c. Wilhelm Kissel.

tion flow of the series-produced models. Furthermore this set-up provided a solid basis for the production of special vehicle bodies, and made it possible to meet even the most exceptional of customer requests with these elaborate bodies, and of earning money by doing so: this was an income that Haspel did not want Daimler-Benz to relinquish without a fight.

Hermann Ahrens was appointed as the manager of this department, having been persuaded to take on the task by the trio at the top of the company: Wilhelm Kissel (Chairman of the Board), Dr Hans Nibel (Board member for development) and Dr Wilhelm Haspel (manager of the Sindelfingen plant since January 1932). Up until this point Ahrens had been responsible for the design of exclusive models for the Horch company, a role that had brought him to the attention of the management team at Mercedes-Benz.

To begin with, the structure of the department was not clear, that is, until April 1933, which brought the arrival of Friedrich Geiger. Both Ahrens and Geiger always considered themselves as engineers, and not simply as designers as we understand the term today: their role encompassed both the styling and its constructive implementation, a concept that reflects rather more the Anglo-Saxon understanding of the term 'design'.

FRIEDRICH GEIGER

Friedrich Geiger.

Friedrich Geiger was born on 24 November 1907 in Süssen, and died on 3 June 1996 in Bad Überkingen.

Friedrich Geiger was an extremely modest and diffident personality, but he was also a remarkable man in many ways. He was the first head of design for the Mercedes-Benz brand, a discipline still known back then as 'stylistics'. Essentially a craftsman and technician, he was also a gifted artist, although he kept his talent as an artist completely under wraps – during his active time with the company, practically no one knew that he also painted enchanting watercolours.

Geiger initially learned his trade in the 1920s as a wheelwright, before going on to study coach building in Meissen. During this time he qualified as a master wheelwright and cartwright. Given that in those days most vehicle bodies were mounted on to a wooden sub-frame, planked with steel, this career path makes good sense. On 10 April 1933 Geiger joined the special vehicle production unit at the Sindelfingen plant, under its head Hermann Ahrens. In particular with regard to the production of special vehicles, Geiger was able to demonstrate convincingly his dual talents as both a technician and an aesthetician.

The next great era began for him in the 1950s, during which he supported Karl Wilferts in the body testing division, where together they built up and managed the Stylistics department. His design of the second 'Mercedes face' with horizontal elements – as opposed to the classic Mercedes-Benz radiator design – set a benchmark in the history of design for the brand. This new front-end design appeared for the first time on the SL models 300SL and 190SL, launched in 1954. Both these models represented a logical continuation of the developments in design that had begun with the 540K Streamliner of 1938.

Just a year after the première of the 300SL in New York, Geiger designed the body for the 300SL Roadster, which made its debut at the Geneva Motor Show of 1957.

Further vehicles created under his leadership include the Coupés and cabriolets of the model series W111 and W112, the 250S to 300SEL 6.3 (W108/109) saloons, the Type 600 (W100) and the 'stroke eight' models (W114/115). Geiger was particularly proud of the Coupé in the W114 model series, a car that he himself drove for many years.

The body of the 230SL (W113) was also designed under his leadership, where the 'Pagoda' roof was promoted by the designer duo Béla Barényi/Karl Wilfert and formally implemented by Paul Bracq. Other cars among today's classics that were created under his leadership include the SL and SLC models of the model series R/C 107, as well as the S Class in the model series 116, and the medium-range 123 series.

Design and engineering went side by side.

The economic recovery that began in 1932 and then took a stronger hold from 1933 on, brought with it a growing interest in exclusive vehicles and thus in the special vehicle production unit. It was here that the many different versions of the supercharged models 380 (W22), 500K and 540K (W29), as well as the Grand Mercedes (W07 and W150) were built, featuring what were often very elaborate special requests.

Between 1932 and 1939 a whole range of elaborate bodyshells for both open and enclosed vehicles was built in Sindelfingen, along with bodies fitted with special protection. Many of the elegantly designed bodies produced during that period under the aegis of Ahrens and Geiger have a timeless beauty about them that has lost nothing of its fascination or radiance, even decades later. Quite a few of the vehicles of that time regularly receive awards in renowned Concours d'Élégance such as that held at Pebble Beach in California each year. Right at the top of the list of these design highlights stands the 'Special Roadster' with its raked radiator grille, which takes to the 'public stage' to enthusiastic applause on a regular basis. No less exciting are the cabriolet variants of the same model, which, with their snugly fitting, lined soft tops, have the added advantage of greater everyday practicality.

Also produced in Sindelfingen in this period were the first cabriolet models with a hard top, aptly known as combination cars or combination Coupés. But individual customer requests, such as special chrome adornment in the form of a protective grille in front of the pointed radiator, or chrome strips emphasizing the vehicle's elegant lines, were also made possible. And let us not forget the positioning of the two spare wheels within the front wings or in the rear of the vehicle, which also had a significant impact on the design

The special vehicle production unit turned the dreams of its discerning clientele into reality, wherever at all possible.

of the body. Or the addition of equipment items such as an internal heater, things that we take for granted today, but which back then were exclusive optional extras.

Ahrens reported that it was almost a regular occurrence for the family of the future vehicle owner to visit for a few days in order to commit time to and receive advice on the choice of body shape, to make their individual selection of colours and materials, and even to determine the vehicle's technical specification. The result in each case would be a unique vehicle, tailored perfectly to an individual lifestyle.

The expertise and flexibility of the special vehicle production unit meant that the specialists in Sindelfingen also became involved in constructing the extremely lightweight bodies that needed to be built at extremely short notice for sporting use in the popular off-road races of the 1930s, creating two-seater models with aluminium bodies that weighed barely 100kg (220lb).

Special requests in terms of body design were quite a normal occurrence for the special vehicle production unit. Questions about aerodynamically designed bodies thus found sympathetic ears among the body-building artists in Sindelfingen. They shied away from nothing, not even from the otherwise seemingly untouchable pointed radiator. Examples here include, as previously mentioned, a touring saloon version of the 500K delivered to a customer in the Dutch East Indies (from 1949 called Indonesia), a 540K Cabriolet produced in 1936, or the 540K with fully aerodynamic body that was supplied to the German Dunlop works in 1938.

CHAPTER TWO

THE RACING COUPÉ

INTRODUCING THE FIRST SUPER SPORT LIGHT RACING CAR

The SSKL ('Super Sport Kurz Leicht' – Super Sport Short Light) was the fourth and final S-series model from the SSKL range of outright competition vehicles, and only a few units were built. However, it is important and relevant to this book as it fits into the SL timeline.

For the first time the chassis used weight-reducing perforations, some of which extended over the entire frame and managed to reduce the weight by 125kg (275lb). The aerodynamics expert Baron Koenig-Fachsenfeld had persuaded the young racing driver Manfred von Brauchitsch to have his 'SSKL' fitted with a streamlined body that he had designed. The light alloy body was manufactured by Vetter in Cannstatt, and fitted on to von Brauchitsch's car. Manfred von Brauchitsch was able to win the race simply because this streamlined car, which he affectionately dubbed the 'cucumber' on account of its shape, had 25 per cent less drag, making it 20km/h (12.4mph) faster than a normal 'SSKL'.

Owing to the great pressure of time, the streamlined body of the 'cucumber' was denied its finishing coat of paint. Consequently, the unusual racing car made its way on to the grid sporting an unpainted silver body, leading to it being referred to as the first Silver Arrow.

The SSKL of 1932, which Manfred von Brauchitsch drove to victory in the Avus race of May 1932.

The 'SSKL' became the glittering highlight of the legendary S-Series, and it was this car alone that would decisively shape the image of the Mercedes-Benz brand. From then on, success on the race track was in the hands of the new Silver Arrows, which, although not suitable for everyday motoring, and beyond the reach of even well-heeled customers, started to make an impact in the production line itself.

THE FIRST SUPER LIGHT COUPÉ

Mercedes-Benz W25 Record Car, 1934

In 1934 Mercedes-Benz' new supercharged-engine racing car, built by the two designers Nibel and Wagner, made its debut; it marked the beginning of the most successful racing period yet in the history of the Daimler-Benz company. Designated by the factory as the W25, it was later called the 'Silver Arrow', and it started its illustrious career by winning the first race at the Nürburgring, in which it was entered.

Immediately seeing its potential, Mercedes-Benz sent the W25 on a record hunt in the same year, in Gyon near Budapest and on the Avus. With its enclosed Coupé-style body, the record car was equipped with the 3980cc, 430bhp M25 B engine. However, it was necessary to modify the body to suit each event. In both record attempts, the usually quite prominent grille opening was significantly reduced and baffled for improved aerodynamic drag, in combination with a more efficient cooling ability

In the W25 record car, Rudolf Caracciola gained an international Class C (3.5-litre category) record over a distance of 5km (3 miles), with an average of 311.98km/h (193.86mph) on the Avus on 10 February. At the end of October in Gyon, he also set international Class C records with 317.5 and 316.6km/h (197.3 and 196.74mph) over a distance of 1km and 1 mile with a flying start, as well as a world record with 188.6km/h (117.2mph) over a distance of 1 mile with a standing start.

When Caracciola dubbed these cars 'racing limousines', a designation that was adopted by the press office and used as often as 'Silver Arrows', he had little idea that it would be the beginning of a model. These 'racing limousines' would become sporting grand tourers: the Super Light, Sport Light Coupé.

Mercedes-Benz T80 Record Car, 1939

The project of the world-record car T80 goes back to an initiative of racing-car driver Hans Stuck, who in 1936 wanted to become the world's fastest man. Stuck originally planned to let Ferdinand Porsche design a record car using two Daimler-Benz 600-series aircraft engines, which had been promised by the German Air Ministry. Stuck reached out with his plans to Daimler-Benz chairman Wilhelm Kissel, and in March 1937 Porsche presented his concept. By the late summer of

The enclosed cab W25 was the beginning of the Sport Coupé.

ABOVE LEFT: **Aerodynamics start taking over the body shape.**

ABOVE RIGHT: **The 1936 version of the W25, also with an enclosed cab area.**

1938 Daimler-Benz had completed the main components of the record car; however, the engine was still not forthcoming.

Porsche estimated that to reach the record-breaking top speed of 550km/h (342mph) Stuck would need an estimated minimum 2,200bhp; however, in September 1938 there was a duel between George Eyston and John Cobb in the American Bonneville area, where both repeatedly set new records with their world-record cars. The top speed reached during those American world-record drives of more than 575km/h (357mph) caused Porsche to set a new target speed of 600km/h (373mph), and for that purpose they recalculated a performance requirement of 3,000bhp.

After much deliberation the engine chosen was a DB-601 inverted V12, which had been earmarked to be used in the Messerschmitt Bf109 fighter plane. Mercedes had modified it to a displacement of 44.5 litres and renamed it DB603, and although still being tested at the time, it had proved an adequately powerful aircraft engine. Complementing the ridiculous amount of power would have been the cutting edge of aerodynamic design during the late 1930s.

A 2.5m-long (8.2ft) scale model was honed and refined while undergoing wind-tunnel testing – even the original down-force fins on the side were reduced in size in order to improve air-flow efficiency; however, the hardest part was to come, which was how to get the power of the engine on the ground. The Porsche designers decided on a vehicle with three axles, with the two rear units being the powered ones; this would bring the total weight of the car without driver and fuel to almost exactly 3,000kg (6,615lb).

The chassis and body were nearing completion in the beginning of 1939; however, the DB603 engine was experiencing several delays, not least the imminence of a Europe-wide war. As the threat of war progressed ever closer, Stuck came to the decision that the original plans to drive the record on the Bonneville salt lake in the US state of Utah were no longer realistic because of the political situation. After several international places were considered, Hitler, who had nicknamed the record car the 'Schwarzer Vogel', meaning 'Black Bird', decided that the land-speed record attempt would be a great coup for Germany if it could take place on German soil. He was even set to paint the car in nationalistic colours, complete with German Adler (eagle) and Hakenkreuz (swastika) additions.

He was, of course, envisioning the Mercedes-Benz T80 as another propaganda triumph of German technological might and superiority over the rest of the world. He saw to it that by mid-1939 a section of the Autobahn near Dessau was

ABOVE: **The T80 record car space-frame.**

The T80 minus the space-frame shell, showing the DB603 engine.

concreted over for its whole width as the intended venue for the record attempt. By October 1939, with only a little fine-tuning still necessary for the completion of the T80, the 'Oberste Nationale Sportbehörde' (Highest National Sports Agency) set the date for the record week at Dessau for October 1940, with the T80 as the main attraction.

But ultimately World War II prevented this from happening, and in February 1940 the T80 was dismantled, the DB603 experimental engine was taken back to the aircraft engine-testing facilities, and by June 1940 the main structure was put away in an underground storage unit. Amazingly the T80 survived the war in storage (albeit without the massive V12 engine), although the car's body and chassis were later separated.

There was some talk after the conflict about reviving the record attempt, but it was deemed too sensitive a time politically to invest the time and money into something so nonsensical, and the T80 Record Coupé was never to test its capabilities. Mercedes eventually put the car's streamlined shell on display with the space-frame and wheels but without the heavy chassis in the Mercedes-Benz Museum in Untertürkheim.

Although ultimately the T80 became nothing more than a white elephant, in order to keep the timeline intact it is

The T80 is now on display in the museum in Stuttgart.

included in the Sport Light Coupé category because it was just that – a planned record-breaking Coupé.

THE INFLUENCES OF PRE-WAR MOTOR SPORT

The W25 1934 Season

Daimler-Benz finally decided in 1933 to develop the all-new W25 to suit the new 'Grand Prix' formula for the 1934 race season. This formula prescribed a maximum weight of 750kg (1,654lb) for the vehicle (without service fluids or tyres) to enable the organizers to limit the power output of the racing cars and thus the top speeds that were possible.

The designers under chief designer Hans Nibel at Mercedes-Benz opted for its well-tried and trusted classic vehicle architecture: the front engine drives the rear wheels via a transmission on the rear axle to distribute the weight more evenly. The 3.4-litre inline supercharged 8-cylinder engine was reused, having already fully proven its worth in racing.

Painted in the German racing livery colour, white, the W25 weighed in at Nürburgring a kilo over the limit, just a day before its first deployment in the International Eifel race; legend holds that the mechanics scraped off the paint, allowing the racer to shine in the silver colour of its unpainted aluminium bodywork. The name 'Silver Arrow' was coined some time later, and gradually caught on over the years.

The combination of slender body, mechanically charged 3.4-litre inline 8-cylinder engine, independent wheel suspension and direct rear-axle transmission made the W25 a top favourite for the upcoming grand prix season. The first race at the International Eifel Race at the Nürburgring on 3 June 1934 resulted in an immediate victory for the formula racing car, with Manfred von Brauchitsch bringing home the W25 in a new course record. Further triumphs followed, including the grand prix at the testing Monza circuit, the Spanish Grand Prix, and a runner's-up

Rudolf Caracciola (65) with a Mercedes-Benz W25 750kg formula racing car.

Mechanics push the two Silver Arrows of Manfred von Brauchitsch and Luigi Fagioli to the starting line of the International Eifel Race on 3 June 1934 at the Nürburgring circuit.

The car for the 1936 season, called the 'short car' because it had a shorter wheelbase than the preceding versions. Further development of the grille can be seen.

place for Fagioli at the Masaryk Grand Prix. Mercedes-Benz was back at the forefront of international motor racing.

The W25 1935/6 Season

Further advanced development of the W25, coupled with the most powerful of the range of engines, the 4310cc M25C, which developed 340kW at 5,800rpm, gave Mercedes-Benz almost total domination of the 1935 race season. Rudolf Caracciola was back at his best, winning six grand prix races, and in doing so he claimed the European championship, a title awarded for the first time that season. In addition, Luigi Fagioli secured three victories. In 1936, however, Caracciola managed only two grand prix wins, Tunis and Monaco, in what was the third season for the modified W25.

RUDOLF UHLENHAUT

Rudolf Uhlenhaut.

Rudolf Uhlenhaut was born on 15 July 1906 in London, and died on 8 May 1989 in Stuttgart.

The Father of the Mercedes Super Light Coupé

Born on 15 July 1906 to an English mother and German father in London, where his father was the head of a subsidiary of the Deutsche Bank, Rudolf lived and attended school there until he was eight years old. Then the family moved first to Brussels, and then Bremen. As a young man, and being a great lover of skiing, Uhlenhaut moved to Munich to study mechanical engineering.

In 1931 the young engineer joined Daimler-Benz in Stuttgart and began his career in the research and development department under Fritz Nallinger. Due to his distinctive skills as a development engineer, after just three years he was appointed head of the department of transport and prefabrication. Also, his family background and his perfect spoken English opened the way for him into the English-speaking world of motor sport, and from October 1936 he became the technical director of the racing department of Daimler-Benz AG.

His first project in this function was to turn a technically inadequate and relatively unsuccessful Mercedes Silver Arrow W25 into a winner. It had had a small number of wins in 1934 and 1935, but the M25 engine had become very unreliable, and the previous chassis developments that had been undertaken to cope with a V12 had made handling abysmal. The young engineer determined that the W25 had too stiff a suspension in too soft a chassis. He therefore set out to develop a completely new car: the W125. His mission was to set the 'cars with the star' back on the road to success.

Never satisfied just to sit at a drawing board, the engineer took to the wheel for thousands of kilometres, mainly on the Untertürkheim test track, but at times also on the road in order to develop a feel for the racing car's faults. In doing so, he not only improved his own driving skills immensely, but this also enabled him to carry out accurate technical fault analysis so he could immediately develop productive corrective measures.

During World War II, Rudolf Uhlenhaut worked in aircraft engine development, and in particular the adaptation of engines to arctic temperatures; however, he never stopped thinking of new ways to create.

The SL is Born

After the war had ended, Uhlenhaut quickly became involved in sports vehicles again, tuning and designing new ways to make engines more efficient, so he could make enough money to survive. An old friend, Michael McEvoy, with whom he used to work on the 'pre-war Silver Arrows', was now a colonel in the Royal Electrical and Mechanical Engineers; deployed to Bad Oeynhausen, he found out that Uhlenhaut was in Messing, and decided to renew old acquaintances.

The conversation soon got round to racing, and McEvoy asked him to build a small racing car. Uhlenhaut planned a frame made of closed tubular triangles, the individual segments of which were only stressed through pressure or tensioning. The construction was new and guaranteed a light weight, but at the same time it was sturdy, and had a high degree of bending and torsional strength.

Unfortunately the difficult times that followed the war prevented the race car going beyond the planning and model stage. However, Uhlenhaut was asked to return to Daimler in Untertürkheim in 1948, and became head of the car-testing department from April 1949. This was his main task, but from 1951 he put his extensive knowledge of his innovative space frame into developing what was to be the sports-car type W194, and later the post-war grand prix car, the W196a.

At the 1955 Le Mans there was a catastrophic accident involving the 300SLR racing car (W196S), after which Mercedes-Benz pulled out of all racing; however, development chief Uhlenhaut would not give up working on and developing fast cars. His intention

Uhlenhaut undertook many thousands of tests personally.

RIGHT: **Uhlenhaut spent many hours in his own home workshop devising and testing new structures for body building.**

was to produce a road-going 'Grand Tourer' on the basis of a 300SLR racing car, and for this he had to build a touring car prototype: this became known as the 'Uhlenhaut Coupé'.

One Victory After Another

Success showed that Rudolf Uhlenhaut was right: four superior victories out of five races! 'The races in 1952 have shown that at top speed the 300SL with a naturally aspirated engine was at the very least a match for its strongest opponents, if not superior to them': this was how he appraised them, not without a certain amount of pride. Despite numerous triumphs, no one in Untertürkheim thought of using the new car in road traffic. Only the pressure of the American general distributor, Maximilian Hoffman, was finally able to convince the Board of Management: the 300SL (W198) series-production sports cars delighted the professional world at the International Motor Sports Show in New York in February 1954. The rest is automobile history, and after the 300SL was voted 'sports car of the century' in 1999, it is far from coming to a close.

As head of technical development, the success of the Mercedes racing cars of the 1930s and 1950s is not least due to Rudolf Uhlenhaut. Furthermore, until his retirement in 1972, all passenger-car models, from the 170S to the W116, went through his hands, including innovations such as the C111. His love for the Coupé shape and design never waned.

continued overleaf

RUDOLF UHLENHAUT *continued*

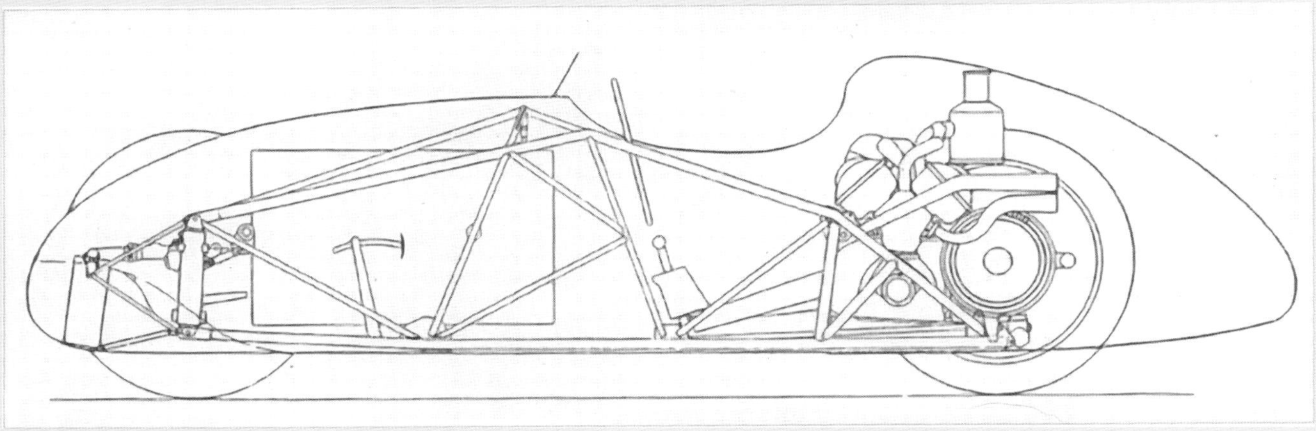

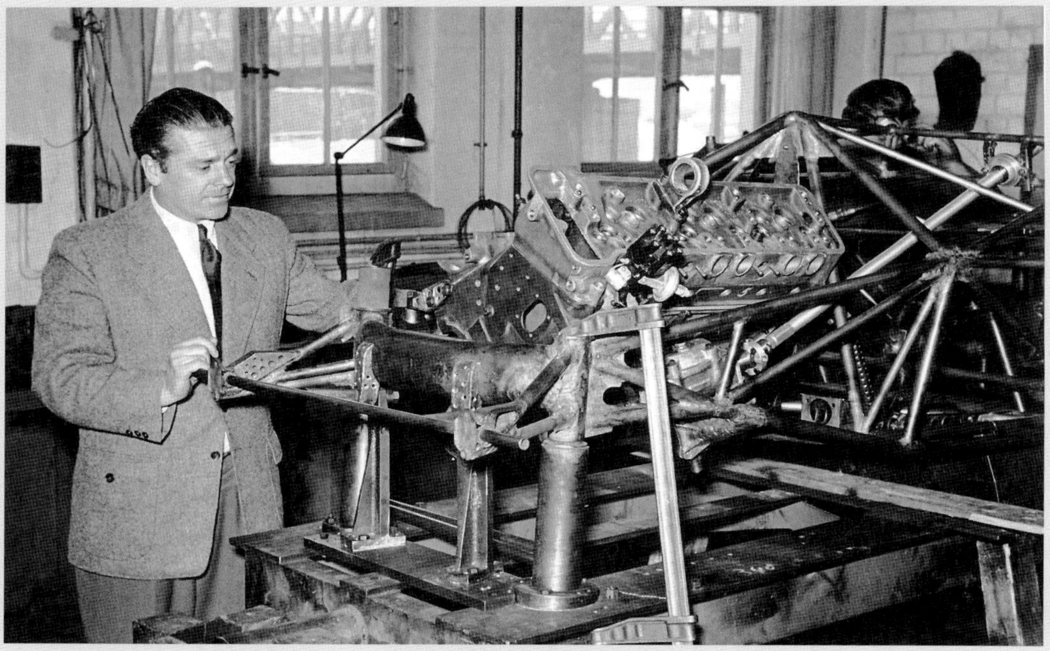

ABOVE: **Uhlenhaut's original 1937 space-frame idea.**

LEFT: **The W194 300SL space frame, with angled engine placement to keep the body line low.**

Uhlenhaut's Exceptional Personal Qualities

In addition to Uhlenhaut's ingenious work, which continues to influence the Mercedes-Benz brand even today, the personal qualities of this exceptional talent also remain unforgotten: whether in the workshop or in the office, he always treated his staff as equals. Thanks to his composure, self-assurance and undeniable competence, he was always on an equal footing with his superiors.

Full, unclad space frame.

The Uhlenhaut Coupé, derived from the W196S.

On 8 May 1989 he died aged almost eighty-three, and it was not only the professional world that mourned him: the former manager was also greatly missed by many of his staff. No one can put it better than Dr Hans Liebold, a project leader on the C111 project under Uhlenhaut:

> You always did your utmost for Uhlenhaut, simply because no one wanted to disappoint him. In his position, he could have been difficult, but he wasn't. Never did I hear him talk down to anyone, he gave respect and received it tenfold.

It was becoming clear that the W25 was losing its edge and was therefore no longer competitive, but help was on hand in the person of Rudolf Uhlenhaut, the new technical head of the motor-racing department. Uhlenhaut and his team of trusted engineers knew immediately that the W25 had lost its supremacy, and even though the 750kg formula, which was counted as an entirely new regulation based on the car's displacement, was due to be in place in 1938, he immediately began to develop a fundamentally new racing car for the 1937 season, to be called the W125.

The W125, 1937 Season

Uhlenhaut's new W125 arrived in the 1937 season. Externally it bore a close resemblance to its predecessor, but the supercharged inline 8-cylinder engine designed by Rudolf Uhlenhaut himself developed a maximum output of 575bhp from its 5.6ltr displacement. That season the car would break all records.

Uhlenhaut was never the paper theory type of engineer, so for the benefit of what was to be the W125 he himself took to testing the W25 under racing conditions in order to gain

The three cooling vents in its front section gave the W125 an unmistakable look.

The redeveloped inline-8 engine displacement was increased to 5.7 litres, which alongside the supercharger increased horsepower by 100bhp.

some practical knowledge of its weaknesses; by doing this he was able to choose a revolutionary chassis design principle for its successor, one with soft spring characteristics and powerful damping. The engine, too, was thoroughly redeveloped. Having raised the displacement to 5.7ltr, the supercharged inline 8-cylinder delivered 435kW (592bhp), around 73kW (100bhp) more than the previous year's model, an output that Grand Prix racing cars only reached again in the late 1980s. The top speed of the W125 was around 320km/h (200mph).

The new Silver Arrow started off with a good omen by winning the very first race it entered, the Tripoli Grand Prix (Libya), piloted by Hermann Lang. With no fewer than seven victories, nine second and six third places, it dominated the 1937 racing season, and Rudolf Caracciola went on to win the Grand Prix European Championship for the second time.

The W154 V12, 1938 Season

In September 1936, the motor-sport body AIACR laid down the new grand prix formula specifications that would apply from 1938. The key points were that instead of a weight only category, each race car was governed by displacement, and from 1938 this would be a maximum displacement of 3ltr for mechanically supercharged engines and 4.5ltr for naturally aspirated engines, and a weight of 400 to 850kg (880 to 1,875lb), depending on engine capacity. These specifications necessitated a completely new car, and even though the 1937 season was still in full swing, Mercedes-Benz designers and engineers had to begin work on what was to be the successor of the successful W125: the W154.

The power available to the drivers was 316kW in the first half of the season, climbing to over 344kW by the end of the year. This was also the first Mercedes-Benz racing car to have a five-speed gearbox. The W154 crouched low over the asphalt, and as well as enhancing the dynamic look of the car, this substantially lowered its centre of gravity and made for excellent road-holding ability.

This new Silver Arrow was an all-round success and gave the Mercedes-Benz racing department its greatest number of victories during this era. The Tripoli Grand Prix resulted in a triple victory for Lang, von Brauchitsch and Caracciola, a feat repeated at the French Grand Prix in the sequence von Brauchitsch, Caracciola and Lang. The British driver Richard Seaman, who had joined the team in 1937, won the German Grand Prix at the Nürburgring ahead of the car driven jointly by Caracciola and Lang, while Hermann Lang took the Coppa Ciano in Livorno, and Rudolf Caracciola the Coppa Acerbo at Pescara.

At the Swiss Grand Prix, the W154 again took all three podium places (Caracciola, Seaman and von Brauchitsch). Rudolf Caracciola was crowned European champion for the third time. Weakened by the death of its top driver Rosemeyer during record-breaking attempts in January 1938, Auto Union was unable to return to winning ways until almost the end of the season.

The W154, 1938 season.

The W154, 1939 Season

In the last racing season before the start of World War II, Mercedes-Benz managed to continue with the W154 where they had left off so successfully in 1938. The first race on the calendar, the Pau Grand Prix, was won by Hermann Lang in a W154 ahead of Manfred von Brauchitsch, making up for defeat the previous year. Lang was again the winner in the Eifel race on 21 May 1939, with Caracciola finishing in third place and von Brauchitsch fourth. On 23 July 1939 Caracciola won the German Grand Prix at the Nürburgring for the fifth time, and at the Swiss Grand Prix the winner was Lang ahead of Caracciola and von Brauchitsch.

Although Lang was clearly the season's leading driver, the AIACR in Paris, the governing body responsible for awarding the title of European champion, was unable to award him the title due to the outbreak of World War II.

A departure from the norm in the series of Mercedes victories in 1939 was the prestigious Tripoli Grand Prix. In an effort to break the dominance of the Silver Arrows, race organizers in the Italian colony of Libya specified a maximum engine displacement of 1.5ltr for its voiturette formula, knowing full well that Mercedes-Benz had no vehicle available that complied with this formula. This was clearly an attempt to give Italian manufacturers Alfa Romeo and Maserati a chance of securing their first victory since 1934.

The W154 (left) with the Tripoli W165 (right), 1939 season.

The W165 voiturette 1.5-litre V8 engine and car was built in just eight months.

Undeterred, racing manager Alfred Neubauer, Rudolf Uhlenhaut and the team set to work, and in just eight months successfully managed to develop a completely new car from scratch, the W165. Better still, the category change ruse was all for nothing for the 'Home' team, as Mercedes-Benz triumphed with a 'one-two' victory for the two Mercedes-Benz W165 cars, giving their adversaries virtually no chance: Hermann Lang won the race, finishing over a lap ahead of Caracciola in second.

The last start by a Silver Arrow car was in the Belgrade City Race on 3 September 1939, in which Manfred von Brauchitsch finished second. By that time, however, World War II had already begun.

THE MERCEDES-BENZ 540K STREAMLINER

The 1920s and 1930s were characterized, in automotive terms, by the steadily increasing speed of travel. The development of fast roadways and long-distance routes reflected this change, while the era also saw the advent of the motorway. The automotive industry took advantage of this progress, and not just with more powerful engines and redesigned suspensions: vehicle bodies, for example, grew more sophisticated in design, and alongside an understanding of aerodynamics, more streamlined.

Against this backdrop, Mercedes-Benz went on to build several vehicles with aerodynamically shaped bodies. The 540K Streamliner, produced in 1938, marked the culmination in this respect. The 540K was Mercedes-Benz's sporty top model in the 1930s, and a one-off Coupé. Customized bodyshell creations, individually manufactured, had always represented the exclusive norm for Mercedes-Benz, and since the introduction of the 'special vehicle production' unit at the Sindelfingen plant, it made possible the realization of such singular ideas.

The term 'designer' as we know it today did not yet exist in those days, but the 'stylists' at Mercedes-Benz created a whole series of aerodynamically shaped bodyshells for the 540K during 1937 and 1938, all of which reflected the concept of aerodynamic flow to a greater or lesser extent. The Streamliner produced in 1938 was not only a masterpiece of design, but also demonstrated the most thorough application of the knowledge gained in the tests in the wind tunnel.

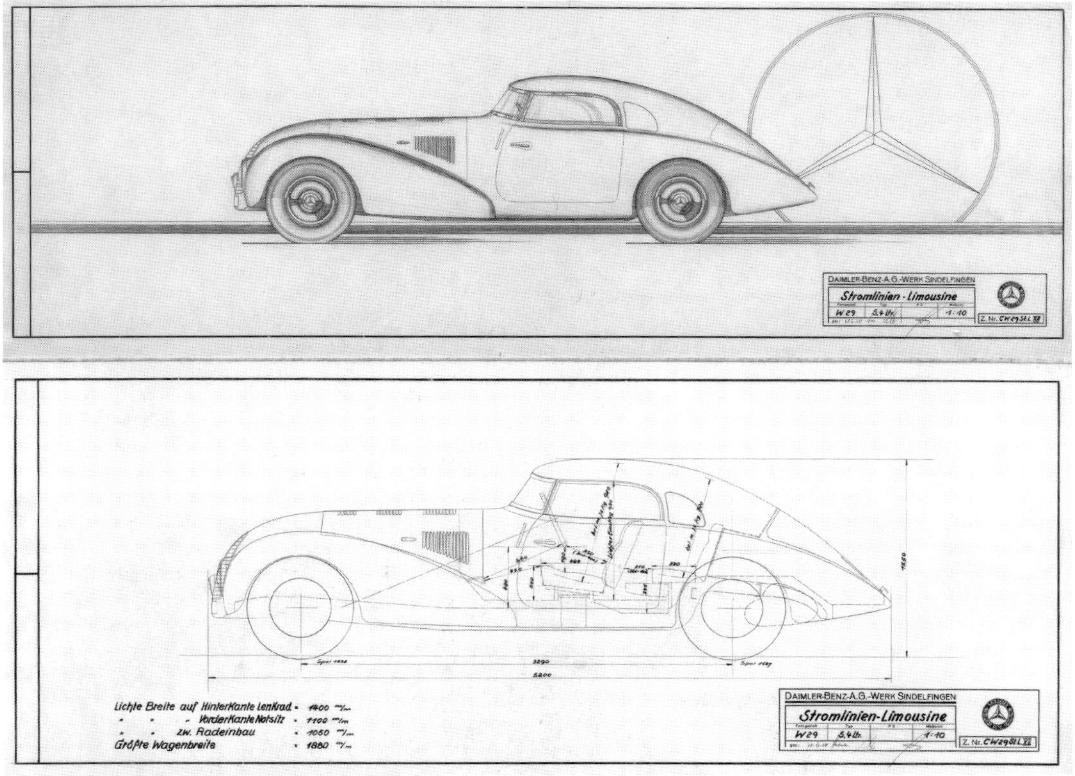

The W29 540K Streamliner design drawing.

In 2014 the W29 was put through modern aerodynamic measurements.

Achieving even higher cruising speeds than the 140 to 145km/h (87 to 90mph) usually associated with a 540K demanded numerous detailed measures. Some of the most important of these involved the car's aerodynamics: a 540K in the standard version, with a Coupé body, achieved a Cd figure of around 0.57 too much for higher cruising speeds. For this, a more streamlined body with a considerably improved Cd figure was required. The 540K Streamliner met this criterion, as wind-tunnel measurements undertaken by Mercedes-Benz Classic in May 2014 went on to prove: it achieved the excellent Cd figure of 0.36. It was this aerodynamic advancement alone that contributed to cruising speeds of 165 to 170km/h (102 to 105mph), and with supercharger a top speed of 185km/h (115mph).

Streamlining the Body Shape

Once the scale model had been tested through the FKFS wind tunnel, the 540K Streamliner was designed to meet these aerodynamic specifications: a shape from front to rear that would allow the air to flow perfectly over it, and to offer as little resistance as possible to the wind. To this end, the windscreens were curved to the sides. The roofline was set low, tapering to a point in the middle of the back and merging from there into the horizontal line of the softly curved rear section. The headlamps were fully integrated. At each point where the air flow risked breaking away from the body, the designers optimized the details, for example by recessing the door handles, omitting the bumpers, and reducing the panel gaps. The under body was also completely panelled, to minimize obstructions to the air flow there.

The requirement to achieve high cruising speeds also dictated an adjustment to the drive-axle ratio, which was lengthened from 3.08 to 2.90. In all other technical details, the car matched the standard version of the 540K.

Just how seriously the builders of the vehicle took their responsibility is demonstrated by the Mercedes star: to take advantage of every opportunity to limit wind resistance, it was not standing proud but was painted on, as in the case of the renowned Silver Arrows Grand Prix racing cars. Also, like these, the streamlined 540K was given silver paintwork. From today's perspective it could be seen as something of a historical irony that the classic, vertical Mercedes-Benz pointed radiator grille was nevertheless still to be found below the bodyshell, and remained a decisive factor in the appearance of the front section.

Of course, practical aspects of cooling and thermal management also played a role here, but a styling element that is as characteristic of the brand as the classic Mercedes radiator is, and always has been, subject to special protection: hardly surprising, then, that the subject was a talking point

Wind-tunnel test in 2014.

at the time right up to Management Board level. This whole process demonstrates the extent to which the automotive industry at the time was changing, and how it balanced on the very threshold between the traditional and the modern.

The resulting overall dynamic appearance of the 540K Streamliner was that of a powerful sports car, the potential of which to achieve high cruising speeds was immediately clear to the casual observer even when the automobile was standing still: the exceptional one-off vehicle caused a considerable stir when it first appeared, and never was Mercedes-Benz mentioned in the press without the 540K Streamliner being mentioned in the next sentence.

Much of the praise around this vehicle should go to Max Sailer. From 1935 onwards he was a deputy board member of Daimler-Benz and responsible for overall vehicle development for the Mercedes-Benz brand, including for its other successful racing and record-breaking vehicles. He was thus very aware of the significance of aerodynamics in motor vehicle construction, and was one of the driving forces behind corresponding projects, also in relation to series-production vehicles.

Tyre Design and Materials

Due to the ever higher speeds at which cars were now travelling, there came a demand for new designs and materials for tyres that would enable them to withstand the more powerful forces to which they were exposed; these tyres then had to be subjected to real-life testing, which was all the more necessary for powerful, heavy and fast cars. The extraordinary 540K Streamliner was commissioned by DDG Co-AG (German Dunlop Rubber Company) in Hanau, and built by the special vehicle production unit in the first half of 1938. In June it was delivered to Hanau by the Daimler-Benz dealership in Frankfurt.

The company immediately put this high-performance vehicle to work, and this is where the 540K Streamliner really came into its own. Far more so than any other vehicle of that era, its aerodynamically styled body and powerful engine made it exceedingly capable of rapid supercharged acceleration to speeds as high as 185km/h (115mph) on German autobahns, in those days still very empty. The 540K Streamliner was ideally suited for this task, and it smoothly

The original 1938 540K Streamliner.

Original rear view of the streamlined bodywork.

sustained cruising speeds of 165 to 170km/h (100 to 105mph) over a considerable period.

The threat of a tyre malfunction was common in these early years, and the drivers themselves were put under extreme tension to concentrate at speeds unheard of previously. They were therefore all the more dependent on a reliable and predictable vehicle that would ensure the driver-fitness safety of its occupants over longer periods of driving at the critical limits.

TYRE TESTING AT DUNLOP

At Dunlop, the vehicle was adopted into the company fleet, where it was looked after by garage foreman Karl Hammes. Hammes was responsible for all test vehicles, managers' company cars, trucks, and even the stables. As soon as the rather involved and time-consuming running-in process required in that era had been completed, this unusual and elegant vehicle was passed on to the respective departments to fulfil its planned purpose: high-speed tyre testing. In a celebratory Dunlop brochure of 1938 we are told:

> A particularly tough challenge is set by our tests with a high-speed streamlined supercharged car on the Reichsautobahn, which enables us to study the performance of the tyres at sustained high speeds. Such tests involve a changeover of drivers, driving at speeds of around 170km per hour. The only stops are for refuelling and for the changeover of drivers, as previously mentioned.

MAX SAILER

Max Sailer.

Max Sailer was born on 20 December 1882 in Esslingen, and died on 5 February 1964, also in Esslingen.

Max Sailer joined the Daimler-Motoren-Gesellschaft (DMG) on 26 November 1902, and remained there, apart from breaks for study, until 1 July 1905. He left to join the Fahrzeugfabrik Eisenach automotive works, but returned to DMG on 1 October 1910. He was an industrious development engineer, who also had a successful sideline as a racing driver. In 1914 he was one of the drivers on the successful team that took the first three places in the legendary French Grand Prix of that year. Sailer, who drove the fastest lap in the race, was in the lead when forced to retire on the sixth lap.

In the Targa Florio of 1921, he took the prize for the fastest production car, followed by a class victory in Sicily the following year. He also won both speed trials in the automotive tournament in Baden-Baden. In 1923 he finished as the best European driver in the Indianapolis 500-mile race, taking eighth place.

He was appointed a director of DMG in 1925, and held overall responsibility for the Daimler-Benz plant in Berlin-Marienfelde from 1927 until 1929. In 1935 he succeeded Dr Hans Nibel as Technical Director and Head of Development for the entire vehicle range. In this role he was then appointed as a deputy member of the Board of Management, remaining on the board until his retirement on 30 June 1942. In this function Sailer was responsible for all vehicle development undertaken for the Mercedes-Benz brand, including the development of a whole series of successful racing and record-breaking cars, particularly in the period from 1936 to 1939. But it was also under his leadership that the diesel engine was first successfully introduced into passenger cars, in 1936.

To ensure that the engine could cope with this exceptional sustained load in the upper range, a series of fluted slots were cut in the upper side, as well as in the trailing end of the bonnet after the flared wheel arch; these allowed air to flow through the engine compartment and then the cooling air to be discharged, so minimizing wind resistance, or drag.

As previously mentioned, the almost empty autobahns, which were still fairly new at the time, offered ideal conditions for testing, and the 540K would often draw crowds as it was employed on long-distance runs – for example to Berlin or Hamburg and back, sometimes even at night. In those days, and with the motorway network far from being complete, this was considered an extraordinary feat of driving. But it was this that made it possible to complete intensive test programmes with high-speed tyres on high-performance vehicles. One of the most common stretches of road to use was the motorway section between Karlsruhe and Göttingen: this corresponds to today's A5 and A7 autobahns.

The 540K during the War Years

Following the outbreak of war on 1 September 1939, the non-official use of motor vehicles within the territory of the German Reich was severely restricted, and the automotive and accessories industries felt the brunt of this. In order still to be able to drive the 540K, for example during the ongoing development work, it was converted to run on liquid gas, as an entry in the vehicle documents dated 21 December 1939, authorized by the Director of Police in Hanau, goes to show. A further entry in the registration document – made by the technical inspection authority of district 5 in Frankfurt on 10 April 1940 – provides evidence that the conversion to run on liquid gas increased the unladen weight from 2,500kg (5,500lb) to 2,580kg (5,690lb). The permissible payload was reduced by these additional 80kg (176lb) to 320kg (705lb).

Fortunately, the 540K survived the period of World War II undamaged, as it had been stored in the garages at the

That the car was not spared during its time at Dunlop is shown by traces of wear and tear on the original components; these were still available to form part of the rebuilt vehicle some seventy-five years later.

Dunlop works. At the war's end it was known to have been used in the Stuttgart area on occasion by a soldier from the US Army, after – rather oddly – having it painted to match the other army vehicles, probably to make it less obvious what he was driving. That is, until one day it was spotted by a staff member, who drew it to the attention of Mr Scheller, the manager of the Dunlop branch in Stuttgart. It was quickly located and returned to the German Dunlop factory, and was subsequently deregistered in Hanau on 21 April 1948. A note in the registration document mentions: 'Vehicle recorded as having been taken off the road in accordance with section 3 of the law of 21 November 1947 pertaining to the misuse of motor vehicles.'

The Streamliner would later be returned to the ownership of Daimler-Benz, but quite when and why it is no longer possible to establish. At this point the streamlined body was removed from its chassis, again without anyone today being able to identify or substantiate the reason for this. The note in the vehicle registration document 'Chassis/Programme' could possibly be an indication that the plan was to fit a different body to the chassis – conversions of this nature undertaken on other models are well documented. These were fitted with bodyshells of a more modern design and sold abroad. Luckily this did not happen to the 540K Streamliner: the chassis, together with some body components and the rear axle, was passed on to the inventory of the museum, where it was furnished in the mid-1950s with a museum list number (known internally as a 'muli' number).

The Streamliner was painstakingly restored to its former glory from 2011 to 2014, taking around 4,800 man-hours to complete; it made its first appearance to the public at Pebble Beach in the USA.

Main body tub restoration.

The sub-structure and ash-frame skeleton of the 540K.

The rear bodywork restoration.

The finished 540K Streamliner on its way to the Pebble Beach Concours d'Élégance.

THE MERCEDES-BENZ 300SL (W194) RACING SPORTS CAR, 1952

When Daimler chairman Wilhelm Haspel regained full control from the 'allied union' in the late 1940s, he quickly expressed an interest in putting Mercedes back into the limelight through motor sport. This was an area in which the company had been particularly dominant before the war, with its mighty W25, W125 and W154 Silver Arrow Formula 1 cars.

A team was put together that included Dr Professor Hans Scherenberg, Fritz Nallinger and Rudolf Uhlenhaut; however, this comeback could only be contemplated for sports-car races and rallies, as a new set of rules was announced for Formula 1, that would come into effect in 1954, and limited resources prevented the development of a competitive Grand Prix vehicle in time.

In 1951 they proceeded to do tests with pre-war single-seaters such as the W154, but quickly found that these cars were too dated and could not stand up to the rivals of the time in any way. Haspel remembered that Uhlenhaut had presented a proposal for a 'prestigious sports car' back in 1948: this had been based on the sports car he had designed in 1946 for Colonel Michael McEvoy, and it was this, and this alone, that enabled the DMG Board to decide to go ahead.

From left: Prof. Dr Hans Scherenberg, Chief Engineer Rudolf Uhlenhaut, and Prof. Dr Fritz Nallinger.

Uhlenhaut and the team knew that world-beating speed was out of the question, so they focused on other attributes needed in an endurance racer. Uhlenhaut had always believed in the three principles of light weight, aerodynamics and reliability, and since the engine and transmission were from the 1,800kg-plus (4,000lb) Adenauer, there was no possibility for weight savings with either component. Excitedly Uhlenhaut set about recalling his design brief – working in his spare time at home and using his kitchen table, he built a frame model from soldering wire, constantly changing and perfecting it until he was satisfied that every segment was either in tension or compression.

The project advanced swiftly, and in a few weeks a drawing had been agreed – and in no more than a further two months a working prototype was built, with a modular framework made up of tiny tubes welded in a triangular grid pattern. It offered an incredibly high level of rigidity for a low weight, and more importantly, its standalone weight was little more than 50kg (110lb).

The Working Prototype

It was no mean feat to make a working prototype as swiftly as they did, with limited resources, and which would be competitive from day one. Having been told they could 'raid the parts bins', they had made use of existing components such as axles, transmission, and a 3-litre inline-six out of the decidedly non-sporting 300 Adenauer sedan. The use of a saloon-car engine in a lightweight race car was not without precedent, as the Jaguar XK120 won many races with the 3.4-litre straight-six from the Mark VII saloon.

As for the bodywork, under the guidance of Friedrich Geiger, and applying what he had learnt from the aerodynamics used on the 540K Streamliner, the team decided initially to use aluminium. However, Geiger remembered that Mercedes-Benz had a lot of aircraft metal they had never used – the very same lightweight aluminium and magnesium alloy that went into the Luftwaffe's infamous Junkers bombers. It was an inspired decision and formed the basis of the new model name, the 'SL'.

The framework alone weighed just 50kg (110lb).

Creating the torsional strength needed for the body, the space frame reached quite far up the sides, and adding conventional doors would have meant chopping into and thereby weakening the frame. Therefore the W194 could not be equipped with conventional doors, and instead a small door was necessary; this started from the main body line and cut into part of the roof, where it pivoted upwards. Little did anyone know what kind of iconic history this would create.

The Junghans chronometers prominently located in the centre of all ten W194 dashboards were war surplus, and in fact were installed in Junkers and the Messerschmitt. To shed a few more kilos and to further keep the weight of the W194s low, all the glass is actually clear plastic. All ten 1952 W194s were hand built.

The headlights were smoothed into the wings, and the roofline was kept low with a sufficiently raked windscreen. Archive records indicate that it had an estimated drag coefficient of 0.25Cd. However, this was probably done using a model in a water tank, as DMG did not have good access to the wind tunnel until 1954 – it had been bombed by allied forces so this figure would not have been as accurate as the wind-tunnel tests.

This early prototype W194 shows the short gullwing door. These doors were later formed further into the body line for ease of access during the running start at the Le Mans 24-Hour endurance race.

To achieve the W194's remarkable aerodynamics the front was entirely smooth with a low-lined bonnet.

RIGHT: **In January 2012 a wind-tunnel test was performed on a Daimler Classics restored car, and it showed this car to have an actual, and much more likely, drag coefficient of 0.36.**

1952 Race Results

As for reliability, the W194 300SL's 1952 success speaks for itself. On their first outing, Gullwings finished both second and fourth in the Mille Miglia. The cars then posted a first- and second-place finish at Bern in Switzerland.

Next, Hermann Lang and Fritz Reiss won the 24 Hours of Le Mans, and the team of Theo Helfrich and Norbert Niedermayer finished second. The W194s then went on to remarkable first-, second-, third- and fourth-place finishes at the Nürburgring Anniversary Grand Prix.

The gruelling 1,600km (994-mile) Mille Miglia; the 300SL finished an impressive second.

Of course, there was one more race the Benz team wanted to win, and in their minds it was the most important race of the year: Mexico's Carrera Pan-Americana. Winning in Europe was one thing, but winning outside Europe was quite another.

The W194 driven by Karl Kling and Hans Klenk won the race, another W194 driven by Hermann Lang came in second, and a third Mercedes, driven by American John Fitch, would have finished third had Fitch not allowed a mechanic to look at the car with a day to go, which disqualified him. Despite that, a one/two finish in Mexico had the desired effect. It was this win that convinced Max Hoffman to demand a sports car (both Coupé and roadster) to pull people into his Frank Lloyd Wright-designed New York showroom. Although mass production of the W194 300SL was initially not planned, Mercedes' new General Director Fritz Konecke confirmed with Max Hoffman that he would consider his request.

At the beginning of 1953 Daimler decided to pull out of racing; the words of the press release went something like this: 'Daimler-Benz believes it is entitled to point out that the Mercedes-Benz sports cars have sufficiently demonstrated

Hermann Lang and Fritz Reiss won the Le Mans 24 Hours in 1952.

LEFT: **Rudolf Caracciola (16) and Karl Kling (18).**

The W194 driven by Karl Kling and Hans Klenk won the race, even after a vulture crashed through the windscreen and knocked Klenk unconscious.

last year that they have sufficient command of the field of international sports cars.'

MERCEDES-BENZ 300SL (W194/11) DIE HOBEL, 1953

Uhlenhaut, not one to procrastinate or rest upon his laurels, still looked to improve the W194. He always considered, not his successes, but what he could have done better, or what he could do to improve something. He was also aware of the pressure from Hoffman to consider a road-going sports car.

Regarding the W194, the aerodynamics had to be improved even more. In the engine, he wanted to replace the carburettor with the new injection technology by Bosch to increase performance; however, that increased performance would also need improvements in drive, safety and stopping power.

The name given to the new model was W194/11: this was because it had the chassis number W194 010 00011/53 with the engine M198 /11; chassis numbers 1 to 10 were assigned to the ten chassis of the 52 300SL – so it was the eleventh W194, and is therefore always correctly called the W194/11.

External Appearance

Externally, the body was changed completely compared with its predecessor: only the basic silhouette was retained, and

The W194 and the W194/11 side by side.

The newly designed mouth of the W194/11.

the car became shorter, narrower, and lower; it was much more streamlined, with smaller headlights. The most striking difference was at the front, the front grille air inlet being much more angular – according to engineers it looked very much like the mouth of a carpenter's wood plane. This is what gave the W194/11 its nickname of the 'Hobel' ('plane' in English).

In order to reduce the drag coefficient further, the track width was reduced by 8cm (3in) at the front and 10cm (4in) at the rear, which made the vehicle almost 16cm (6.3in) narrower. Together with lowering the roof, this reduced the frontal area by approximately 9 per cent. By lowering the front end, it also became necessary to add a bonnet bulge in order to accommodate the engine valve cover that now protruded above the body line even after canting the engine on its side; a second bulge was added purely for aesthetic balance.

On the side of the vehicle there were grilled openings behind both the front and rear wheel arch, and these 'gills' were by no means only for the sake of improved appear-

Flank-side picture showing the differences in body profile.

BELOW RIGHT: **The new M198 fuel-injected engine.**

ance: Uhlenhaut had found that it was better in terms of air flow not to dissipate the heat from the engine and tyres via the underbody, but laterally via the body sides, which were surrounded by a lower air pressure, enabling fast transit of warm air. This was later proven in 1954 when the fifty-second Carrera Pan Americana W194 was modified with these gills, with the same positive results. The wheel arches were also enlarged to accommodate 16in wheels. A chrome trim strip was added above the sill line: this was unusual for a race car, but hinted at a future road car.

The Engine

The W194/11 had the same engine as was fitted in the 1951 W186 300 Adenauer (M186) with 115bhp: when this engine was fitted in the original W194 it was designated as the M198, but in the W194/11 it was designated as the M194. A number of changes were made, including an improved block that could cope with much higher horsepower.

As car-design manager for Mercedes, Dr Hans Scherenberg was able to bring to the W194/11 project his ample experience in petrol injection, which he had gained during aircraft engine construction in the war. The W194/11

PROFESSOR HANS SCHERENBERG

Professor Hans Scherenberg.

Professor Hans Scherenberg was born on 28 October 1910 in Dresden, and died on 17 November 2000 in Stuttgart.

It is not hard to describe Professor Scherenberg as a full-blooded engineer. He was fascinated by the world of mechanical engineering at an early age. He was born in Dresden in 1910 and grew up in Heidelberg; after attending grammar school, he devoted himself to the study of mechanical engineering at the Stuttgart and Karlsruhe Colleges of Technology.

At the age of twenty-five he joined Daimler-Benz as a newly graduated engineer, and by 1935 he was working in the research department, collaborating initially over the first diesel car in the world, the 260D. After this, and for many years, he worked on questions concerning increasing power. He was engaged in the further improvement of the pre-chamber system on the diesel engine, in the development and control of fuel injection in conjunction with valve-timing on aircraft engines, as well as experimental design.

The considerable successes he achieved in obtaining higher engine power at great altitudes through the correct matching of supercharger, valve-timing and fuel injection led to the award in 1942 of a doctorate in engineering. The subject of his thesis was 'Valve-timing in four-stroke, high-altitude aircraft engines'. In 1943 he was appointed senior engineer and head of the aircraft engine test department.

After the war Scherenberg initially stepped away from Daimler-Benz and worked at Adolf Schnürle Motorenkonstruktion in Stuttgart, alongside Dr Adolf Schnürle, where the further development of the two-stroke diesel engine was of prime importance. In 1946 he was collaborating with the Gutbrod-Werken in Plochingen, where, two years later, he took over as Head of Development and Manufacture. It was thanks to him and his team that the Gutbrod 'Superior', with a Robert Bosch GmbH fuel injection system, came on to the market.

The car was a technical marvel, and was hailed as one of the most contemporary designs in small vehicles of the early 1950s as regards concept and progressiveness.

In 1952, at the age of forty-one, Dr Scherenberg returned to Daimler-Benz, where Professor Nallinger appointed him Head of Car Design in Untertürkheim. This was at the beginning of an extremely important period, when innovations in technology would continue to rebuild the strength of Daimler-Benz in a still young federal Germany.

In the car field, the models in the 180, 190 and 220a range had a lasting effect on automobile manufacture: their self-supporting 'Pontoon' bodywork, the frame floor unit, the single-joint swing axle and also the sub-frame that combines the elements in the front wheel suspension, were trend-setting achievements by the engineers at Daimler-Benz.

Working alongside Rudy Uhlenhaut, Dr Scherenberg's technical knowledge further influenced examples of technical progress in the Daimler-Benz racing and sports car endeavours, especially concerning the W196 and 300SLR – and the 4-cylinder 190SL sports car. At the same time, the standard production version of the dynamic high-performance 300SL sports car was fitted with a direct petrol injection system and demonstrated impressively the advantages of this system in practical operation.

In 1955, Dr Hans Scherenberg was appointed deputy member of the Board of Management by the Supervisory Board. He was put in charge of the manufacture of large engines and aircraft engines, the preliminary development of diesel combustion processes, and design strength.

became the first four-stroke engine with direct petrol injection installed in a Mercedes car.

Further developments to the M198 included the following: the compression ratio was increased, the arrangement of the spark plugs was changed, the valves were enlarged and their control times adjusted accordingly, and of course all the necessary preparations for installing the injection system were made. The engine, although remaining 2996cc, now produced a massive 215bhp.

Testing the W194/11

The W194/11 was finally completed early in 1953, and in anticipation of the 1954 season, Mercedes' racing team manager Alfred Neubauer arranged a test session for one of the original 1952 300SLs and the new prototype at the Solitude racing circuit near Stuttgart. Mercedes had to hire 150 policemen to close off the public roads that comprised most of the historic track.

The fastest lap of the day was posted in the 00011/53 prototype by the youngest driver, Hans Herrmann, who had made his F1 debut in 1953. He completed the 11.7km circuit in 4min 52sec, faster than any of the Mercedes veterans, including Karl Kling, Hermann Lang and Rudolf Uhlenhaut.

It was considered that there were perhaps three of these W194/11 test models, and the various photos prove a number of differences between them.

Early in the next chapter there is an image showing the dark-painted 'No. 11' next to a real W194, a W198 and an

Most pictures are of a silver vehicle with relatively narrow gills in the front and three chrome strips along the rear gills. *Top*: The exhaust exits in the lower part of the right gill at the front. A few pictures show a silver vehicle with wider front gills and four chrome strips on the rear air outlet. *Bottom*: Here the exhaust comes out of the body below the right gill and below the long chrome strip.

The interior of the W194 (*top*) and the revised interior of the W194/11 (*bottom*).

SLR. In this picture you can only see the front gills of the mentioned features of the W194/11, and these correspond to the second version described here. In contrast to the other pictures, this car still has a chrome-plated mask around the front air inlet, and a registration number plate.

After prototypes and test mules have done their job they are usually destroyed – however, once Uhlenhaut had finished with one of the prototypes, it was slightly modified as a company car for director Ing. Karl Wilfert, and painted black with added trim on the front grille. Thankfully Mercedes-Benz kept the original W194/11 version and put it on display in their museum.

The Hobel never raced, but the racing success of the W194 did spawn a brief return to Formula 1 in the shape of the W196 – but more importantly it introduced the shape of an SL Coupé, and with its new 'mouth/grille' shape it redefined the Mercedes brand.

Project W198 began in September 1953, and in eighteen months was ready for the market.

Registered as a road car for Karl Wilfert.

Before the war, Mercedes sold a total of forty-one cars in the USA. Of the 1,400 W198 Coupés built in total, the largest part, about 1,100, reached the USA. More than 80 per cent of the vehicle's total production of approximately 1,400 units were sold in the USA, making the Coupé the first Mercedes-Benz widely successful outside its home market, and thoroughly validating Hoffman's prediction.

THE W196 GRAND PRIX CAR

Although not a Coupé, the W196 is included in this book as it played a large part in the design process of future Super Light Coupés, as well as becoming the foundation of what came to be called the 'Uhlenhaut Coupé' (see below).

Mercedes-Benz's re-entry into Grand Prix racing coincided with the establishment of new regulations that were heavily biased against supercharged engines, which were limited to only 750cc.

Mercedes had invested a lot of money in its team of engineers; Fritz Nallinger oversaw the project, ably assisted by Rudolf Uhlenhaut, who headed a team of engineers including Hans Scherenberg, Ludwig Kraus, Manfred Lorscheidt, Hans Gassmann and Karl-Heinz Göschel. They put all their knowledge into producing the W196 with the intention of crushing the opposition. It seems that fourteen units of the W196 were assembled during its two seasons of activity.

The handling characteristics of the cars continued to be a problem for their whole lifetime: different wheelbase lengths of 2,337mm (92in), 2,223mm (87.5in) and finally 2,159mm (85in) were tried, with mixed but inevitably unsuccessful results.

The original W196 'Streamliner' was dressed in a contoured body made entirely of aluminium, which gave it a classic car look. The first tests were made using a 1:5 scale wooden model in the Stuttgart Imperial College wind tunnel. The bodywork, now referred to as 'Type Monza', was used on high-speed circuits such as Reims in France, Silverstone in the United Kingdom (the former disused aerodrome), Monza in Italy, the Nürburgring long route and the Bremgarten circuit in Switzerland. This body was mainly used to reduce the drag generated by the car, thus achieving a higher maximum speed.

However, from the German Grand Prix on the Nürburgring in early August 1954 onwards, an open-wheel (monoposto) version also formed part of the line-up. Its tubular space frame was light and sturdy, and its suspension with torsion bars, and a new single-joint swing axle at the rear, as well as the giant, turbo-cooled, and at first centrally arranged Duplex drum brakes, were unconventionally good.

FRITZ NALLINGER

Fritz Nallinger.

Fritz Nallinger was born on 6 August 1898 in Esslingen, and died on 4 June 1984 in Stuttgart. He was the fourth child of DMG board member Friedrich Nallinger, and his early years revolved around automobile design; at the age of thirteen he received his first patent for automotive headlights, which he sold to Carl Zeiss. He graduated from school at the age of eighteen and was immediately enlisted into military service, where he became a pilot.

Having had a fair amount of experience with the mechanics of aircraft engines during his time as a World War I pilot, he decided to study mechanical engineering at the Karlsruhe University. After completing his studies at the age of twenty-four, he started his professional career in the design office of Benz & Cie after recommendations from his father Freidrich Nallinger, who had previously left the board of DMG and also worked at Benz & Cie.

In these early days he played an important part in the development of all-round independent suspension for passenger cars. He also spent time helping with the development of diesel engines, working closely with W. Lippart of Bosch; they advanced the technology of pumps and injectors, and introduced the first 'glow plug' technology.

In his spare time, alongside his father, he also drove car races as a works driver, with some success. At the automobile tournament in Baden Baden in 1925 he finished in second place behind the legendary Rudolf Caracciola.

After the merger between Benz and Daimler in 1926, Fritz Nallinger moved to Untertürkheim as one of the first full-time Daimler-Benz AG engineer designers. He took over the management of the experimental facility, overseeing marine, rail, aircraft and heavy vehicle engine development under Ferdinand Porsche.

Within only a couple of years, Ferdinand Porsche resigned his position as technical director, and was succeeded by Hans Nibel. This was very fortuitous for Nallinger's career, as Nibel and Nallinger had been the best of friends for many years, as well as associates through Benz & Cie. Nibel gave Nallinger free rein to develop his own ideas on future vehicle and engine concepts, in particular on development work in the experimental operations department.

He started the first experiments with the Vollschwingachsen ('full swing axles') chassis, which were used for the first time in the 'small Mercedes' W170 in 1931. At the same time he was working on the development of the fuel-efficient, high-speed diesel engine, which was released in the type 260D in 1936; and his work with Arthur Berger and Albert Friedrich produced the first ever direct injection gasoline aircraft engine, which produced 1,000bhp. The LZ 129 *Hindenburg* was the first airship to be fitted with a 16-cylinder version of one of his engines.

In 1935, Nallinger was appointed Chief Technical Officer, and took over the overall management of large engine construction with the design and test department for aircraft, marine, railcar and army engines. In 1940 he became a full member of the Executive Board responsible for the entire Daimler-Benz programme.

During the early war period of 1939 to 1942 Nallinger developed the DB600 series of engines, the first X-shaped inline engine with 24 cylinders and rotary valve control, which went on to develop close to 2,500bhp (1,800kW). During his tenure, until 1945, 100,000 aircraft engines were produced.

From the end of World War II until the beginning of 1948 his mandate with Daimler was suspended because of a special commission from the French government to work on the further development of large aircraft turbine engines at J. Szydlowski in

Pau. However, by May 1948 he had resumed his duties as a board member and technical director of Daimler-Benz AG, now with overall responsibility for design, testing and development of all vehicle lines of the house.

The following years of his tenure were marked by many technical milestones, including self-supporting bodies, sub-frame technology, single-joint pendulum rear axle, recirculating ball steering, valve-controlled short-stroke engines, fuel injection, automatic transmission and disc brakes. During this time a large number of new passenger car models were developed, which significantly impacted all international automotive engineering.

In the 1950s, Daimler-Benz returned to Grand Prix racing. A team under the leadership of Fritz Nallinger, together with Hans Scherenberg and Rudolf Uhlenhaut, his closest technical employees, developed a new racing car: as a W196 it became one of the most successful of the post-war epoch. In 1963 the Type W100 600 was introduced, a top-of-the-range model that followed the tradition of the 'big Mercedes' of the pre-war period, in which most of the technical innovation was developed by Nallinger and his team.

Fritz Nallinger frequently sent his brightest engineers to work with universities on the continuous improvement programmes, particularly on fast-changing production technology and advancements in design and construction. What became known in the 1980s as 'Kaizen' or 'betterment' was for Fritz Nallinger in the mid-1930s the result of scientific/technical collaboration between scholars and engineers. It had such an impact on everything that was done at Daimler-Benz that the results could still be felt many decades after his retirement.

Fritz Nallinger retired at the end of 1965. Up to that point, more than 300 patents were made in his name.

Fritz Nallinger and Rudolf Uhlenhaut beside the W196R.

W196R Type Monza Streamliner.

BELOW: **A later picture of the Sir Stirling Moss 722 W196R, and the standard W196 body style.**

The two versions of the W196R were quite effortlessly interchangeable. Chassis number ten, for instance, glittering with former glory in its brand-new aluminium body one day, was entered with open wheels in the 1955 Argentine Grand Prix (driven by Hans Herrmann, Karl Kling and Moss to fourth place) and the Dutch Grand Prix (with Moss at the wheel, finishing as runner-up), and fully streamlined again, performed tests in Monza. Which version was used depended upon the peculiarities of the circuit, the strategy chosen, but also the likes and dislikes of the respective driver.

The W196 'Streamliner' had the unfortunate tendency to understeer, and far too much. Its wheelbase was modified a few times to try to solve this problem, but without success. It was driven by Fangio and Kling, as well as by Stirling Moss and Hans Herrmann.

In just twelve Grand Prix races, the Mercedes W196 achieved eight pole positions and nine wins. The car also helped Fangio to win the F1 World Champion title in 1954 and 1955.

THE MERCEDES-BENZ RACING-CAR TRANSPORTER

It was not just the legendary Mercedes-Benz Silver Arrows that attracted attention in the early 1950s. With the 'world's fastest racing-car transporter', Mercedes-Benz also caused a sensation off the racetrack.

Preparations for a return to motor racing also involved setting up a service vehicle for trackside repairs and maintenance, and constructing appropriate trucks to transport the racing cars. Racing manager Alfred Neubauer recalled a large 28/95bhp Mercedes touring car, which at his suggestion DMG had converted into a racing-car transporter in 1924. Its original purpose had been to take an 8-cylinder Mercedes racing car to the Monza circuit, rather than have it drive there under its own power.

In the early 1950s, Neubauer planned development of similar state-of-the-art high-speed racing-car transport. The specifications for the transporter were simple: it had to be fast and reliable generally, but also fast even fully laden, with a grand prix car or SLR racing sports car on its back. The transporter would need plenty of power, but also had to be fitted with appropriate brakes.

The one-off vehicle was built using tried-and-tested components: the 300S donated its X-form tubular frame as the basis, and the engine came from the 300SL. The aerodynamic body contributed to a top speed of 165km/h (103mph) and gave the vehicle an imposing appearance. At 3,050mm (120in), the wheelbase was also impressive.

By mid-1954 the rapid transporter was ready, painted in the brand's blue livery. For racing department employees it

A 28/95bhp Mercedes touring car converted to a transporter.

was a blessing, since it gave them longer prior to an event to get the cars race-ready and transport them to the venue. They were also able to return a damaged or defective car back to the factory more quickly, giving more time for repairs.

The 'blue miracle', as it became known, was a sensation on the roads and motorways of Europe; indeed, in the paddock it attracted almost as much attention as the racing cars themselves. There was no better way to put the fear of God into the opposition than to arrive at a race track with a transporter that was almost as fast as the race cars themselves.

After the withdrawal of Daimler-Benz from motor sport in 1955, the rapid transporter even went on tour to the USA and was shown at numerous exhibitions. It returned to Europe in 1957 and was intended to be put into the Mercedes-Benz Museum collection, along with the 300SLR already on display. However, the two vehicles together were too heavy for the museum structure, so the once proud racing transporter served time as a test and support vehicle on the Untertürkheim test track until repairs were no longer cost efficient. On the instructions of Rudolf Uhlenhaut, the vehicle was scrapped in December 1967.

In 1993 the decision was taken to rebuild the one-off vehicle. However, since there were few sketches or plans for the racing transporter, these had to be reconstructed in meticulous detail first, using as much of the archived information as possible.

The transporter at the trackside was enough to breathe fear into the opposition.

The 're-imaged' transporter painted in the original brand's blue livery.

The experts had experimented, working out the steering and shift geometry, redesigning the wiring harness, constructing the cab's rear window and shaping the metal panels – and after almost 6,000 man hours and seven long years, the racing car transporter was finally presented at the Goodwood Festival of Speed in southern England in 2001.

Its Coupé design with its SL-style front grille permitted it to be a part of this book. It was also the 'commercial' vehicle that encouraged the decision that buses and most commercial vehicles manufactured by Mercedes-Benz would sport the same grille, commencing with the O321H bus.

The O312H commercial vehicles received the new, open mouth front end.

THE UHLENHAUT COUPÉ

The Coupé version of the 300SLR racing sports car was developed in 1955 with the intention of creating a closed vehicle for endurance racing, thus reducing the stresses and strains exerted on the driver. Against this backdrop, two chassis of the 300SLR were fitted with Coupé bodies.

Unfortunately the closed version was never used for racing. On the one hand this was because the sixth Carrera Pan-Americana, the race for which the Coupé would have been highly suitable, had to be cancelled in August 1955 after objections were raised by the Mexican government. It was also because of the catastrophic events at the 1955 Le Mans 24-Hour race when eighty-three spectators died: as a result of this, Daimler-Benz withdrew from racing altogether from October 1955.

The fact that the 300SLR Coupé was not just left to gather dust was down to Rudolf Uhlenhaut, who ultimately had also created this driving machine.

An excellent driver himself, Uhlenhaut covered some incredible distances and made numerous journeys across Europe in one of the two examples of the car. This proved to be an impressive demonstration of the reliability and high everyday practicality of this top-class 300bhp racing sports car.

One concession that was made for road use was the huge exhaust silencer fitted on the right-hand side, which helped to reduce the ear-piercing sound effects to a more bearable level. This was the version of the 'Uhlenhaut Coupé', as the car is generally known today, that was subjected to an endurance test of over 3,500km (2,175 miles) in 1956 by journalists from the Swiss magazine *Automobil Revue*. In his test report, published in the issue dated 12 December 1956, the test driver was nothing less than enthusiastic about the qualities of the 300SLR:

> We are driving in a car that overtakes the vehicles of other road users in a matter of seconds, for which 200km/h on a quiet motorway is a stroll in the park, a car whose cornering safety seems to defy the laws of centrifugal force, a car that uses less petrol at 160km/h than many a saloon travelling at a more modest speed, but also a car that can never be bought, and which no average driver would ever buy, either.

Uhlenhaut covered thousands of miles in the Coupé.

There have already been vehicles offering similar or even better performance. These have included supercharged racing cars, which devoured their 150 litres of fuel over a distance of 100km, which could only be mastered by a few top drivers, and which after every race required minor or sometimes more extensive maintenance work.

The 300SLR has none of the sensitivity of its predecessors. Our test car cruised through towns and villages in Switzerland, Germany and Italy, tackled steep mountain roads at full throttle, endured the severest of acceleration and braking trials on the track at Monza, covered long motorway stretches at an average speed approaching 200km/h, reached a top speed of 284km/h, once even 290km/h, and in the meantime served as a pure means of transport without suffering even the slightest breakdown.

The fact that Daimler-Benz has complete confidence in the durability of what is currently its most powerful model is already reflected in its willingness to loan an SLR to 'AR' for an endurance test. The 12,000km showing on the speedometer when the vehicle was handed over, clocked up by Rudolf Uhlenhaut on trips across Europe and as far north as Sweden, are even stronger evidence of the fact that this technically remarkable car, which is happy to use any commercially available premium grade fuel, demonstrates a level of reliability that is unique in the field of high-performance vehicle construction.

We could hardly have imagined anything less exciting than the high-speed trial. We waited at four a.m. on a September morning on the Munich–Eching motorway, until the police had cordoned it off. After two warm-up runs, off we went. How does the car handle at 290km/h? As straight as a die, without even batting an eyelid. This was taking sensationalism to the extreme. That's because the power of the 300SLR is not too high for either the car or a driver who knows how to make the most of it sensibly. Even on our narrow, congested roads, in a car with the performance and safety of the 300SLR, while observing conventional road etiquette, it is still possible to achieve average speeds that seem Utopian.

The significance of such a racing sports car amounts to more than either its successes or the excitement it arouses in fans of sporting masterpieces. It shows rather more that automotive engineering still has some unexploited technical opportunities up its sleeve.

An automotive manufacturer could hardly wish for a better evaluation of its products.

300SLR Coupé Specifications 1955

Wheelbase	2,370mm (93in)
Front track	1,330mm (52in)
Rear track	1,380mm (54in)
Length	4,350mm (172in)
Width	1,750mm (69in)
Height	1,210mm (48in)
Vehicle weight	1,117kg (2,463lb)
Maximum speed	284km/h (176mph)
Engine type	M196S
Displacement	2982cc
Maximum output	310bhp at 7,400rpm
Fuel system	Direct injection, Bosch 8-plunger injection pump

The 'Uhlenhaut Coupé' is now part of the vehicle collection at the Mercedes-Benz Museum, and even today still attracts a great deal of public and media interest when it appears at events.

CHAPTER THREE

THE SPORTS COUPÉ

THE SL NAME

When the SL model-range car was introduced, Mercedes-Benz made no announcement as to what the abbreviation 'SL' meant, so inevitably there was some initial confusion as to whether 'S' meant 'Super' or 'Sport'. The 'L' stands for 'leicht', which, as a German adverb, may be translated as 'easy'; however, no one would believe that the car would be referred to as either a 'Super Easy' or a 'Sport Easy', so it was assumed that 'leicht' stood for the German adverb meaning 'light in weight'.

The Super Light bodyshell may or may not be the reason for the SL name.

A German car magazine in 2012 declared that the abbreviation 'SL' 'was personally signed off by Rudolf Uhlenhaut' as 'Super Light'. However, this contradicted the information in a book called *Mercedes-Benz 300SL* written by Engelen, Riedner and Seufert, which was produced in close co-operation with Rudolf Uhlenhaut and stated that the abbreviation always meant 'Sport Leicht'; Mercedes-Benz even used 'Sport' on their company website until 2017. But then, just to confuse matters further, Mercedes-Benz started to refer to the SL name as 'Super Leicht' again.

THE 1954 300SL GULLWING

The 300SL Gullwing was the first true sports Coupé Grand Tourer. The 300SL W198 became one of the most iconic cars in the history of automobiles from the moment it hit the International Motor Sports Show in New York on 6 February 1954. What the E-Type was to Jaguar, and the DB5 was to Aston Martin, the 300SL Gullwing was to Benz: this vehicle alone came to define the entire Mercedes-Benz experience. If there was a downside, it would be that its cost was in the 'supercar range' at DM29,000: this was double that of a Jaguar XK140 of the same year. In France one could buy ten Citroen 2CVs for the same money.

The 300SL Coupé was born straight out of the Mercedes' sports programme, which had been revived in the early 1950s with the aforementioned W194. Ultimately it was a detuned road-going Grand Prix car aimed at the quickly rising post-war upper classes; however, it became an excep-

All four incarnations of the first SL Coupé (from right to left): W194, W194/11, W198, W196 Uhlenhaut Coupé.

tional car that not only marked its place in time, but also in the history of the automobile.

It was called the 300SL due to its 3-litre engine, and as the W194 before it, the W198 had Uhlenhaut's innovative tubular frame; this distributed the weight of the car evenly and in a balanced way, while increasing its rigidity. Its 1,285kg (2,833lb) body was made from steel, but the bonnet, doors and bootlid were all a special type of magnesium aluminium alloy. And if any customer thought the car was too heavy, they could opt for an all-aluminium body, which decreased weight by 80kg (176lb); however, the high price limited the numbers built to only twenty-nine for this option. The 'Super Leicht' body was aerodynamically and breathtakingly beautiful; even during early tests, it achieved the title of the 'fastest production car in the world'.

By far the most salient feature was the unusual top-hinged doors: taken from the W194 racing car, these were nicknamed 'gullwing' in English-speaking countries. This unusual design solution was by no means a publicity stunt, although it was indeed used to the maximum during marketing and display – but as had been the case with the W194, from a construction point of view this was an absolute necessity. To keep the strength integrity of the over-height tubular space frame, which weighed a mere 50kg (110lb), conventional doors were simply not feasible. In the early W194 the gullwing doors were little more than a hatch where the side window would have been, but this was impractical in races, where it was necessary to get in and out of the vehicle quickly, so the gullwing door was extended below the waistline; this also gave it a slightly more 'birdlike' stance.

To solve the problem of getting into and out of the seat easily, Uhlenhaut designed an ingenious steering wheel that broke at the knuckle so as to allow access for the driver's legs. However, the gullwing doors did not allow for conventional sliding glass, so they were made removable; the occupants were then responsible for storing them in a pocket provided for this purpose.

The streamlined body concealed several other novelties: while all other super cars were still fuelled using carburettors, for the first time a Bosch fuel-injection system was used in a production car; this resulted in an increase of around 40bhp as compared with the carburettor version W194. It also produced a mere 15ltr/100km (18.8mpg), which was very reasonable if compared with the 20ltr/100km (14.1mpg) of a Ferrari or Jaguar of the same period.

Its perfect weight distribution, coupled with its independent rear suspension, led to a tremendous driving experience, unlike any other. The twin overhead-camshaft 6-cylinder engine was inclined towards the side in order to ensure a flat and streamlined front design. The lightweight construction kept the weight of the complete car, together with spare tyre, tools and fuel weight, to only 1,295kg (2,855lb), and depending on rear axle transmission, a maximum speed of between 235km/h (145mph) and 260km/h (160mph) could easily be achieved.

The International Motor Sports Show in New York on 6 February 1954.

The W198 side by side with the W194.

The M198 showing its innovative fuel-injection system.

BELOW: **The M198 twin overhead-camshaft engine was inclined at an angle to help improve the aerodynamics.**

From August 1954 until May 1957, 1,400 units were built in Sindelfingen, twenty-nine of them with a light-alloy body; one test vehicle was built using a GRP body. This individual car can be easily recognized by two features: there are additional indicators on the front mudguards, which had also been carried over from the 220a, and there were bigger gaps between its door panels, so there is no flush surface when the doors are closed.

300SL Gullwing Specifications 1954–1957

Model	W198 I
Production	Aug 1954–May 1957
Units produced	1,400 (of which 29 with light-alloy body)
Wheelbase	2,400mm (94.5in)
Front track	1,385mm (54.5in)
Rear track	1,435mm (56.5in)
Length	4,520mm (178in)
Width	1,790mm (70.5in)
Height	1,300mm (51in)
Vehicle weight	1,515kg (3,340lb)
Engine type	M196S
Displacement	2982cc
Maximum speed	260km/h (162mph)
Acceleration	0–100km/h in 10sec
Maximum Output	310bhp at 7,400rpm
Fuel system	Direct injection, Bosch six-plunger injection pump

MAX HOFFMAN, US DISTRIBUTOR

A number of hyperbolical myths surround Max Hoffman's input into the early stages of the W198's construction, and these should be corrected.

Hoffman's Dream Car

It was said that the W198 was Hoffman's 'dream car', and that it was only as a result of his demands that it was made; however, this is simply not true. Hoffman was a US distributor for only a year and had no authority to make such demands – although according to the minutes of a contractual meeting in September 1953 he did manage to ruffle a few feathers amongst the board members with his outspoken criticism of their 'model policy'. He also asked about the possibility of an 'open-top sports car with a Mercedes star on the bonnet', knowing the American public would love such a vehicle.

However, the oft-repeated assertion that he paid a large deposit, there and then, to a cash-strapped Daimler-Benz AG for 1,000 W198 units, was incorrect: there is absolutely no evidence of this whatsoever.

W198 Sales and Popularity were all down to Max Hoffman

Although the part that Max Hoffman played in getting the W198 recognized in the USA is undeniable, it was not entirely his doing. The Gullwing Sport Coupé was already in the consciousness of the American people due to the success of its sister, the W194, in the Carrera Pan-Americana race in Mexico, and with his marketing acumen he knew it was time to make the most of this enthusiasm. Yes, around 80 per cent of all W198 (1,400) were delivered to the USA; however, by 1957 Hoffman had broken his contract with Daimler, and subsequently it fell to 'Studebaker-Packard', with its network of 2,500 dealers throughout the USA, to provide for the distribution of both the W198 Coupé and Roadster as well as the later W121 (190SL). The import was eventually taken over by the newly founded 'Daimler-Benz North America'.

The story does not stop there, and Max Hoffman did indeed get his wish for his 'open top Mercedes'. Initially it was essentially a mini version of the 300SL, but more related to the W120/121 saloon. It was built from 1955, in the form of the W121, a 4-cylinder version called the 190SL, but its immediate success sounded the death knell for the 300SL Coupé, and production slowed to a stop in May 1957. For those who still wanted the 3-litre, Mercedes decided to continue to build the W198 in Roadster form only, although it was offered with a hardtop for an extra DM1,500 for those who wanted it with both a Coupé and open-top feel.

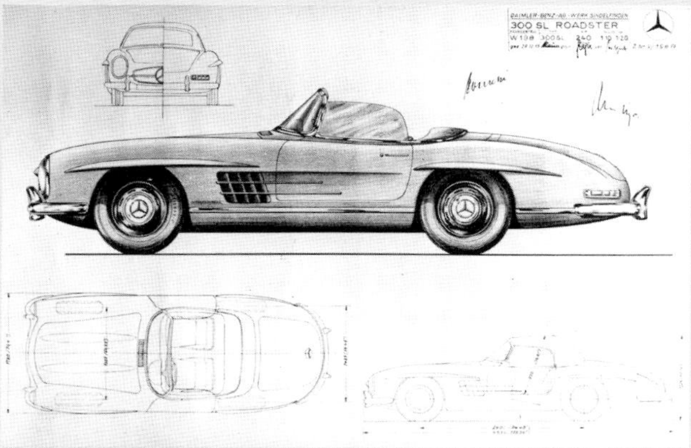

ABOVE LEFT: **A Hoffman dealership in the USA.**

ABOVE RIGHT: **The designs for the 300SL roadster also signed off by Hoffman.**

THE 1960 MERCEDES-BENZ W118/W119 PROJECT

The origins of the Mercedes-Benz W118/W119 project – the compact Benz that never was – lie in the 'Wirtschaftswunder', or post-war German economic miracle. Between 1950 and 1959 the country's living standards virtually doubled, while the GDP increased by almost 8 per cent per annum. Car ownership grew by 700 per cent between 1945 and the mid-1960s, while in 1954, the turnover of Daimler-Benz was over a billion marks each year.

In February 1953, under the direction of Fritz Nallinger, the Daimler-Benz board decided to build a car that was 15–20 per cent less than the 170V in terms of materials and labour costs. It is said to have been developed from two existing models, the 170V and 170D (the W136), after the 170S had been replaced by the new 180 (the W120), the 'Ponton-Mercedes' in the autumn of that year.

By 1956, the vehicle internally called the W122 had reached considerable maturity and had what it took to be a great success; however, it was not to be, and it was shelved later in 1956. On the one hand, Daimler-Benz had taken over Auto Union, and there was therefore a certain conflict of interests between a large DKW and a small Mercedes-Benz. On the other hand, the models of the W111 series were about to be launched, and their new safety concept made a W122 series, on the conventional platform of the W120 Ponton series, appear outdated.

From today's perspective, the appearance of the 122 series is extremely interesting, and it has been included in this book as it was the first production car to consider using the Sport-Light grille. Although it didn't proceed beyond this date of 1956, development continued on what was to be called the W118/119, which had a Coupé option, once again using the SL grille.

Not one to 'let go' of a concept easily, in 1958 Daimler-Benz's chief engineer Fritz Nallinger asked Ludwig Kraus of the 'Construction Development' to develop an in-house mid-sized car: the result was an extremely elegant, front-wheel-drive saloon in two- or four-door guise. The initial idea was for it to be powered by a 1.5-litre 'boxer' engine (the M118), but the prototype would eventually gain a newly developed 1.7-litre inline high-compression engine as the M119. (This code was used later for a V8.)

When it was unveiled in about 1960, it seemed logical that it would be made by Auto Union, as they had extensive experience of building small cars. However, there was also the issue of their F102, due to be launched in a couple of years, and because of the agreement between Daimler and the Auto Union, the W119 was shelved in favour of the F102 and the upcoming F103.

Design model for a possible Mercedes-Benz W122 model series, dating from the mid-1950s. It did not reach the series production stage (the inset shows a slight frontal change).

ABOVE LEFT: **W118/9 prototype Coupé with a variation on the SL grille.**

ABOVE RIGHT: **The W118/9 Coupé rear took its cues from the W113.**

Had the compact Mercedes-Benz made its debut in 1963, rather than the F102, its looks alone would almost undoubtedly have been a sales advantage in their own right. There was none of the W111's imposing flamboyance: instead there was low-key coachwork with a large glass area, and a notable lack of the 'traditional' radiator grille – more than one observer has compared it with the W113 'Pagoda'. A further controversial aspect of the design was the engine layout, but Ford's 1962 P4 Taunus had demonstrated that the average middle-class German motorist would have been ready for a medium-sized front-wheel-drive saloon car.

Fritz Nallinger, who was responsible for research and development as a member of the Executive Board until 1965, continued to push hard for a smaller Mercedes, but the road to a Baby Benz was arduous. As was the case ten years earlier for the birth of the SL, the decisive impetus would come from the USA.

On the evidence of the surviving photographs, the Mercedes-Benz W118/W119 would have tempted thousands of up-and-coming accountants and lawyers away from their Neue Klasse BMWs. But a 'Baby Benz' would not come to fruition until the mid-1970s, when the impact of the OPEC oil crisis meant that it became imperative to offer a more fuel-efficient model that would also serve as a 'second car'.

In 1976 work commenced on the W201. It made its bow in November 1982 as the 190 and 190E, and these were arguably the first compact Mercedes-Benz since the demise of the 170V nearly three decades earlier.

THE PININFARINA COUPÉ

The 113 Series 'One-Off' Pininfarina Coupé, 1963

With the W198 (300SL) and the W121 (190SL), Daimler had achieved a strong foothold in the North American automotive market. Having discontinued production of the W198 Coupé in 1957, they concentrated on continuing the SL body and grille shape in a 'Roadster with additional hardtop' style, firstly with the W121 (the 190SL) until 1963, and then with the W113 (the pagoda SL). However, times were changing, and there was a marked decline in the fashion of the open-top sports car. It is supposed that this was in part due to the proliferation of quality, factory-installed air-conditioning systems in standard vehicles – but it was also due to the constant tightening of many federal safety regulations, and these included measures to prevent 'roll-over' accidents. At one point North America threatened to ban convertibles completely.

Daimler responded to this with the W113. This was the first sports car with a 'safety body', based on Béla Barényi's extensive work on vehicle safety: it had a rigid passenger cell, and designated crumple zones with impact-absorbing front and rear sections built into the vehicle structure; it also included the innovative 'Pagoda' removable hardtop safety roof. The interior was 'rounded', with all hard corners and edges removed, as in the W111 sedan, to come into line with stricter 'passive safety' regulations.

The Pininfarina 113 Coupé, as presented at the Paris Motor Show.

Brochure pictures of the 113 Coupé.
PININFARINA

Even so, Daimler were concerned enough to consider reintroducing a Coupé body into the line, and commissioned Italian 'carrozzeria' Pininfarina to create a design for a 230SL Coupé of their own, while retaining enough of the original lines to make the car instantly recognizable. Several of Pininfarina's stylists pitched their ideas for the revised 230SL Coupé. Eventually it was young American designer Tom Tjaarda who was awarded the assignment.

In 1964, at the 51st International Paris Show, the silver Mercedes-Benz 230SL Coupé Pininfarina was brought before the public. It was well received by the audience, and about thirty potential customers turned to Pininfarina with a request for a production car. However, the Coupé remained a single copy. For reasons unknown, this was to be the car's only public appearance, and it was not followed up by even a small production run.

The 1970 Mercedes W109 300SEL 6.3 Coupé Pininfarina

This model is included in this Coupé book purely because it was a one-off, and it ended up being a Coupé with an SL-style grille. However, it had nothing to do with Mercedes-Benz. In truth, having seen what Sergio Pininfarina had done to the W113 a few years previously, a wealthy multinational executive from Holland (not 'Heineken', as has been reported) did ask Mercedes-Benz to build one on a special basis for him. But they refused, and Italy was his next port of call.

It was said that the client loved the reliability of heavy, solid Mercedes cars, but craved something unusual. He purchased, and took delivery of a W109 300SEL 6.3, and delivered it straight to Turin without a brief. The Pininfarina design team had a free hand.

The wheelbase, track, overall length and the height of the doors remained unchanged; however, the A-post was repositioned further back in the profile of the car, and the front windscreen was adjusted to a much sharper angle, while the rear screen was positioned further forward, creating a more Coupé-like size interior. A completely redesigned steel roof was made by hand, as was the bonnet, boot and wings. The front doors were extended, while the rear doors were absorbed into the body form.

Brochure pictures of the W109 Coupé.
PININFARINA

The combination of Mercedes' greatest saloon car, 400,000 guilders (about 100,000 US dollars), and the world's renowned automotive design studio should have been a recipe for success – but it was not to be. The result was a shape to forget, and everyone tried to – the car wasn't even added to the Pininfarina history books. It looked as though the Pininfarina team had conjoined the front end of a 1965 Ford Galaxie to the rear end of a Rolls-Royce Camargue, which Pininfarina had a hand in designing. Mercedes-Benz refused even to talk about it, and the businessman's family did not want to be associated with the car, even refusing to travel with the owner.

Even though the drivetrain and underpinnings remained that of the W109, the interior was all Pininfarina. The firewall and dash remained as the original, but the seats, both front and rear, were completely remodelled; they were upholstered in cognac/almond-coloured leather, contrasted with a 'very Pininfarina' emerald green carpet.

Whatever your opinions of this 'one-off' Coupé, from a perspective fifty years on, to some extent it was ahead of its time and much maligned for it. At the time Mercedes-Benz wallowed in the SL-style Coupé concept, and hadn't even considered using a large, luxurious saloon as a base for the

The front SL-style grille was hand-made and specially constructed for this car, giving it that official Mercedes Coupé appearance.

Pininfarina influences can be seen in the Bruno Sacco C126 design.

300SEL 6.3 Pininfarina Coupé Specification 1970

Sold/number built	1970/1
Construction	All-steel body
Engine	
6332cc, V8, 2 valves per cylinder, Bosch mechanical fuel injection	
Max power	250bhp @ 4,000rpm
Max torque	369lb ft @ 2,800rpm
Transmission	Four-speed automatic
Drive	Rear-wheel drive
Suspension	
Front independent, double wishbone, air spring and anti-roll bar	
Rear swing arm with air spring and anti-roll bar	
Steering	Power-assisted rack-and-pinion
Brakes	Ventilated discs with servo
Weight	1,900kg (4,190lb)
Performance	
0–62mph	6.6sec
Top speed	225km/h (140mph)
Fuel consumption	21ltr/100km (13.5mpg)
Price new	400,000 Dutch guilders approx. (£45,946) ($100,000)

Coupé – but even when they did, it wasn't difficult to recognize the similarities in design.

THE 107 SERIES SLC COUPÉS, 1971–1981

Before the W198 Super Light Coupé, Daimler had always produced a marketable Coupé from their high-end saloon range; however, the specialness of the 300SL proved to Daimler that customers were excited by a sport Coupé. The 300SL changed the way forward from that moment on. It introduced not just one new Mercedes to the model range, but two: the SL Roadster and the SL Coupé. The last saloon-derived version, the W111/112, was discontinued

107 Series SLC Coupés: Units Produced 1971–1981

350SLC	13,925
280SLC	10,666
450SLC	31,739
450SLC 5.0 & 500SLC	2,769
380SLC	3,789

in July 1971, so it was time to continue the 'Super Light Coupé'.

Although Paul Bracq and Giorgio Battistellas can be credited with instigating the early design drawings of the R107 shape, the final shape credit goes to Joseph Gallitzendörfer, under the auspices of Friedrich Geiger. It was thought that the early renderings were too close to that of the W113, and Daimler wanted to move forwards with a more Teutonic style, more in line with the 'new generation' of Mercedes family automobiles, including what was to be the first real 'Sonderklasse', the W116. Friedrich Geiger said: 'Our European designs should appeal to American eyes, not the other way round.'

Heated debates rumbled on through the late 1960s at the Daimler Board concerning the new SL. Hans Scherenberg was very aware that the North American Safety Board could put an outright ban on all open-top automobiles, and this would shut down the American market to the SL range overnight, which in turn would result in potential losses.

A number of manufacturers were introducing either Coupé versions of their sports cars, or the Targa-style two-seater. For example, BMW introduced the 911 T-top in 1965; and when Triumph decided to replace the TR6, they did so with the TR7, a two-seater fixed-head Coupé – even their new two-seater sports car, the Stag, had a roll-over bar.

Mercedes had started developing various design studies – the Battistella/Bracq/Sacco SL/X, for example, and even the C111 range – and in early Bracq drawings of a potential W113 replacement Scherenberg seriously considered a T-bar option for the R107. However, after much debate with the board he hedged his bets by offering up a fixed-head version.

Daimler presented the Type 350SLC at the Paris Motor Show in October 1971, and production would commence

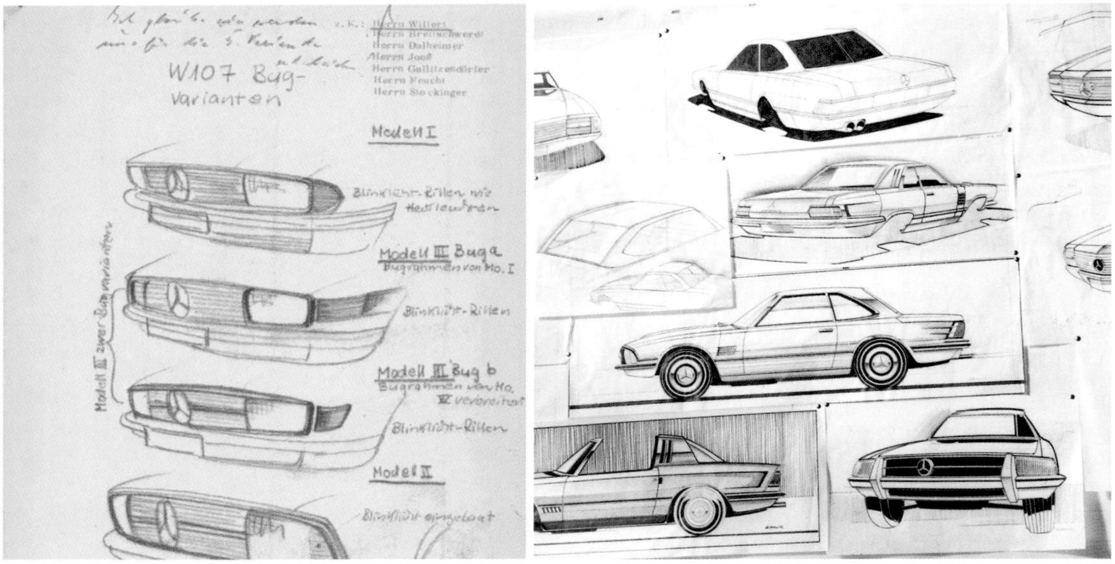

Brainstorming multiple designs have always been a Mercedes thing.

Final rendering of the C107 by Joseph Gallitzendörfer.

around February 1972. In contrast to its predecessors, the new Coupé was neither based on a limousine of the upper class, nor was it an uncompromising sports automobile: it was based on its sister model presented only six months earlier, the R107SL.

It became very clear over the nine years of production of the R113 – where it started as a sprightly sports car and ended up as a luxury 'Grand Tourer' – what customers wanted and expected. No longer was it sufficient just to produce a dynamic sports car that sacrificed all for straight-line speed. Passive and active safety were the new watchwords of all manufacturers, and customers were beginning to expect it.

Although the R113 in the guise of the 280SL was still selling remarkably well, the body was based on that of the W110 (Fintail) and was no longer considered 'up to date' in either innovation or safety standards. It still had the old single-joint swing-axle set-up at the rear, which, although in its time was ground-breaking, by now was falling behind in road-holding capabilities. The W114 had already been introduced into the range in 1968, with its vastly superior semi-trailing arm set-up.

Daimler presented the Type 350SLC at the Paris Motor Show in October 1971.

Gone was the iconic V-shaped radiator grille, and in its place was an opportunity to highlight their success in the motor-sport arena: the continued use of the open mouth, with the Mercedes star placed full centre.

Tentative attempts at fitting a V8 engine to the W113 had also failed due to weight and size issues, and Daimler were desperate to add a V8 sports car to the range.

The W114/5 had introduced the so-called 'new generation models', and was to be the harbinger of the first dedicated luxury 'Sonderklasse' automobile, the W116; so in line with the Daimler philosophy of model 'vertical affinity' and 'horizontal homogeneity', the new SL had to shadow these models in both style and innovation.

From the very beginning the brief for the new SL series was to be more of a grand touring, cross-country cruiser, incorporating prestige, comfort, speed, reliability, and above all else safety, over and above its predecessor.

It was at this time that the nomenclature was changed a little, because the R107 belied its SL moniker in that at around 1,600kg (3,530lb) it wasn't even 'light', let alone 'super-light' – so it was often referred to in the media as a 'Sport-light' as opposed to the 'Super-light'.

The last Mercedes to have created such waves of emotion as did the R107 at its release in the spring of 1971 was the W198, and in the same way it had its supporters as well as its detractors. Not everyone appreciated its simple, modern, Teutonic, wedge-shaped design – even its SL-style grille and horizontally framed headlights were much maligned in the press – but what came to be recognized as time went on was its timelessness: its forward-looking design remained relevant for a whopping eighteen years, longer than any other Mercedes of the time, only surpassed more recently by the G-Wagen.

In terms of dimensions, the R107 outperformed its predecessor by a few centimetres: the wheelbase was 6cm (2.4in) longer, the overall length was increased by 9cm (3.5in) and the outer width by 3.5cm (1.4in). The R107 employed the exact suspension systems of the W114/15 saloons, giving it a narrower track width on the front and rear axles, and making it less stocky looking than that of the W113. The wheels were located further inside, giving the overall visual impression of the body a less sporty look, but more subtle and elegant.

The new double-wishbone independent wheel suspension with the maintenance-free ball joints was used at the front, and the semi-trailing arm construction – called 'diagonal pendulum axle' – at the rear. In contrast to that of the /8 ('stroke eight'), the SL used a recirculating-ball steering system with power assistance as standard, and also rode on wider wheels.

Many of the details were revolutionary in their way, too: the open mouth-like radiator sat above a second elongated mouth to keep the large V8 well cooled, but also allowed a through-flow of air that, with the newly developed cowl panels at the A-pillars, serving as water-deflection gutters, guaranteed good visibility in the rain, and also kept the side windows clean in bad weather. Wide, wraparound front direction indicators improved their visibility from the side, and having played with a few design ideas such as side air-ducting around the rear tail-lights to keep them clean, a less

The R107 at its release in the USA.

frivolous idea of using castellated profiled rear light lenses was all that was needed to maintain a high percentage of visibility even when exposed to heavy dirt and road grime.

The many safety-oriented construction details that were used for the first time in the R107 naturally transferred to the C107. The fuel tank was relocated above the rear axle to protect it from rear-end shunts. The extremely strong frame, coupled with a firmly inclined windscreen, made the body incredibly strong in the event of an 'overturn accident', but also gave the automobiles an airy, free look that a rollover bar would have lost.

With development in 'passive safety' testing the interior was completely revised: similar to that of the W113, the wooden accoutrements and toggle switches were replaced by a strongly padded, deformable dashboard, concealed or flush switches and controls, as well as the new four-spoke security wheel with impact absorber and broad impact cushion provided for maximum crash protection.

The washboard pattern in the lower area of the body flanks was also introduced to help prevent dirty water from whirling up from the front wheels, and to keep it away from the door handles and side windows.

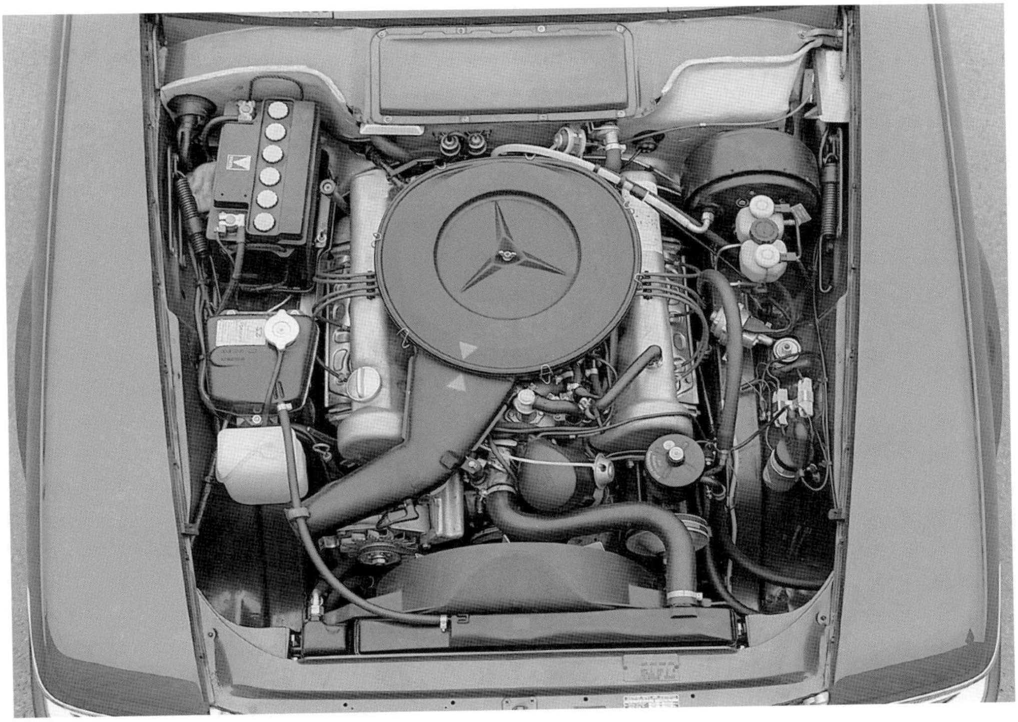

The M116 V8 engine.

None of the W113 engines were used in the R107; the sohc 6-cylinder used previously had seen better days, and the new emission regulations would never have been achieved. Even though there was a new dohc 6-cylinder (M110) in development, it wasn't yet ready – but the R107 had been designed with only one engine in mind, and that was the M116 as used in the W109 300SEL 3.5.

THE SPORT-LIGHT COUPÉ 350SLC

Six months after the R107 Roadster was introduced, the family friendly version, the 350SLC, was presented at the Paris Car Show in October 1971. The Coupé used the Daimler's internal designation model code of C107.

Exterior Design

Except for the hard roof of the SLC, both variants were identical up to the door's rear edge. The differences showed themselves in the rear half of the car. The wheelbase was elongated by 360mm (14in) in comparison to that of the SL, and this allowed a larger interior and accommodated four full-sized seats. The resultant proportions, with the rear axle placed further back, meant that many found the SLC Coupé to be the prettier car.

With its excellently proportioned lines, many found the SLC prettier than the R107.

The design of the rear side window is particularly characteristic, and again not without controversy. In order to visually balance the C-post body-to-glass area, and also to enable the window to retract fully out of sight, it was necessary to split the pane, which is not that big anyway, into two sections: the front piece can be fully sunk into the body, but the rear piece remains. It is backed with a kind of plastic blind, which prevents occupants being viewed from the outside, but allows them to look out to the outside, although the view is limited.

Interior Design

The interior is just as new as the exterior, and here, too, like the R107, the primary concern is passive accident safety. The pretty dashboard is made of painted sheet metal; the two large round instruments and exotic wood parts give way to a modern, foamed instrument binnacle; and the traditional steering wheel has a round impact surface and a modern four-spoke valance.

The improved heating and ventilation system also makes the generation change clear: it is a complex, air-controlled system that is particularly pleasant and easy to control. A new feature is the 'surface heating' on the vehicle sides, in which warm air is conducted into and through the doors, thus reducing the incidence of cool spots and minimizing condensation build-up on the side window glass.

To make it easier for passengers in the rear to get in and out, the C107 seats use automatic vacuum-operated locking backrests, which allows reasonably easy access to the

The innovative blinds gave privacy to the rear, but were angled sufficiently for the driver to be able to see behind.

relatively spacious rear. This is similar to the seats of the Coupés of the W111 series and the 8-series Coupé, which the new 350SLC replaces.

The Engine

Only eighteen months after producing the 3.5-litre M116 engine 350SLC, Daimler introduced the 4.5-litre M117 450SLC, offering a vastly improved 225bhp. The same engine, which had been adapted for the US exhaust emission regulations with less compression and 195bhp, had already been available in the North American model since July 1972.

The front seats were high-class, attractive and unlike those of the normal sports car.

The rear seat offered a good deal of room for two people.

As a consequence of the oil crisis in 1973, the SLC was also offered with a 2.8-litre, double overhead camshaft, fuel-injection engine (the M110). It had already stood its test in the W114/5 'dash-eight' series for the previous two years. It was also to be offered in the first Sonderklasse W116.

The Three SLC Coupés

Thus three SLC Coupés, each with a different engine, were available, and only an attentive observer was able to differentiate between the three versions. The 280SLC could be recognized by its slightly narrower tyres. Type 450SLC was characterized by an inconspicuous front spoiler applied at the rear low end of the front apron, thus increasing the rate of air flow considerably.

The first 5-litre, the 450SLC 5.0 released in 1978, and the later 500 models presented in 1980, also carried the black foam rear spoiler, sometimes dubbed a 'rubber sausage', on the rear edge of the boot lid.

The M110 straight-six engine.

The 'rubber sausage' spoiler compared to a 280SLC.

Between November 1975 and February 1976 the fuel-injection system of all three engines was modified in order to correspond to the now stricter exhaust emission standards in most European countries. The electronically controlled Bosch 'D-Jetronic' was replaced by the newly developed, mechanically controlled Bosch 'K-Jetronic'. In all three cases the conversion was connected with slight power reductions. In the 2.8-litre engine as well as in the 3.5-litre engine the compression was lowered at the same time.

In order to simplify maintenance, both V8 engines were equipped with a breakerless transistor ignition and hydraulic valve lifters. In the 2.8-litre M110 engine the compression was increased to its former value, and with the help of some further measures, the former power output was reached once again.

The 450SLC 5.0 Coupé, 107

At the Frankfurt Motor Show (IAA) in September 1977, a new top-of-the-range 450SLC 5.0, 107 was presented. It introduced and promoted the new generation of 'all alloy' V8 engines. The new engine had the bore enlarged to 97mm, and it weighed 40kg (88lb) less than its sister 4.5-litre iron block. In part this was made possible by having no heavy bore liners, but instead using an innovative alloy called alusil; when this was etched, a very hard silicon substance was brought to the surface, which created a non-porous bearing surface. Horsepower increased to 240bhp, also increasing torque by around 10 per cent.

The weight-reducing measures were not limited to the engine; a further weight reduction of more than 80kg (176lb) was achieved by using aluminium for the bonnet, boot-lid and both bumpers. Introducing light-alloy wheels further helped its unladen weight ratio.

Unusual as it was for Daimler-Benz to utilize add-on parts, the new rubberized boot spoiler wasn't for any type of visual impact: engineers deemed it necessary on this occasion as it significantly reduced negative lift force at both the front and rear axle.

Surprisingly, AMG saw the 450SLC 5.0 Coupé as having rally-winning potential; however, the displacement capacity of 5025cc was not so well chosen with regard to certain aspects of race homologation. After discussions with Daimler-Benz, the bore was reduced by 0.5mm, resulting in a total piston displacement of now 4973cc. This modified engine with reduced displacement was also used in the standard

The new M117 5-litre.

production cars from May 1979 onwards. Considering the 450SLC 5.0 Coupé had a production run of only two years, it sold reasonably well at 2,769 cars.

THE COMPLETE 107 RANGE UPDATED

At the Geneva Motor Show in March 1980 the complete 107 range was updated. The all aluminium-engined 450SLC 5.0 was renamed the 500SLC, replacing the 450 range completely. A lot of its early exclusivity was lost, however, since there now existed a 500SL, as well as the 500SE and a 500SEL from the 126 S-Class range, with the same engine and almost identical driving performance.

The 350SLC was cancelled in favour of the 380SLC. The new 3.8-litre engine was based on the time-tested 3.5 M116, but was also given the all-aluminium block. Only the 6-cylinder engine of the 280SLC remained unchanged in the programme.

One of the very last 500SLCs.

The all aluminium-engined 450SLC 5.0 was renamed the 500SLC, and replaced the 450 range completely.

C107 Specifications 1971–1981

Production	June 1971 to September 1981
Engine type	M110 (6-cylinder) M116, M117 (V8)
Dimensions	
Wheelbase	2,820mm (111in)
Front track	1,452mm (57in)
Rear track	1,440mm (56.7in)
Length	4,450mm (175in)
Width	1,790mm (70.5in)
Height	1,330mm (52.4in)
Vehicle weight	2,050kg (4,520lb)

The three-speed automatic transmission was replaced by a four-speed version with torque converter, as used in the 126 range.

The interior as well as the steering wheel was adapted more in line with the plush style of the newly released 126 S-Class saloons.

From the outside, except for the model type decal on the boot lid, there were almost no differences to the preceding models; however, all three SLC types were now equipped with the rubberized front spoiler known from the 450SLC 5.0. However, the black (rubber sausage) rear spoiler remained exclusively for the 500SLC.

In 1981, and only eighteen months after this last big model improvement, the SLC Coupés of type range 107 had to yield to their successors: the Sonderklasse-based C126.

After a production time of ten years, 62,888 cars had been produced, of which just 1,636 were the 450SLC-5.0 and 1,133 were the 500SLC; it was the last time that Daimler-Benz would use a sports car as the base for a Coupé. The R107 however, went on to be produced until August of 1989.

THE 5-LITRE SLC CARS IN RALLY COMPETITION

Even though Mercedes-Benz cars were seen in rallying during the mid-1950s to the mid-1960s – cars such as the legendary W198 300SL, then the W111 220SE, the W113 230SL and finally the W111 300SE – their lack of any great success kept them out of the limelight.

In the London-to-Sydney rally Andrew Cowan, Colin Malkin and Mike Broad were victorious in a W123 280E.

Tony Fowkes and his co-driver Peter O'Gorman in their Mercedes-Benz 280E during the south-eastern Europe stage of the London-to-Sydney rally.

It wasn't until 1977, twelve years after their last race, that they again had some success, albeit with a privately owned team. The UK-based team, consisting of Andrew Cowan, Colin Malkin and Mike Broad, was victorious in a W123 280E in the 18,000km (11,185 miles) London-to-Sydney Rally, and a similar 280E of Fowkes and O'Gorman came in second.

Following the success of this privateer team, Mercedes-Benz made the decision to expand its efforts in rally competition once again with a full works team. However, at the time, the WRC was dominated by small saloons such as the Fiat 131 Abarth and Ford Escort RS1800, and Mercedes-Benz certainly had no small sporty saloon. What it did have, however, was a large, heavy and expensive luxury Sport Coupé in the C107 SLC, and under the leadership of Erich Waxenberger the first 450SLC was prepared.

The 1978 Rally Season

To set their place in the 1978 rally season, Mercedes-Benz entered the Kenya Safari Rally with a full 'works team' of four W123 280Es. The team was only marginally successful, with the car of Sobieslaw Zasada and Blazej Krupa finishing sixth, but it did give Daimler some experience with how rallying had changed. It also – and even more importantly – gave added kudos and a marketing ploy to show how durable their cars were, even in 'standard' form.

ERICH WAXENBERGER, THE 'BAVARIAN HURRICANE'

Erich Waxenberger was born on 9 April 1931 in Miesbach, Bavaria; he died on 18 July 2017 in Stuttgart. His father and sister ran a DKW concessionaire in the town of Miesbach. His father was also an enthusiastic motorcyclist, and would often organize and take part in races during the summer months; in winter they would race on the frozen lakes around the south of Bavaria.

The same excitement gripped Erich from a very young age, and he had a thirst for knowledge. His father taught him to 'think outside the box', and demonstrated the importance of adapting mechanical solutions in order to achieve optimum speed in difficult environments. He also showed him how the pilot's balance and movement was of the utmost importance: controlling one's own core body movements would give you the edge in the control of your vehicle. His father took him skiing regularly from the age of four, in the belief that there was no better way to learn balance, and Erich never forgot this.

Erich studied at the Academy for Applied Technology in Munich, and graduated from his course in mechanical engineering as both the second youngest and second best graduate. He sat his last exam on Friday 11 June 1953. Two days later, on the very next Monday, he started work at Daimler-Benz in the Untertürkheim passenger car testing department, primarily concentrating on vehicle assemblies. Daimler-Benz remained his only employer for forty-three years, just as it was for his later boss Rudolph Uhlenhaut. Encouraged by Uhlenhaut, Erich took every opportunity to hone his skills, and he and Uhlenhaut drove fast cars, and went skiing and sailing together as much as they could.

In 1956, only two years after he started working at Daimler-Benz, Waxenberger was officially transferred to the chassis development department. His primary concern was with the development of the three SL series of those years: the 300SL in its

ABOVE: **Erich Waxenberger.**

The 3rd International ADAC 1,000-kilometre race at the Nürburgring, 26 May 1957. Lindberg and Waxenberger reach third place in the category GT cars over 1600cc.

gullwing version, the 300SL Roadster and the 190SL, then in its development stage. The development of another SL, a 190SL with a 2.2-litre 6-cylinder engine and petrol direct injection, initially named the W127 series, and with a 3-litre injection engine named the W104 series, was added to his list of projects by Fritz Nallinger.

The W127 was considered a potential 'Alpine Rally' contender, but even though it managed to lap the Nürburgring 25 seconds faster than a regular W121, it was shelved due to cost and tooling difficulties, and it was decided that production of the W127 could not realistically begin before 1960. So instead, Nallinger proposed to continue development of the engine for the upcoming W113: this became known as the 230SL, and featured designer Béla Barényi's famous 'pagoda' roof.

Test drives continued to the Stelvio Pass or the Grossglockner alpine route as a part of the standard programme during the summer months, and were very much to the liking of the young engineer.

In 1963 the W113 series – the so-called 'Pagoda' SL – was launched, and Erich also supervised this model in the testing department for its potential use in rallying in 1963 and 1964, and prepared the model especially for these competitions.

The 'Pagoda' with the most exciting potential was also created under Waxenberger's guidance: a 230SL with the 6.3-litre M100 V8 engine taken from the Mercedes-Benz W100 (600). His dream was to be able to fit a V8 into an SL, as the ultimate in sports cars.

Using the legendary Nordschleife (North Loop) of the Nürburgring, with the adapted W113 shod in racing tyres, he clocked a best time of 10min 30secs (not bad when you consider the record today is just 6min 45secs, set in July 2018). However, the high front-axle loads exerted by the heavy engine caused severe front-end pitching under hard braking and extremely severe understeer, so much so that after only nine laps the front tyres were worn out, the rears only lasting a couple of laps more.

Waxenberger was not exclusively a theorist: he was an extremely pragmatic engineer and hated giving in to a failure, a fact that immediately attracted attention. On the occasion of the 1980 New Zealand rally, Björn Waldegård departed the track in his 450SLC and ended up driving through a barbed-wire fence; the wire wrapped around the front rim and the rear driveshaft, and caused both right-hand wheels to block. Erich Waxenberger flew in immediately by helicopter, and ripped off the barbed wire with his bare hands, his face contorted with pain – but it wasn't just physical pain, it was the pain of desperation.

Among those watching was head engineer and member of the Board of Management, Professor Fritz Nallinger. There were critical murmurings, and questions as to whether the vehicle would go again, but hearing them, Nallinger replied drily: 'Let him be, Waxenberger always finds a way!'

Waxenberger was, beyond everything else, a true Bavarian in nature. He may have had a seemingly direct arrogance, but with it he brought a bold integrity in his work, which in his time with Daimler-Benz earned him great respect as an engineer and innovator.

Erich Waxenberger finally retired on 1 July 1996, leaving behind a legacy of indefatigable, hands-on leadership.

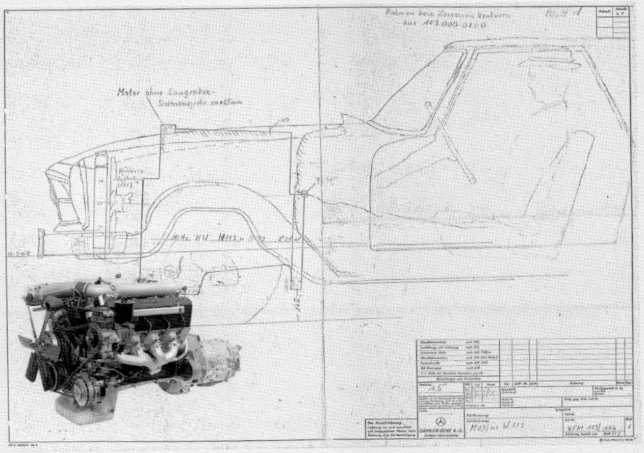

The only working test V8 W113.

LEFT: **Working drawing of the W113 (inset: the M100 V8 engine).**

Although in theory 'SL' was supposed to stand for 'Sports Light', the C107SL Coupé was far from this – but as the flagship of the Mercedes-Benz range, the thinking at the time was that its V8 engine and inherent comfort made it a fast and comfortable tourer, which essentially meant that crews would suffer the minimum of fatigue over long rallies.

The fixed roof of the SLC also added to the rigidity of the body frame and gave the car superb handling, and together with the comfort of the long-wheelbase Coupé, meant that crews would suffer the minimum of fatigue over long rallies.

The C107 series had been released in October 1971 as the 350SLC with the 200bhp (147kW) 3.5-litre M116 V8; subsequently the 225bhp (165kW) 4.5-litre M117 V8 was added to the range as the 450SLC.

The Rally Version C107

Previously all 107 models used engines with alloy cylinder heads on cast-iron cylinder blocks; however, in September 1977 a new, all-alloy 5025cc, 240bhp (177kW) V8 engine was revealed, developed specifically for the rally version C107. This special version of the 107 Coupé was prepared in order to homologate the SLC for the 1978 World Rally Championship, and together with a lightweight aluminium bonnet and boot lid, the new engine also assisted in reducing the substantial weight of the big Coupé; the resulting car became known as the 450SLC-5.0. It also received a black rubber rear spoiler, along with a small front-lip spoiler.

With little more than some under-shell skid plates, extra lights and roll-cage protection fitted, these cars were entered into the gruelling month-long 30,000km (18,640 miles) 1978 Vuelta America del Sud (Tour of South America) as the debut event for the new 450SLC-5.0. Only about one third of all the entered cars survived the gruelling rally; however, three out of the four SLCs entered completed the event, with first place for the car crewed by Andrew Cowan and Colin Malkin, second place for the SLC crewed by Sobieslaw Zasada and Andrzej Zembruski, and fourth place for the Coupé of Timo Makinen and Jean Todt (later FIA director and president). Third place went to the 280E Mercedes of Tony Fowkes and Klaus Kaiser.

The 1979 World Rally Championship

Massive factory support under the leadership of Eric Waxenberger backed the effort behind several entries in the 1979 World Rally Championship, and the 450SLC-5.0 was homologated this time as a Group 4 rally car, having had its engine power increased to around 300bhp (220kW). In order to help reduce the substantial weight of the C107 chassis, aluminium doors, bonnet and boot lid were produced for the 5.0, and further weight reductions followed by stripping out all unnecessary interior fittings. The three-speed automatic transmission was preserved, as it was considered the only Daimler-Benz unit capable of withstanding the torque of the M117 engine.

Full 1978 works team, including Waxenberger's 450SLC.

Andrew Cowen and Colin Malkin went on to win the 1977 London-to-Sydney rally.

Mikkola and Hertz celebrating first place at the Bandama Rally in 1979.

Three 450SLCs and three 280Es were entered in the African Safari Rally, and even though the SLC driven by Björn Waldegård and Hannu Mikkola led for much of the event, they finished second overall, 48 minutes after a Datsun 160J. Andrew Cowan and Johnstone Syer finished fourth in a 280E, and Björn Waldegård and Hans Thorszelius achieved sixth place in their SLC; Vic Preston Jnr and John Lyall retired after breaking a rear axle in the last works SLC.

However, much greater success was achieved at the 5,500km Bandama (Ivory Coast) Rally, with a clean sweep with four 450SLC-5.0s: Mikkola and Hertz took first place, Waldegård and Thorszelius second, Cowan and Kaiser third, and Preston and Doughety fourth.

The 1980 Season

Following the 1978 and 1979 successes, an even greater effort went into the 1980 season. Some even considered it unfairly excessive, and Daimler started receiving some bad press. At a time when Ford were winning world championships with relatively simple, straightforward cars, it was reported in the press that unlike any other manufacturer, Mercedes serviced their cars by helicopter, and that the budget the Mercedes works team had per event was more than Ford and Fiat had for the whole season.

Even Erich Waxenberger, who was known to be somewhat of an eccentric extrovert, also came in for plenty of 'media stick'. On one occasion, during the 1980 Safari, Arne Hertz injured his hand, and everybody around told Waxenberger that a navigator could not be replaced – but in Waxenberger's book giving up wasn't an option, so he got into Arne's seat and told Hannu Mikkola to 'Get moving!' Mikkola, not wanting to argue with the strong character that Waxenberger was, did as he was told; but at the finish line of the next stage the team was disqualified.

As the year progressed it was becoming obvious that the big SLC was not so suited to the shorter and tighter European rallies, and the Portugal Rally resulted in a best place of only fourth for Waldegård and Thorszelius. In the 5,300km Safari Rally, where success was expected, rear suspension failures saw a best of only third place to Vic Preston Jnr in a 450SLC-5.0. In the Acropolis Rally the power of the 5-litre, coupled to the new four-speed automatic transmission, resulted in shredded tyres on the rocky roads, with the highest placing again going to Vic Preston Jnr, but this time down in fourteenth place.

Three-quarters of the way through the 1980 season, and in line with the production version, the C107 received an updated engine: output was increased to 329bhp, despite a slight reduction in displacement to 4975cc, and from then on it became known as the 500SLC; this also meant that the Mercedes would be changed from a Group 4 to a Group 2 car. These Group 2 500SLCs could be identified from the Group 4 450SLC 5.0 by the round, black wheel-arch extensions.

Although the 500SLC only went on to compete in a further three events, it was introduced so it could attack the 1981 season.

For the Rally of Argentina, Mikkola and Hertz managed second place; however, the two other 500SLCs suffered broken drive shafts. In the Rally of New Zealand, Mikkola finished third and Waldegård fifth. In the same event Cowan suffered rear brake problems.

The final event contested for the 1980 season was the Ivory Coast Rally, which was far better suited to the big Mercedes, and they did not disappoint: just eleven cars finished, and out of these first place went to Björn Waldegård, second to Jorge Recalde, and fifth to Vic Preston, all in 500SLCs. However, because they did not enter every event for the 1980 season, Mercedes finished a rather disappointing fourth overall in the championship.

Rally Cars for the 1981 Season

Towards the end of 1980, Mercedes-Benz registered four new works rally cars for the 1981 season (S-EH 1418, 1419, 1420, 1820); two of these started life as Group 2 500SLCs, while the other cars were converted to Group 4 450SLCs.

Waxenberger also proposed a move to the much shorter and lighter SL platform, as the shorter wheelbase allowed for better response in cornering. There were even rumours that Mercedes had plans for a mid-engined version 107, though if a prototype existed it would have been destroyed.

A number of prototype R107s were built. To lighten the car, the windows were all replaced with lexan (polycarbonate), while the roll-cage material was changed to a high-strength aluminium. A large, high-rise handbrake was fitted in front of the plastic Recaro racing seats to assist in rotating the big Benz; it also retained the 722.3 automatic transmission.

The End of the Mercedes Works Rallying Team

But this time Waxenberger's enthusiasm was not enough. Even though Mercedes, in preparation for the following year,

Invar Carlsson in Portugal 1980 shows black wheel extensions.

Waldegaard, Ivory Coast Rally 1980.

The original prototype R107 in period (*top*), and a more recent image at the Goodwood festival of Speed (*bottom*).

had managed to recruit winning driver Walter Röhrl and Ari Vatanen on a ten-year contract, it was not to be.

In December 1980, having just returned from the Bandama rally where his two 500SLCs had finished in first and second place, Erich Waxenberger was invited to present his case to the Daimler management board for the funding of the next five years of rallying. With his usual jubilant enthusiasm, he promised to deliver Daimler-Benz the World Rally Championship in time for the 100th anniversary of the automobile in 1986. The one small problem was that a single sceptical board member had asked the new driver Walter Röhrl what he considered his chances were of winning the Monte Carlo rally for the next year – and of course, erring on the side of caution, Röhrl spoke honestly and declared to the member that he expected to finish within the first five. Having reported this back to the board, it put Waxenberger's proposition on not such a sure footing as he had thought.

After a great deal of debate, they finally agreed to fund just one car instead of two for the forthcoming rallying activities. Waxenberger was furious, having prepared four cars for the following season, as well as having managed to secure the two world-class drivers Walter Röhrl and Ari Vatanen. So Waxenberger called the board's bluff, and declared he would prefer to stop all rallying activities completely than do half a job. Of course, he expected the board to concede to his demands and call him back – but he had no one on the board to support him, and that was that: the case was closed. The reigning world champion Röhrl, his co-driver Geistdörfer and their Finnish colleague Vatanen were out of a job, and that was the end of the Mercedes works rallying team.

As abrupt as it might seem, Röhrl's honest answer and Waxenberger's threat might not have been the only reason that the board cancelled the rally project. It was rumoured that Daimler-Benz's budget for a single rally was equal to that for an entire season for other car manufacturers, and given that Mercedes cars were selling at a very healthy pace, there was no reason to sink large amounts of Deutschemarks into something they could not guarantee would show them in a good light. In actual fact they feared that a less-than-stellar performance could even have a detrimental effect on Mercedes as a brand.

Furthermore competition was no longer like it had been in the 1950s, when Ferrari, Jaguar and Mercedes were battling for supremacy; now, in the early 1980s, rallying was inherently a competition of all makes and models. This was compounded by the fact that, if an Opel or a Fiat could very easily beat a grand Mercedes, in the eyes of the public it would not look so good for Mercedes – and as was proved by the derisive write-ups of the previous year, the press would make the most of it. Headlines in big bold letters that read '*Fiat and Opel better than Mercedes*' was not a gamble the board was prepared to take any longer.

At the Waxenberger board meeting, the writing must already have been on the wall. The half-hearted attempt by the board to grant him the money for just one car was already the sign that he had not presented his case convincingly enough. They probably knew that Waxenberger's impetuosity would give them all they needed, a somewhat graceful way to get out of it, and now they could blame Waxenberger for not accepting their offer.

It has been said that it was the attitude of Mercedes that led to the problems. Even though they were by far the richest team, throwing millions of DMs at the sport didn't guarantee them wins, and they often made basic mistakes. The opposition and the press enjoyed this, and didn't refrain from mentioning it whenever possible. For example, as has been mentioned, Mercedes serviced their cars by helicopter, and on one occasion, when delivering a brand-new rear axle to the breakdown scene, it slipped the winch because it hadn't been tied on safely and fell to the ground, shattering into pieces. Everyone laughed and gloated incessantly for weeks afterwards.

Nor did having an inexhaustive budget equate to wins. Mercedes entered the 1980 Rally Portugal but finished 44 minutes off the pace, and when they entered the 1980 Acropolis with a four-car team, only one finished, and that was down in fourteenth place.

Waxenberger and Waldergård, Acropolis Rally 1980.

Goodwood Festival of Speed with Roland Asch.

Roland Asch leaves the track and damages the SL prototype.

BELOW RIGHT: **Early Giorgio Battistella sketches of the SLX, with a small plaque in the rear parcel shelf clearly denoting '230. Coupé'.**

BOTTOM RIGHT: **Giorgio Battistella working alongside Paul Bracq.**

But the company hasn't forgotten its rallying projects, and one of the prototype 500SL rally cars has recently appeared in a Daimler-Benz promotional video, in which it was careening full pelt through the desert. And another of the prototypes met an unfortunate end at the Goodwood Festival of Speed with Roland Asch at the wheel during a demonstration run. They also often appear at official events and staged displays at the Daimler Museum.

THE SLX COUPÉ DESIGN STUDY, 1965

In the early 1960s Karl Wilfert initiated a project for a car that was purported to be the spiritual successor to the Gullwing W198. He reached out to Italian stylist Giorgio Battistella to work alongside Paul Bracq and Bruno Sacco to produce a mid-engined super sports car. Later on it was referred to by Daimler-Benz as the SLX, but in reality there doesn't seem to have been an official name or designation for the programme. While researching this subject there have been several code designations, including X, SL X, SL-X, 700 SL, 300SLX and even C101/111. In one of the Battistella sketches there is even a nod to the 230SL with a small plaque in the rear parcel shelf clearly denoting '230. Coupé'.

By the spring of 1965 a full 1:1 model had been built in wood, and testing began in the wind tunnel. However, following a reappraisal of priorities in the wake of the change of technical directorship from Fritz Nallinger to

The wooden SLX model is usually displayed at the museum.

Wind-tunnel lift and side-wind tests of the SLX.

Hans Scherenberg at the end of 1965, work on the car was suspended.

All was not lost, however, as with Scherenberg's appointment, a new engineering-focused generation assumed command at Untertürkheim, headed by his friend and colleague during the racing years, Rudolf Uhlenhaut. Uhlenhaut's intuitive hands-on approach to Mercedes' engineering was matched by his outstanding skill behind the wheel as a test driver – and something special was to come.

The SLX may have been shelved permanently, but its design concept made way for project C101, which was presented only three years later, designed by Bruno Sacco and Josef Gallitzendörfer.

THE 1969 C111 EXPERIMENTAL COUPÉ

At the International Motor Show (IAA) in Frankfurt in September 1969 the journalists got to see a model that was nothing short of a supercar, the like of which had never been seen before from the Swabian company. Even the expectant, hard-to-please journalists were shocked to their core when the automobile was finally unveiled.

Crowds gathered around the sleek, compact, wedge-shaped car, resplendent in its metallic 'Weissherbst' orange, its gullwing doors erect like a bird about to take flight – but

The International Motor Show (IAA) in Frankfurt in September 1969.

what shocked them the most was that this stunning automobile was nothing more than a research vehicle. It was never to be seen gracing the front window of any main dealership. Even at the earnest behest of many customers, some of whom sent blank cheques to Stuttgart to be sure of securing one, Daimler-Benz refused point blank to put it into production. The potential dream car of the 1970s was just that: a dream.

For most of the 1960s rumours proliferated that Mercedes-Benz was planning to launch something phenomenal, which would bring them back to the forefront of racing. Speculation reached fever pitch when automotive journalists caught Daimler testing a mid-engined racing Porsche and a racing Lotus Europa Coupé on their Untertürkheim test track – but still no one guessed what was really going on.

Untertürkheim test-track testing of the first bodied C111.

Under the auspices of head of passenger-car development Rudolf Uhlenhaut, and head of pre-development Dr Hans Liebold, work had begun as far back as 1967 on what was originally coded as the C101. The fascinating design was created by a team under Joseph Gallitzendörfer, while Bruno Sacco, who had recently moved from pre-development to styling, coordinated body development for the spectacular sports car. At its release at the IAA, to avoid a conflict with model designations trademarked by Peugeot with a zero as the middle digit, it was renamed the C111.

The Ultimate Experimental Coupé

From the very start, the C111 was conceived purely as an experimental, test vehicle, the main objectives being to test, first, the integrity of the bonding and adherence of glassfibre-reinforced plastic for automotive body shells, and second, the Wankel engine. Although Mercedes-Benz had been experimenting with the Wankel engine principle since 1962, it needed extensive road-testing of Felix Wankel's unconventional propulsion system, the rotary piston engine, before it was fitted in their production cars. The first test drive of the first complete vehicle took place at Hockenheimring on 15 July 1969.

From the day of its release, the C111 concept became the absolute dream car of the 1970s. Its iconic character was reinforced by the unusual metallic orange paint finish, called 'Weissherbst'. The name stemmed from the glowing orange/rosé colour of Germany's popular wines. The vehicle displayed at the IAA show in Frankfurt was the first C111 in this spectacular paint finish; however, the other vehicles in the first series, which were used as demonstration vehicles during the show, remained in their original white paint finish, only being repainted in 'Weissherbst' a few weeks later.

Media Feedback

The C111's engineering lived up to the promise of Bruno Sacco's futuristic styling, and this admiration was reflected in the media. Paul Frère wrote in the motoring magazine *Auto Motor und Sport*, issue 8/1970: 'The four-rotor version would not only be the most comfortable and smooth, but also the fastest car of this kind. I am firmly convinced that there would be thousands of customers for such a car around the world.'

Toy manufacturers were producing the C111 in all scales, hoping upon hope that Mercedes-Benz would put the C111 into production. They also did a police version.

Dazzling in the unusual 'Weissherbst' colour.

The *Deutsche Auto-Zeitung* called it: 'The car that takes your breath away!' And the motoring magazine *Road & Track* wrote the following in November 1969: 'If we tell them how much we like it, maybe they'll produce it.'

A New Engine

On 26 October 1961, Daimler-Benz signed a licence to explore the potential of the new rotating combustion engine conceived by Felix Wankel. Work on the Mercedes Wankel was directed by Wolf-Dieter Bensinger, designer of the engine used in the Gullwing 300SL. Among other engineers on the project were Hans-Otto Derndinger and Heinz Lamm.

The first Daimler-Benz Wankel built was the 450cc chamber volume, KA-series with three rotor units, initially using carburettors. However, most of the test-bed running took place with a specially adapted Bosch fuel-injection system direct into the intake/compression side of the chamber, where the nozzle is at all times shielded from combustion temperatures and pressures. This direct-injection fuel system was a unique and important contribution to Wankel advancement made by Daimler-Benz.

In 1967 the KC-series engine was designed and built, followed in December 1968 by the KE series. The KE's rotor and housing were widened by 5mm to 75mm, to bring the displacement of a single chamber to 600cc. Vast improvements were made to the design of the rotor housings and the intermediate sections between the rotors. The triple-rotor version of the KE was called the M950. The total displacement of the three chambers around one rotor assembly was 1800cc, making the swept volume of the three-rotor engine three times 1800cc, or 5.4 litres. Even though this developed around 220bhp, Hans Liebold suggested the low-end torque range did not provide sufficient power for a saloon car, but would suit a small sports car.

Body Design

Early in November 1968, the Daimler-Benz central design office prepared to start work on a mid-engined Coupé, designed around the compact Wankel engine.

Rudy Uhlenhaut introduced the first three-rotor Wankel engine.

The new Coupé was designed from the driver's seat outwards. Starting with the necessary ground clearance, they added the driver's seated height to arrive at an overall height of 1,125mm (44.3in). Next, a heavy roll-bar structure behind the seats was established, and behind that, the siting of the Wankel engine with its attached five-speed ZF transaxle. This determined the placement of the rear wheels. The front-wheel distance forwards was set by the length needed for comfortable leg distance to the control pedals.

Chassis and Frame Design

Designed strictly for the three-rotor Wankel engine, the first chassis had a 2,499mm (98.4in) wheelbase. All later chassis had room for a possible four-rotor engine, provided by a wheelbase of 2,621mm (103.2in). The rear track was 1,392mm (54.8in); the front track was 1,379mm (54.3in) with Michelin touring tyres, and 1,440mm (56.7in) when equipped with wider wheels and tyres that might be suitable for racing.

Several types of frame were assessed, including the tubular frame design of the W198 300SL. However, engineering estimates showed that the car's overall weight would be higher than needed with this style of tubular frame; also, a racing-style monocoque frame would not be as well suited to a car that was intended chiefly for road use, requiring appropriate interior space and ease of servicing. Furthermore, crash protection for the side-mounted fuel tanks and the occupants would not come up to expectations.

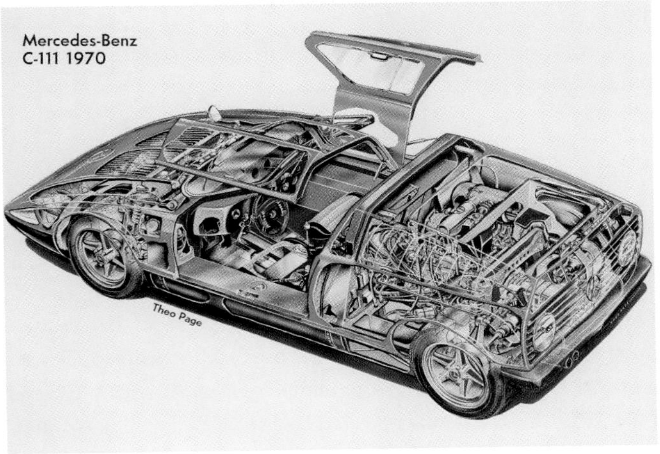

Detailed drawing of the C111 platform frame.

The choice therefore fell on a third alternative: a platform frame with deep side sills, which would provide both torsion and beam stiffness. When this frame was first used in the C101 it was intended to have triangular stiffening webs from its roll-bar arch down to the rear frame extensions; but with the mid-engine mount position, these would have blocked access to the spark plugs and the exhaust system, so diagonal bracing tubes were used instead. However, further computer analysis showed that the rear of the frame of these first C111s lacked around 18 per cent of its achievable stiffness, so it was extensively redesigned for the second and subsequent C111s.

The main chassis frame was not dissimilar to that of the 1964 version of the Ford GT40: deep-sided with a high cowl structure, it was fabricated of steel of 0.8mm and 1.0mm thickness; it weighed a little over 130kg (206lb).

The deep outer sill forming the frame contained a 60ltr (13gal) fuel tank on each side, which for crash-testing purposes went through various incarnations from corrugated aluminium to rubber bladders.

Brakes and Steering

Brakes were borrowed from the 300SEL 6.3 sedan; a brake servo was used for the road-test vehicles but not for the track cars.

Most production Mercedes-Benz cars of this era were provided with a recirculating-ball steering gearbox; however, the C101 front end was different. It was designed around the concept that the front-wheel steering axis should intersect with the surface of the pavement exactly at the centre of the tyre where it contacted the road. Conventional designs offset this axis/road intersection between 10 and 25 per cent to achieve a lighter steering action at low speeds, but this 'zero offset' geometry as used in the C101 enabled maximum stability under heavy braking, which was more important for test purposes.

The First Test Runs

The heavily disguised car's first trip on the open road, on 16 April, was shared by Rudolf Uhlenhaut and his forty-two-year-old engineer Hans Liebold; due to its crudely shod, metal body panels engineers referred to it as the 'tin box'. In little under a month it had its first test runs at both the

The disguised test version of the C111, known as the 'tin box', driven by Hans Liebold.

Nürburgring and Hockenheimring, but first impressions were not favourable: weak performance, poor handling and terrible shifting – and that was only the start.

The rear suspension of the very first test chassis used off-the-shelf parts from the W108 saloon models in 1968, and although some improvement was achieved using wider racetrack tyres on the rear semi-swing axles, Enke and Löffler decided it wasn't anywhere near good enough and went back to their drawing boards and keyboards. The newly upgraded IBM computer system plotted 300 different linkage combinations to pinpoint the one that would do the job best.

The engineers suspected that at least some of the instability problems experienced were due to the crude body shape of the 'tin box', and they decided to put it into the new full-scale wind tunnel. Trimming the high wings and rear flanks with tin shears along pen-marked lines allowed the tests to continue, and resulted in a marked improvement of rear stability.

Body Development

The body development group headed by Werner Breitschwerdt and Karl Wilfert was already creating something a little more professional. 'Our objective,' recalled Wilfert, 'was a functional car with low aerodynamic drag. It was to be without lift and without movable flaps or spoilers.'

A clay model of the car went into the Daimler-Benz wind tunnel at Sindelfingen in only a matter of weeks. Due to the placement of the engine, the most important areas of the test automobile would be the air scoops, and these airflow requirements strongly influenced the body design. Large scoops were placed at the rear to force cool air around the engine and engine oil coolers, but a large scoop in the front deck also enabled the coolant radiator to be placed in the front deck; air entered through the lower deck and flowed out through a grilled area in the upper deck below the windscreen.

The front suspension also influenced the body stance: its 'MacPherson strut'-style, coil-over shock absorber needed extra clearance over the front wheel arches, and so forced the cowl line high and led the stylists towards a high belt line and a tapered wedge shape.

By the end of January 1969, only two months into the project and after countless wind-tunnel tests of the full-size clay model, styling was completed.

Body Manufacture

Wanting further to explore the possible use of GRP (glassfibre reinforced plastic) in body manufacture, Breitschwerdt and Wilfert decided to outsource the body builds to Rastätter Waggonfabrik, a company west of Stuttgart located near Daimler-Benz's large truck plant at Gaggenau. As producers of fibreglass truck bodies, they were well equipped to build the C101. The Sindelfingen clay model was immediately

Several clay models were built at 1:1 (full size) and 1:5 scale for wind-tunnel tests, as well as body bucks.

shipped to Rastätt to begin the complicated body-making process.

Fibreglass was laid over the clay model to form a 'female mould', which unfortunately destroyed the clay model in the removal process. Within this female buck a complete, heavy body 'male' shell was laid; this 'intermediate body' was then refined and painted, and equipped with wipers, lamps and licence plates for the approval of Daimler-Benz management. This 'male' body then served as the master mould for the final set of female body moulds, and from these, the final, single-piece fibreglass bodies were made, from the nose to the roof spine and on to the sides of the rear wings.

On 15 July 1969, the final body of a C101, having been glued, riveted and screwed into place, was ready for the track – but first it was removed to Daimler's FKFS wind-tunnel complex. This time it was tufted with ribbon to help show how air flowed over the body, to see how well its shape worked.

The way in which the windscreens were glued in place, flush with the body surface, went a long way to contributing to the excellent drag coefficient reading of 0.335 – but just as importantly, stability had been vastly improved over that of the 'tin box'. At 250km/h (155mph), the C101 experienced a 30kg (66lb) downforce on the front wheels, and a lift of only 10kg (22lb) at the rear. The Sindelfingen stylists' brief of downforce without add-on spoilers had been achieved.

Unexpected Problems

In the interim, road tests of the 'tin box' had continued in earnest at Untertürkheim and at Hockenheim following the

The clay models were all but destroyed by the fibreglass laying process.

The C111/1 undergoing ribbon flow tests in the FKFS wind tunnel.

installation of a new nose cone, and this extensive testing had highlighted a few unexpected problems.

The rear-mounted oil coolers weren't getting the expected amount of cool air, and the engine compartment was becoming unbearably hot. Also the system of venting the warm front radiator air at the base of the windshield was making the glass hot, which in turn heated up the interior to intolerable levels.

The solution was to lengthen the front end by several centimetres to relocate the spare tyre: this made room at the very front for the coolant radiator with an oil cooler ahead of it. Air was now taken in through a black-painted inlet in the elongated nose, while the slatted grille in the front deck that had formerly been the air inlet became the outlet; the effect was that warm air from the radiators was ejected successfully, keeping both the cabin and the engine area a great deal cooler.

Sporting Style

In a historical nod to the racing W198 of the early 1950s, the seating and door inner surfaces were upholstered in houndstooth cloth in orange/black and white/black. Although the side windows were fixed, they had lever-operated vent flaps, and a knob between the seats operated the narrow rear window to slide open or closed. Considering the width of the sills, it was decided to follow the W198 once again and fit 'gullwing'-style doors.

The original three-rotor Wankel engine produced an adequate 220bhp; however, this was not considered enough to propel the 1,000kg (2,205lb) C111 in the sporting style desired, so it was given a number of Stuttgart-style tweaks, as a result of which its output soared to 330bhp gross, and 270 to 280bhp at 7,000rpm. This made it by far the most powerful Wankel engine ever installed in an automobile.

Release to the Public

It was decided by the board that the C101 would be released to the public at Frankfurt's IAA, the international auto show, in September. Said Fritz Naumann:

> We worked through the nights, the mechanics in shifts, Liebold and I with our own timetable. I put a bed in my office so I could snatch a few minutes' sleep from time to time. In one month I recorded 165 hours of overtime. Whether it was paid I cared not; I was totally besotted with the C101.

Only a month before the IAA the Daimler-Benz management board decided to change the name of the C101 to C111. Peugeot had long since protected their three-digit-type designations using a 0 in the middle, and Daimler-Benz didn't

Houndstooth check in orange/black and white/black was available for the show cars.

There was no possibility of wind-down windows, so side flaps were available for extra air.

want to create any legal difficulties even before the C111 was revealed.

Further Testing

Even in its early form, testing had proved this to be a formidable automobile. The 1969 C111s would accelerate from a standstill to 100km/h (60mph) in 5sec, and were geared to reach 265km/h (165mph) at 7,000rpm in fifth, which they would attain easily, given sufficient distance.

Due to the C111's eager throttle response, downshifting of the ZF transmission became a problem for the test drivers. One of Liebold's engineers came up with an ingenious solution, adding a simple linkage and a supplementary throttle pedal low and to the left: this had a lower operating ratio than the main pedal. This novel two-stage accelerator allowed for test engineers to make quick and smooth downshifts, and also did away with the over-revving problem.

Following the accelerator upgrades, further test drives at Hockenheim of three separate cars revealed that the C111's three-rotor Wankel spread its power over a broad range: from 1,000rpm idle, the power climbed smoothly at first and then thrust the C111 forwards with a sense of unbridled energy, its torque levelling off between 5,000 and 6,500rpm before peak output was reached at 7,000. At 7,500rpm the injection pump decreased fuel supply to limit over-revving.

Indoors, under test, the engine sound was 'excruciatingly noisy and well beyond human endurance', as one engineer put it; from the outside, the engine had a deep metallic ringing like that of a two-stroke at speed. From inside the car its 'just adequate' level of sound-suppressing material left it 'singing like a huge electric motor'.

At Hockenheim, Uhlenhaut would hurl the 'tuned' C111 through its fast bends at speeds that generated a cornering acceleration of 1.5g, gleefully gluing his passenger against the side of his seat. The precise yet supple suspension allowed stunningly fast cornering, with precisely neutral handling on both fast and slow turns. Even the 'touring' version, on the same track, would generate close to 1g in cornering; this was unsurpassed by any other road car at that time, and achieved by very few even to the present day. The lack of a rear anti-roll bar caused the car to understeer strongly.

Testing at Hockenheim.

BELOW: **Rudy Uhlenhaut taking a cake and tea break from testing.**

Those test drivers who had the privilege of putting the C111 through its paces leading up to its reveal in September 1969 had only two complaints: one was that the Wankel engine, even when tuned for maximum power, lacked torque below 4,500rpm; the other was that its wedge-shaped body, high wing lines and narrow windows weren't ideal for visibility. However, Daimler-Benz had a solution: the C111/II, and surprisingly soon, in 1970.

Even knowing that the C111 would only ever be an experimental test machine, and having driven it around the Black Forest, racing driver Paul Frère summed up his feelings:

> There is no doubt that this is a very fast road car, and what is more important, it is a car that can be driven consistently fast, for it is utterly safe and very restful. In this it completely fulfils its aim, which is not to be a racing car, but a worthy successor to the immortal gull-winged 300SL: it is the fastest practical automobile of its time.

At a time when the average output of normal cars was somewhere around 52bhp, the C111/I of 1969, with its three-rotor Wankel engine, achieved 206kW/280bhp and could accelerate from a standing start to 100km/h (60mph) in 4.9sec; comparable cars such as the Ferrari Daytona and the Lamborghini Miura could not reach anything close to this speed because of unfavourable air resistance.

THE 1970 MERCEDES-BENZ C111/II

The C111/II was first presented at the Geneva Motor Show in March 1970, only six months after the first series. Significant improvements to the bodywork meant an improvement in visibility for the drivers, as well as an aerodynamic efficiency to 0.325Cd.

In place of the tri-rotor Wankel engine was the quad-rotor Wankel engine with an output of 258kW/350bhp. A slight improvement was made to the standing start – 0 to 100km/h (0–62mph) was cut to 4.8sec – but the top speed of 300km/h (186mph) was a vast improvement.

A new variable intake system increased torque up to 540Nm. The four-rotor engine was equipped with a single ignition and direct injection. Other characteristics included a new configuration of the suspensions, which allowed wider rims, the first anti-lock braking system, and a leather interior.

Mercedes-Benz engineers pushed the Wankel engine to the very limits of its design, and even though many engineering design problems of the Wankel engine principle were solved, the engine's poor degree of efficiency – due to the elongated, variable combustion chambers of the rotary-piston principle – was simply inherent in the design, and impossible to overcome with technical modifications. The problem was, that in a Wankel engine, the fuel burns within the space between the convex side of the rotary piston and the concave wall of the piston housing, rather than in the cylindrical combustion chamber of a reciprocating-piston engine.

To counteract this, engineers installed a post-combustion system in an effort to reduce the proportion of unburned

The C111/II was introduced at the Geneva Motor Show in March 1970.

Quad-rotor Wankel engine.

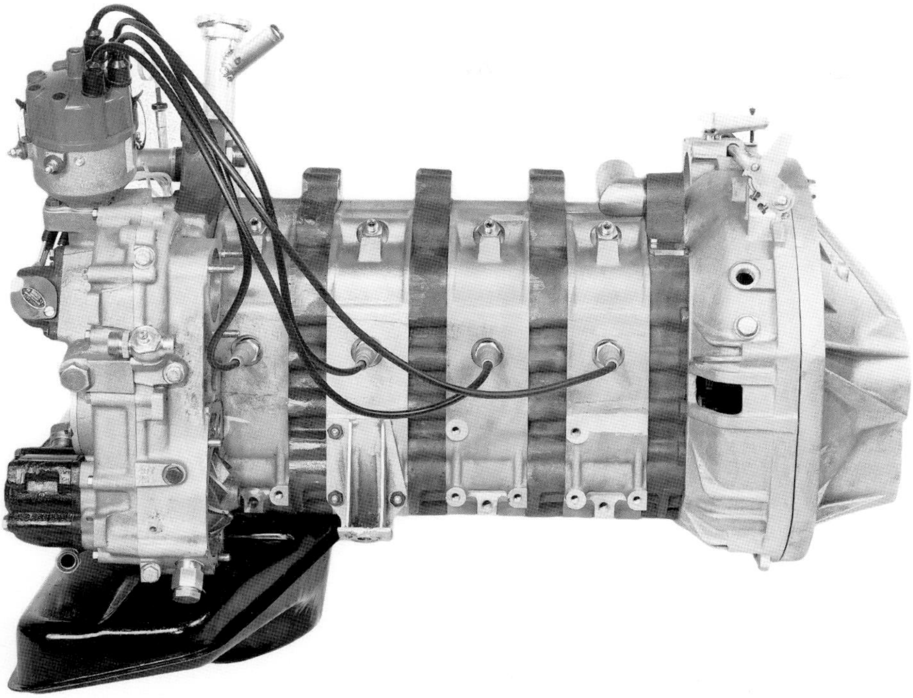

hydrocarbons. This improved matters a little, but one of the side effects was that it created popping and flaming from the exhaust. The poor thermodynamic fuel efficiency of the rotor, as compared with a reciprocating-piston engine, resulted in significantly higher fuel consumption for the same output.

The more stringent emissions legislation appearing all over the world, but especially in the USA, was to prove an added complication. Dramatic Wankel failures in Audi/NSU saloons in the late 1960s almost sunk the Audi company, and Mercedes wanted to avoid the same fate. The 1970 C111/II was the last Mercedes-Benz fitted with a Wankel engine. The last engine mount was the 4-cylinder rotary engine DB M950 KE409. The car's developer, Dr Hans Liebold, said: 'The Wankel engine was not yet mature enough to be handed over to customers in line with company standards.'

THE 1976 MERCEDES-BENZ C111/IID

By 1973 the growing importance of fuel-efficient engines had become clear, not least as a result of the oil crisis, presenting good opportunities for thrifty diesels. In an attempt to disprove the diesel engine's reputation as loud and lacking dynamism, the test department fitted the C111/II with a 3-litre 5-cylinder diesel engine taken from the 300D 3.0 of the W115 series ('stroke eight').

This revolutionary new diesel 5-cylinder engine, with advanced Bosch fuel and electronics systems, was fast and super powerful compared with all others before. Mercedes needed a light and sporty prototype chassis to really prove how amazing this new diesel was to the world. Thus the C111/IID was born.

Adding a Garret AiR turbocharger and an intercooler to the original OM617LA production engine of 59kW/80bhp now produced 140kW/190bhp at 4,400rpm and 373Nm/275lb ft of torque. A five-speed manual transmission with rear-wheel drive and experimental Michelin tyres on 15in rims helped to put the power on to the road.

The car accelerated from 0–100km/h (62mph) in 6.5sec and up to a top speed of 278km/h (173mph): an impressive speed for a petrol engine, let alone a diesel.

In June 1976 the C111/IID delivered a convincing performance on the test circuit at Nardò in Italy: over the space of sixty hours, four drivers set sixteen world records, among them thirteen for diesel vehicles, and three for cars with any

The slightly revised 'tin box' (top); the C111/I (middle); and the C111/II (bottom).

The OM617 5-cylinder diesel with garret turbo fitted in the C111/II.

type of engine. The three world absolute records recorded by the C111/IID are as follows:

5,000 miles with an average speed of 252.540km/h (156.921mph)
10,000 kilometres with an average speed of 252.249km/h (156.74mph)
10,000 miles with an average speed of 251.798km/h (156.46mph)

Their average speed was 252km/h (156.6mph) over a distance of 10,000km (6,200 miles), proving that a Mercedes-Benz diesel engine is also more than capable of a constant high speed.

The C111/II in the test pits for refuelling at the Nardo test track.

BELOW: **The C111/II in full swing on the Nardo test track.**

The first three C111 test-bed versions provided research and development data for around eight years. The Wankel engine may not have been a successful detour, but many other innovations used in Mercedes production automobiles started life in the C111 – for example, zero-offset front suspension was used in the 116 and 126 S-Class, and the ABS antilock brake system became standard in all automobiles worldwide. Advancements in diesel-engine development changed overnight, while using wind-tunnel technology to achieve efficient drag, lift and stability of airflow provided huge benefits.

The success of the C111, and the surprising record success of the lightly modified C111/II in Nardò, prompted the engineers to strive for new heights; however, this also sounded the end for the road-going automobile. Although retaining the C111 moniker, the C111/III and C11/IV became 'proper' record-breaking racing cars.

The C111/III full record-winning team (top), with the car at full speed (bottom).

C111/I and C111/II Specifications 1969–1971

Model	C111/I	C111/II
Production	Apr 1969	Feb 1970
Units produced	6	6
Wheelbase	2,620mm (103in)	
Front track	1,380mm (54in)	1,410mm (55.5in)
Rear track	1,370mm (53.9in)	1,445mm (56.9in)
Length	4,200mm (165in)	4,440mm (174.8in)
Width	1,800mm (70.8in)	
Height	1,125mm (44.3in)	
Vehicle weight	1,100kg (2,425lb)	1,240kg (2,734lb)
Engine type	M 950F Wankel	
Displacement	3 × 600cc	4 × 600cc
Maximum speed	300km/h (186mph)	
Acceleration	0–100km/h 4.8sec	
Maximum output	280bhp @ 7,000rpm	350bhp @ 7,000rpm
Fuel system	Direct injection, Bosch 4-plunger injection pump	

Twelve years would pass before another experimental, road-going Coupé vehicle was developed.

THE 1991 C112 EXPERIMENTAL COUPÉ

In the wake of other manufacturers producing a 'supercar' for the road market, and with the success of the C111 concept range from a little over a decade previously still ringing in their ears, in the late 1980s Daimler decided that it was time to build a supercar of their own, albeit fashionably late to the party.

It was not until the success of the C11 Group C Sauber racing car in the 1990–91 season, piloted by Michael Schumacher, that Mercedes engineers had a base with which to work. Some of the Group C Sauber success was down to the remarkable ABC (Active Body Control) system, and engineers were keen to fit the system into a normal saloon to test its viability for public roads. Initially the engineers planned to mount the system on a W201, however neither the Daimler nor the Sauber engineers could come up with a design that would suit this humble saloon. So putting their collective engineering minds together, they agreed to build a supercar – though hedging their bets, they used the term 'experimental vehicle' once again.

Instead of using the original M119 V8 as put in the C11, it was decided to test another more recent development: their M120 6-litre V12 petrol engine. This particular high-powered engine was used for two primary reasons: one, so that the engineers could demonstrate how the active suspension worked while driving at high speeds, but also to test it under great load, as it was to be used in the upcoming W140 S-Class.

The ongoing brief was that this new supercar should also fit into a socially acceptable environment, and be practical to use as a road-going automobile; it was to be luxuriously appointed, but should also be capable of being homologated for all world markets, from Switzerland with its strict noise regulations, to California with its demanding emissions limits. Bruno Sacco commented:

> When the C112 theme was being developed we didn't get lost in the maze, tempted to be too trendy. It possesses a well-defined tradition, anchored in the past but coherently linked to design concepts developed over the last fifteen years. We tried to continue with what we retain as our design philosophy.

The Group C11 Group C Sauber next to its spiritual sister the C112.

The M120 6-litre V12, tightly packed middle to rear.

Multiple design concepts were investigated in both 1/10 and 1/5-scale form, many with sharp flowing lines and large side air intakes, which overstated the rear engine placement that had become common with many other late 1980s supercar concepts. However, Harald Leschke and his designers employed a purer, more architectonically harmonious shape, which even echoed some of the proportions of the C111/III.

The Chassis

Created by an élite twenty-man engineering team under Karl Hoehl's technical direction, the chassis of the C112 was built at the experimental department at Sindelfingen, following design and safety influences of the original Sauber-Mercedes Group C racers. The riveted and bonded aluminium monocoque chassis tub ran back as far as the engine bay, and weighed a little under 60kg (132lb) in its bare form. The high rear bulkhead formed an enclosed fuel tank, from which two internal electric pumps drew fuel.

The three major bulkheads were joined by a central backbone running between the seats, which increased stiffness in bending and added a high level of impact resistance. A light tubular cage was added to the tub as a support for the roof and doors.

Water pipes were routed through the chassis backbone to the engine. A substantial welded-steel framework extended to the rear, alongside the engine, to carry the rear suspension mounts; it was bolted to the monocoque structure so it could be removed for service or repair.

Once complete, the bare chassis was fitted with slave wheels and shipped to Turin's 'Carrozzeria Cossiola', where the outer skin would be built to form the final shape.

High-Class Aerodynamics

The C112 'ground effect' aerodynamics were based upon the underbody venturi diffuser system pioneered by Lotus in the late 1970s, and used in the successful Group-C Sauber C11. In this system an inverted (compared with an aircraft) air-channel section in the floor reduced drag and increased downforce by making use of negative pressure air running under the vehicle. The problem for the design team was that

The design similarities of the C111/III can be seen in the C112 (bottom).

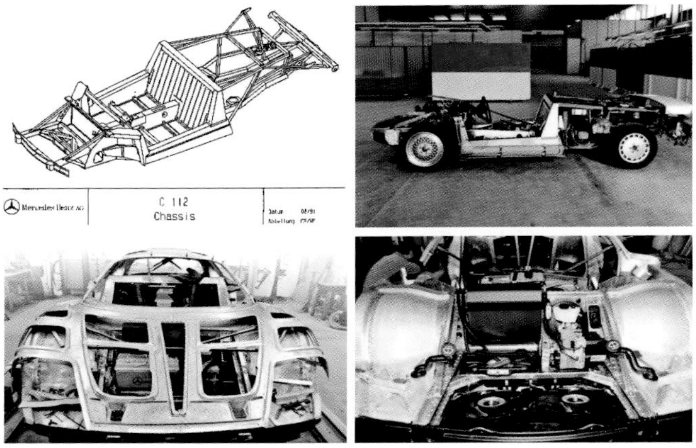

ABOVE LEFT: **The three-bulkhead structure design was an advanced version of the C111.**

ABOVE RIGHT: **The front spoiler extended to reduce front-end lift at speed.**

in 'track use', as with the C11 Sauber, this venturi system worked perfectly; however, in 'road use', with ever-changing road conditions, it would have its problems.

The C112 was also equipped with a unique feature to enhance aerodynamic stability: both its rear and front spoilers would adapt to driving styles and environments. During a normal driving situation, both front and rear spoilers remained hidden; however, at speeds above 250km/h (155mph) the front spoiler would descend enough to increase air flow and reduce lift of the nose, and the rear spoiler would elevate and turn to a 65-degree angle to increase downforce at the rear. Coupled with the venturi diffuser, this 'active' aerodynamic system successfully increased the overall downforce to around 1,000kg (2,200lb).

The aerofoil acted to increase downforce and also as an air brake.

In critical situations where brakes were applied suddenly, the rear spoiler would further extend to 45 degrees to act as an airbrake, trebling the normal drag value to 0.90Cd. Even from the top speed of 300km/h (186mph) this spoiler enabled the C112 to stop within 100m (330ft).

To maintain a low aerodynamic drag, there were only three main air inlets: the nose scoop supplied cooling air to both the front brakes and the coolant radiator, while the flank air intakes supplied cooling air for the rear brakes, the engine bay and an engine oil cooler.

Although common on many supercars of the time, Mercedes-Benz successfully avoided the use of 'flip-up' headlamps in favour of headlamps that were hidden behind transparent fairings, similar to those of the C111/III; the main reason for this was that it could degrade the drag coefficient, therefore secondary lamps were integrated into the Kevlar front bumper.

Pioneering Form

Maintaining a forty-year tradition the C112 received 'gull-wing doors', although this time they employed servo-assisted, hydraulic-operating cylinders adapted from those used to activate the flip-up roll bar on the SL roadster, to open or close the doors at the press of a button or by way of an infrared remote. A manual back-up system guarded against failure, and each door was designed so that it could also be forced open in case the car was upside down.

The rear bodywork consisted of a simple hinged aluminium engine cover to enable easy access for maintenance. Aluminium panels were riveted to a steel subframe to form the side flanks and around the rear tail-end with its articulated aerofoil. The whole of the rear end of the body, from the bumper line up, was formed around a tail-light array. The bumper section was formed from Kevlar matting, and flowed seamlessly around the venturi diffusers.

Engineering Marvel

Daimler found out that BMW were planning on bringing out a V12 engine version for their 7-series range way back in the mid-1980s, and had commissioned Kurt Oblander to develop their own version soon after. They even seriously considered adding a V12 version to their 126 S-Class line-up. However, it was decided to stay with an uprated 5.6-litre version of the 5-litre M117 instead, and to keep the new M120 engine for their upcoming 140 S-Class range.

The all-new M120 60-degree V12 engine was constructed in a high silicon/copper content aluminium alloy, enabling the block to remain without a liner, like that of the M117, and keeping weight to a minimum. Positioned behind the seats in the C112 this 5987cc unit developed 408bhp at 5,200rpm;

The nose and side scoops added better cooling to radiator and engine, while the fared-in headlights added to the C112's excellent drag coefficient.

The venturi aerodynamic channels can be seen clearly, as can the 'gullwing' doors.

it accelerated from rest to 100km/h (62mph) in just under 4.9sec, and it was purported to have a top speed of over 300km/h (190mph). Its power was put to the road via a six-speed ZF-style transaxle taken from the Group C cars.

Innovative Suspension

The C112 inherited the anti-lock braking (ABS) and anti-spin control (ASR) system used in the S-Class 126, as well as the five-link double-wishbone system used on the W201. However, what set the C112 apart from any other exotic sports car was its additional computerized, intelligent handling system.

For the rear, key inputs from the ECU would fine tune the handling by means of hydraulically operated toe-control arms; this so-called 'cybernetic' steering automatically compensated for irregularities in the road surface as well as pilot input. When driving at less than 60km/h (37mph) the rear wheels would steer in the opposite direction to the front by 3.5 degrees, and when driving faster than 60km/h the rear wheels would turn at the same angle as the front to ensure optimum road grip and chassis stability at all times.

The springing of the C112 was via steel coil springs and shock absorbers. However, this was also modified according to road and driving conditions by a comprehensive electronic system called 'automatic body control' (ABC). The system was manually adjustable from understeer, through neutral to oversteer characteristics by the driver. However, the chosen setting was continually monitored in real time by the ECU to preserve perfect balance – in fact, even though the C112 sat three times higher than the C11 Group-C cars, the ABC could neutralize body pitch and roll, keeping the body dead level at all times. Adding in the 'active aerodynamics' previously mentioned, this made the C112 a very formidable automobile.

Unlike its Spartan C111 predecessors, the C112 was luxuriously appointed, and despite its aluminium chassis, its creature comforts added to its overall bulk: its curb weight was a substantial 1,600kg (3,530lb) compared with the 1,100kg (2,425lb) of the C111.

The C112 is Revealed

At the IAA Frankfurt in August 1991 the C112 was revealed to a tremendously excited press and public. However,

Cybernetic steering, or four-wheel steering, improved precision steering but also maintained chassis stability.

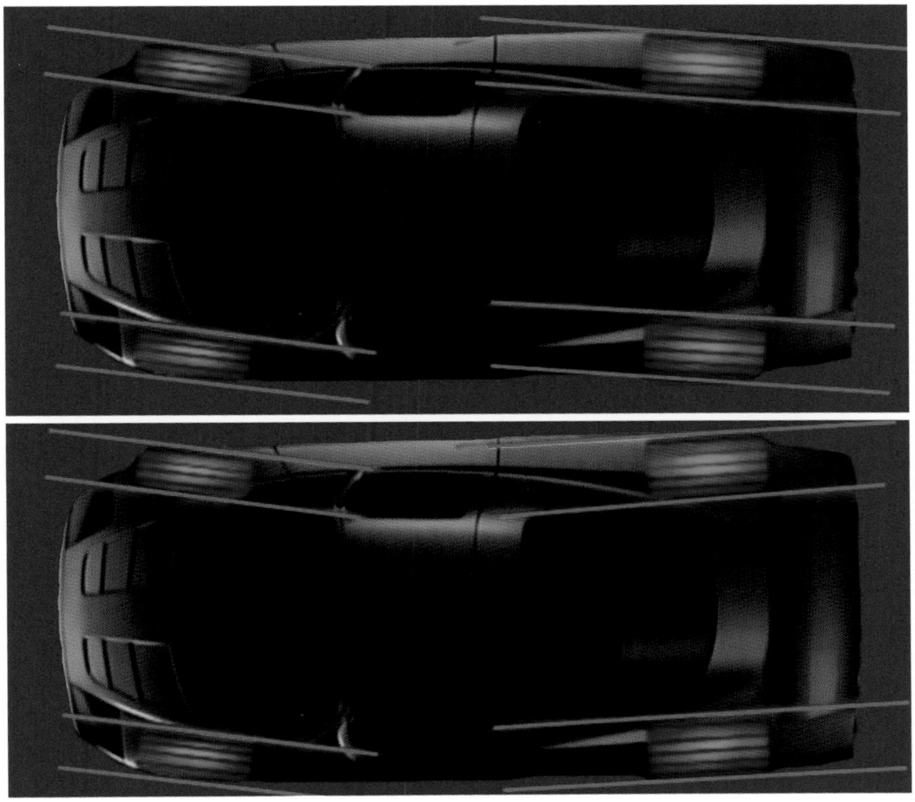

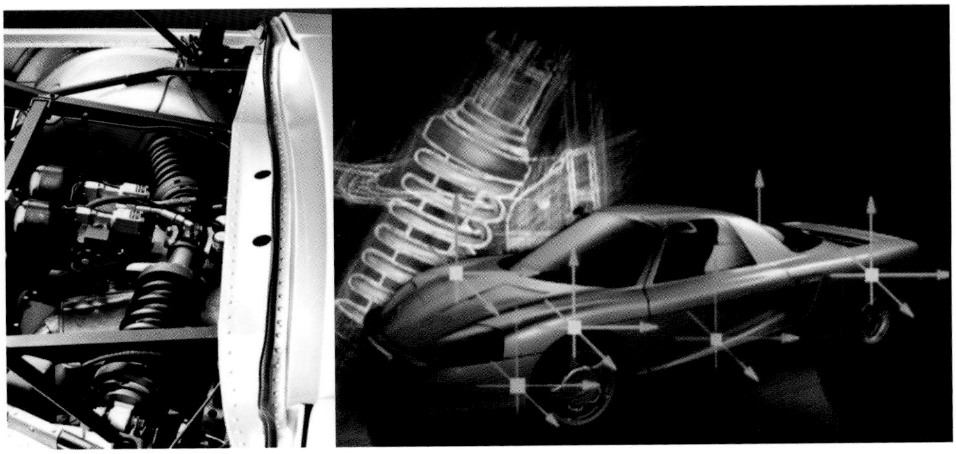

The ABC kept the body level at all times.

despite hundreds of official requests and 1.5 million DM in deposit cheques, its fate had already been sealed.

As a supercar, it was indeed late to the market; however, some high-ranking members of the board also thought that Daimler did not need to prove anything by building one. Even though it was production ready, having been built to conform to multiple markets, including the tough US market, they no longer had 'Hoffman'-style independent suppliers to make it a worthwhile investment. There was talk of Peter Sauber's new factory in Switzerland building a small number of road cars to customers' orders, but the Head of Passenger Car Division Jurgen Hubbert decided

C112 Specifications 1991

Model	C112
Production	1991
Units produced	1
Wheelbase	2,700mm (106in)
Front track	1,625mm (64in)
Rear track	1,600mm (63in)
Length	4,616mm (182in)
Width	1,976mm (78in)
Height	1,200mm (47in)
Vehicle weight	1,550kg (3,420lb)
Engine type	M120V12
Displacement	5987cc
Maximum speed	250km/h (155mph) governed
Acceleration	0–100km/h (62mph) 5.9sec
Maximum output	408bhp at 5,200rpm
Fuel system	Bosch LH-Jetronic

there were too many contractual issues to consider, and shelved the idea.

The creation of the C112 was initially the idea of Werner 'Mr Mercedes' Niefer, but by the time the project was complete, he was no longer around to be able to defend its position, and new people brought with them new ideas. The C112 therefore remained an 'experimental vehicle'.

THE 1996 F200 IMAGINATION COUPÉ

The F200 Imagination concept study was presented at the Paris Motor Show in October 1996. Its development and build were due to a co-operation between the 'Advanced Design' and 'Advanced Engineering' departments, and it epitomized the Mercedes-Benz tradition of building experimental automobiles to develop and test innovation for potential future use. Its primary objective was the development and testing of ergonomic computer systems, where all common driver commands and controls were transferred into an electronic based 'fly-by-wire' technology.

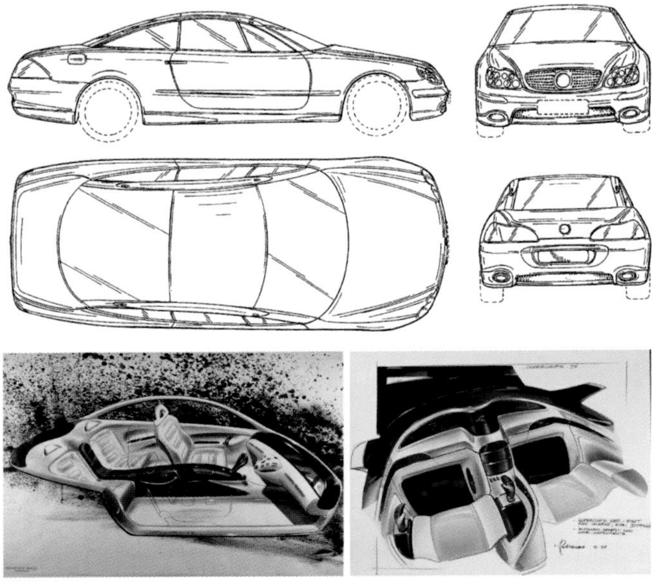

Early sketches and design ideas for the F200.

Computer-Controlled Systems

The F200 no longer had either a conventional steering wheel nor floor pedals; the conventional mechanical elements normally used by the driver were now replaced by electronic pulses and hydraulic actuators, as the driver controls all movements of his vehicle by means of 'sidesticks', similar to gaming 'joysticks', which were located on the door trim and on the central console. If the driver pushes the sidestick forwards, the F200 Imagination accelerates. If he moves the lever to the right or left, the vehicle steers to the right or left. If he pulls the lever back, the vehicle brakes, and if desired, after stopping, drives in reverse. Control could also be passed to a passenger who also had their own set.

The computer-controlled system was a precursor to an auto-pilot, pilot assist-enabled vehicle seen more recently such as 'lane control', where a computer compares the driver's steering commands with pre-set values and thus makes sure that the car does not veer off a given path, even in a critical situation. The development of this system showed that drive-by-wire systems could very easily offer many advantages in terms of safety, comfort and costs.

In the F200 the control system was also connected with the 'active body control' (ABC) system, which had already been successfully trialled on the C112. Like the supercar, the system compensated for the leaning movements of the body when driving through bends, and adapted the

Fly-by-wire joysticks on both front seat areas.

characteristics of springs and shock absorbers to the actual driving situation. It also retained the electro-hydraulic rear spoiler of the C112, assisting with both downforce and braking force.

Innovative Features

The F200 also included some innovative passive safety features. For example, in addition to the seat, side-airbag system, a new type of 'side-airbag curtain' was introduced. These so-called 'window-bags' activated within a millisecond of the impact and would deploy from the roof line, from the A-post to the C-post, protecting both front and rear occupants, and protecting all occupants in the case of a side impact.

The panoramic, electrochromic glass roof of the car provided a light, friendly atmosphere inside; it could be darkened by push button, and thus regulated both the amount of heat and light entering the interior. It was later used in the Maybach 62 Limousine.

The stainless-steel roof trim concealed a total of four multi-positional, micro-electronic cameras, which, combined with the LCD displays on the dashboard, made both exterior and interior rear-view mirrors redundant. A fifth camera faced to the rear and automatically connected to the dash display to provide a reversing view.

A new kind of hinge was developed for the 'winged doors', which used hydraulic cylinders to open the doors at an angle of 30 degrees upwards. This system facilitated the use of wider door openings for ease of access, as well as requiring less space for the doors to open in tight parking spaces. Locking operation of the doors was by push-button from inside the car and by a magnetic card from outside. A similar door was used in the SLR McLaren launched in 2003.

The headlight system featured a variable light distribution offering 'optimized vision in every situation'. Six individual reflectors in each headlamp, each with a separate LED bulb, are automatically switched on and off by sensing situation speed, and also other road user proximity so as not to dazzle oncoming traffic. When taking corners, the light follows the

The panoramic glass could be adjusted for clarity.

The F200 showing its winged doors; something similar was used on the SLR McLaren.

wheel angle set by the driver, enhancing safety for night-time driving. At high speeds on motorways an additional spot reflector is engaged to better illuminate the roadway far ahead.

The rear lights did not miss out either, and the very compact tail-light unit incorporated nine separate functions. The unobtrusive turn signal was a slender, arched neon tube of high luminosity and long life. This system went on to be developed further, and was used first in the W211 E-Class.

A voice recognition system initially developed for safe hands-free mobile phone use went on to be used in the

A rear view of the F200.

1996 facelift W140; it was known as the Linguatronic system.

A Pioneering Research Vehicle

In the sum of its characteristics, the F200 Imagination was always a pioneering research vehicle, particularly in regard to its electronics systems: if these were to play a bigger role in future cars they needed to be subjected to intensive testing before they went into production.

Although some innovations implemented in the F200 seemed rather pointless at first glance, these ideas have to be explored: the steering, braking and accelerating joysticks may not have been a serious alternative to steering wheels and pedals, but they did open up new dimensions in respect of driving dynamics, ride comfort and handling safety. Further development of these very 'fly-by-wire' systems have contributed to the success in viability of more recent 'driverless' vehicle concepts, as well as 'lane assist' systems. Moreover, as previously mentioned, many systems deployed in the F200 were in fact further developed, to be used in later Mercedes-Benz automobiles.

CHAPTER FOUR

THE SONDERKLASSE COUPÉ

THE 126 S-CLASS SALOONS

The Mercedes-Benz S classification within a model range had always been the ultimate in luxury and technology. However, with the introduction of the 116, Mercedes-Benz introduced a completely new stand-alone range of 'Sonderklasse' vehicles. The second incarnation of this new S Class was the 126 range, and it raised the bar even higher.

Launched in September 1979 after six years in development, and following a global realization that fuel was a limited resource after the scare of the 1970s fuel embargos, for the first time in Daimler-Benz history it wasn't adequate just to produce a standalone luxury vehicle: it also had to be one that was socially acceptable in terms of efficiency, ecological benefits and safety. The 126 was to be the champion in the areas of safety, technology and efficiency – it would be the

The 126 in 1979 at the IAA.

car that would take Mercedes-Benz into the next decade, not only in the hearts of loyal customers but also in the mind of the public.

Efficient Energy Concept

This Mercedes was developed under the brand's new 'efficient energy' concept. The aim was to reduce fuel consumption by at least 10 per cent over the outgoing W116, and to do this it would be necessary to reduce its component weight drastically; every piece of interior was reconsidered and redesigned, the weight of the heating system was reduced from 43 to 38kg (95 to 84lb) and the front seats from 36 to 33kg (79 to 73lb).

Around 50kg (110lb) was reduced from the bodyshell itself by using high strength but thinner steel, and high strength aluminium, and the increased use of ABS plastics in non-structural areas reduced weight by around 20kg (44lb). Much of the weight reduction was, of course, due to the new all-alloy and part-alloy engines. Depending on the vehicle, they saved between 60 and 280kg (132 and 617lb).

Although often used for racing cars and general aerodynamic specifications, the wind tunnel was not often used for 'production run' vehicles – but at the insistence of Bruno Sacco, 126 clay models spent many hours in the recently upgraded wind tunnels at Sindelfingen, undergoing on-site fine body reshaping. They were then followed, for the first time, by fully complete pre-production 126 cars, also to find the optimum shape for reducing aerodynamic drag on the finished product. The S-Class saloon came on the market with a world-record air resistance (drag coefficient) of 0.36: this corresponded to an improvement of 14 per cent over the 116, which had a drag coefficient of 0.41. At the time, no other luxury car in the world could get anywhere near that figure.

In a further effort to reduce weight and drag, for the first time in Mercedes-Benz history a luxury saloon was launched without the traditional chrome bumpers.

Crash Protection Systems

Mercedes-Benz wanted the W126 to be one of the safest cars in the world, and so used the latest science in its passive

Clay versions were made to aid design as well as improve aerodynamics after extensive wind-tunnel testing.

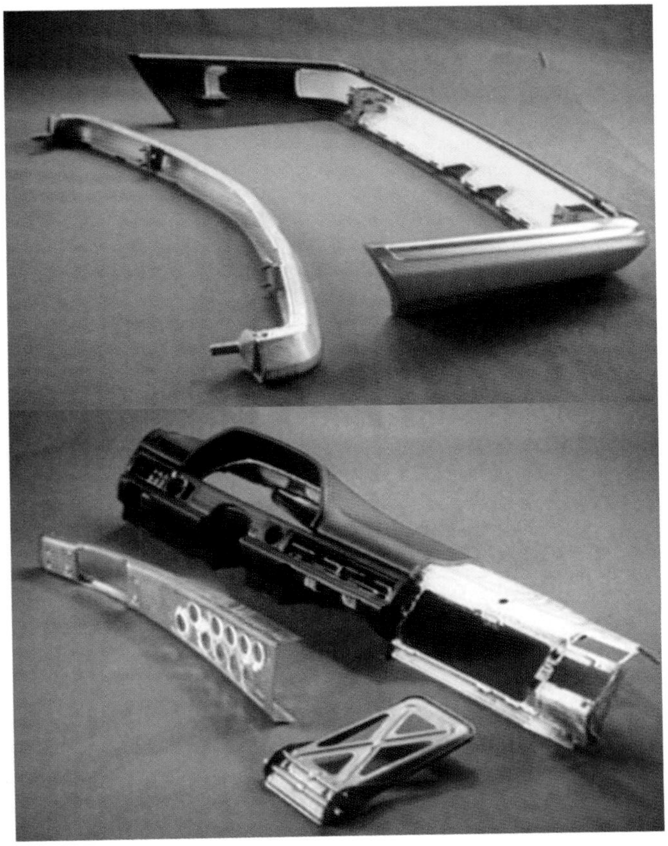

Lightweight plastics were used for bumpers for the first time on a Mercedes, and lightweight alloys were used wherever possible to reduce weight.

as well as active crash protection systems. It was the first Mercedes to incorporate an airbag and to feature traction control, both of which are taken for granted today. Its W116 predecessor might have been the first passenger car fitted with an anti-lock braking system (ABS), but the new W126 was the first to offer seatbelt pre-tensioners. This clever system tightened the seatbelts of occupants when the car's sensors predicted circumstances that could result in a crash.

Extensive crash testing and simulations proved the value of these life-saving technologies. The S-Class went on to win

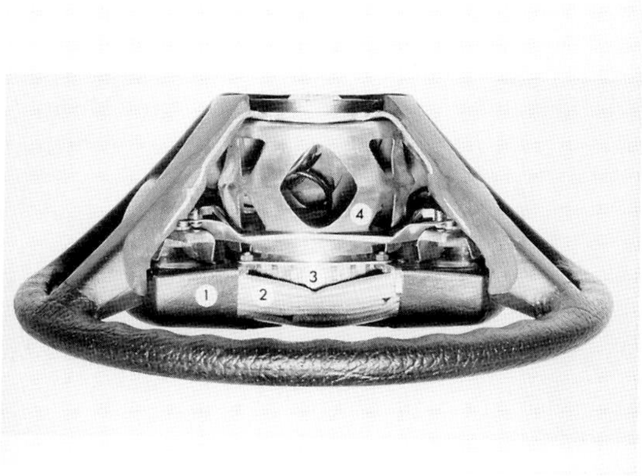

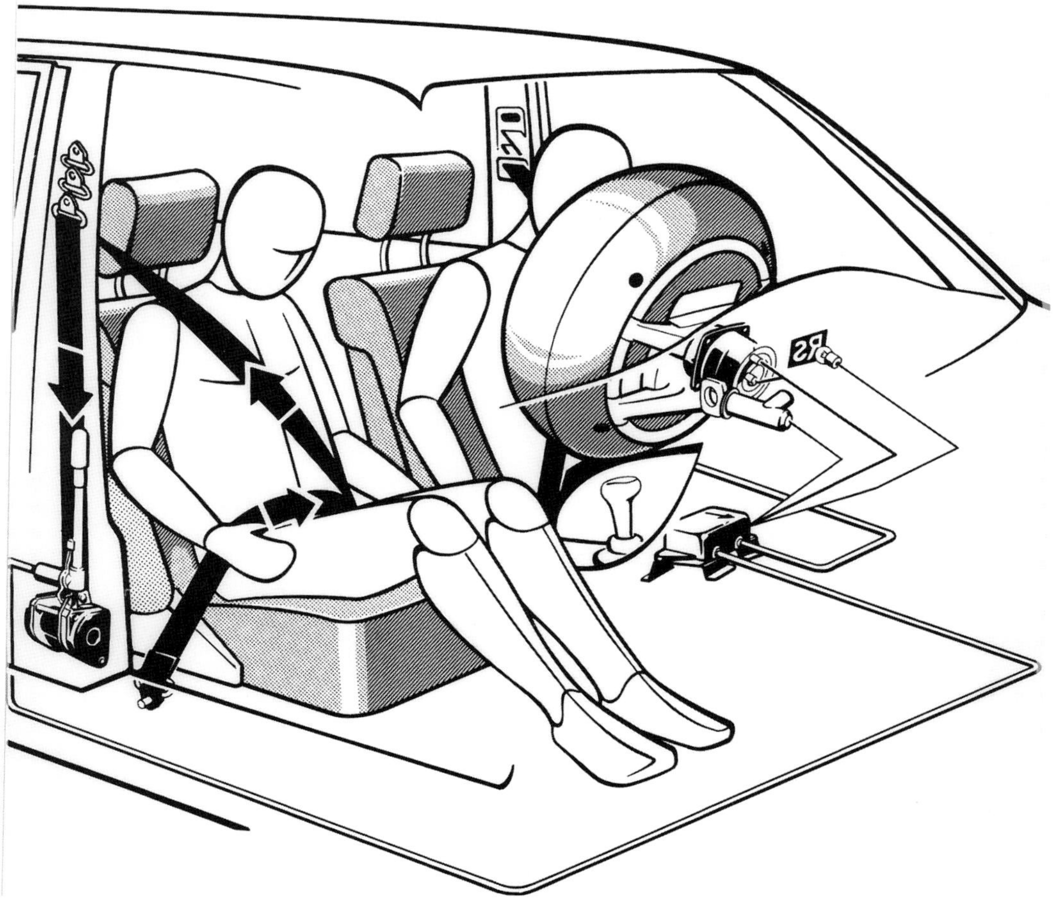

The 126 was the first vehicle ever to offer seatbelt pre-tensioners and airbags.

the US Highway Loss Data Institute's 'Safest Passenger Car of the Year' in 1988 and 1989.

THE 126 SERIES S-CLASS COUPÉS, 1981–1991

Before the Uhlenhaut Coupé and consequently the W198 300SL production version, the Coupé form had always followed the traditional 'cut' saloon: it was presented with saloon-type design elements, such as the saloon-style radiator grille, and was luxuriously appointed. With the introduction of the so-called 'Sports-Light Coupé' Mercedes-Benz had not only introduced a completely new concept in design, but had also, by using the open-mouthed grille arrangement of the sports cars, introduced an additional recognized brand element.

The 1980s had brought an element of indulgence in the finer things, and customers had already started to notice that while owning a Mercedes marque was an indulgence in itself, the SL Coupé cars did not seem to offer the luxury that their price tag might have intimated. The SLC C107 was 5,000DM more expensive than the SL R107, yet offered little more than a roof. Consequently Daimler, having put on their marketing head, decided that they wanted to return to the more luxuriously appointed Coupé of old, but keep the sporty style – and the best way to do this was by means of the brand new model line of Sonderklasse cars.

The first true S-Class model was the 116. However, although drawings were made with the intention of producing a Coupé version, it was decided it was already too close in design to the C107, especially as they had decided to keep the now recognizable image of the wide open-mouthed Coupé grille.

Brainstorming had started on what was to be the replacement to the 116 as early as 1971, and even as early on as this, it had been decided that the 126 S-class would include a Coupé version. Said Bruno Sacco:

> Mercedes-Benz Coupés attracted a clientèle that consciously opts for a body with flowing lines, and sees their vehicle as a logical extension of a lifestyle often characterized by beauty and elegance.
>
> The C126 will be the epitome of elegance on four wheels.

At the IAA in September 1981, the new Mercedes 380SEC and the 500SEC were the undisputed stars of the show.

External Appearance

Although Mercedes-Benz no longer wanted to use the SL platform as the base of the Coupé, there was some discussion as to whether the new Coupé would follow the saloon-style grille or keep the now recognizable 'Sport-Light' version. Although there are no full frontal pictures available, early 1976 clay models show hints of the original grille; by March 1977, however, the 'Mass Konzeption' drawings penned under Bruno Sacco showed the 'Sport-Light' grille.

Ultimately the new Coupé needed to symbolize not just the Mercedes spirit, but that of the S-class also. Although only the second incarnation of the 'Sonderklasse' range, it needed to emphasize tradition, robustness, reliability and innovation.

The base of the four-door chassis of the W126 was reduced by 85mm (3.3in), primarily for design proportional integrity, but also to improve handling; it was also lower, wider and with a lower centre of gravity. Despite the significant proportions of this Mercedes Coupé (4.93m/16ft in length), the aerodynamics were studied closely and individually refined.

Early model of the 126 Coupé with hints of the W111.

The enthusiasm of the people at the IAA for the new C126 is clear to see.

The traditional grille of the Mercedes was replaced with the SL-style open-mouth grille, while the imposing three-pointed star took centre place, giving a much more aggressive and yet at the same time a sleeker stance.

Externally, even the exterior mirrors received special care to contribute best to aerodynamic and acoustic efficiency. The side windows were flush fitting and without a B post, giving an almost natural elegant flow to this prestigious Coupé.

A remarkable construction detail was the aerodynamically optimized door handle recesses: although disliked by Bruno Sacco, he was overruled by the engineering department, who insisted that their aerodynamic shape served a multitude of purposes: they directed wind, noise and turbulence away from where the door glass met the rear quarter light, particularly necessary due to the lack of a B post. In any case the vehicle's aerodynamics were optimized for lower fuel consumption.

The bonnet profile rose smoothly from the grille to the windshield, camouflaging the wipers, which would have detracted from the eye but also from the aerodynamic efficiency. The overall result of this sleek body gave a remarkable Cd value of 0.34, a 15 per cent improvement over that of the C107, and around 10 per cent better than the saloon versions of the 126.

The Interior

Unlike the Mercedes 107 SLC, the Mercedes C126 offered four defined seats with a decent amount of legroom at the rear also, especially when compared with the direct competition of Aston Martin, Porsche, Maserati and Jaguar.

The interior appointments of the C126 were all but identical to those of its saloon sisters, although, as was common with European vehicles, much more was available as options than with the saloon bodies. Equipment such as the electric seat adjustment, cruise control, electric windows and electric mirrors were standard, added to which was the innovative 'seat-belt butler', which automatically offered the belt on a motorized arm to both passenger and driver.

The Engines

Unlike the saloon version 126, Mercedes-Benz decided that it would not diminish its prestige value by adding any of the 'small' 6-cylinder engines to its range. Thus the C126 was only available as the 380SEC (3.8-litre) V8, which produced

Although not frontal, these early 'mass konzeption' drawings clearly show hints of the SL grille.

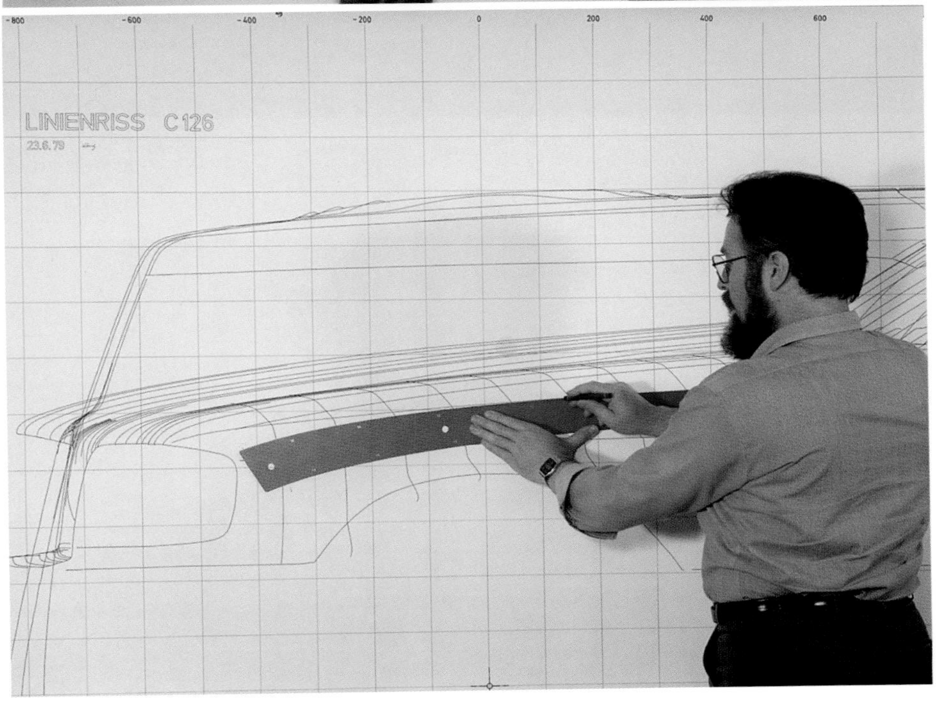

204bhp, and the 500SEC (5.0-litre) V8, offering 231bhp. Both engines were offered with the 722.3 four-speed automatic transmissions. The V8 engines, already known in principle from the 116 saloons and the SLC models, had been thoroughly redesigned within the 'Mercedes-Benz Energy Concept' in order to reduce consumption and pollutants.

Although specifications were good for the time, being relatively heavy they were not 'blisteringly' fast; rather, they were distinguished more by driving pleasure than by pure performance. It should also be noted that the other priority in the development of the C126 engines was the reduction of consumption; so even though both engines were slightly less powerful than their 107 predecessors, their torque availability responsiveness had been vastly improved, as had their overall fuel consumption due to the improved KE-Jetronic fuel-injection system.

The early model version of the C126 undergoing wind-tunnel tests.

The two bumpers as well as the side protection strips were shaped, as in the saloons. The front apron, however, was pulled further down, with integrated fog lights to avoid having fog lamps in the main headlamps as in the saloon.

The front screen edges allowed an efficient air flow up the screen (A) and the 'slipper'-style door handles (B).

Bruno Sacco alongside a 1:5-scale model.

Automatic 'seat-belt butlers' offered the seat belt forwards so front passengers didn't have to reach behind for them.

The S-Class body permitted four comfortable seats.

The M116 engine inside the 380SEC.

GENERATION TWO C126

Four years after the debut of the SEC Coupé, the model range underwent an extensive package of refinements. In September 1985, again at the Frankfurt show, a completely revised range of S-Class saloons and Coupés were introduced. The 380SEC was replaced by a 420SEC with a 4.2-litre V8 developing 218bhp; the 500SEC retained its engine, albeit with modifications and a boosted 240bhp. The C126 also received some additional equipment and fittings, such as the seats: although remaining electrically controlled, they now had 'position memorization'. The Mercedes ASR system was also added, thus increasing even more the level of active safety of the SEC.

The ageing 'Mexican hat'-style aluminium wheel rims were replaced by a new fifteen-hole design, and the previously fluted plastic side cladding (Sacco boards) was now almost flat and slightly more enveloping with better integrated body trim.

The most spectacular innovation in the engine range was a 5.6-litre 8-cylinder unit, which was developed by lengthening the stroke of the 5.0-litre V8, and which unleashed an output of 272bhp. If required, an even more highly compressed version was also available that delivered a mighty 300bhp, although it was not possible to combine this unit with a closed-loop cat emission-control system. Even without the catalytic converter this 'ECE version' still met the emissions standards stipulated by the Economic Commission for Europe. The models fitted with this engine variant – the 560SEL and 560SEC – were, in their day, the most powerful Mercedes-Benz production cars ever built. The new 'top of the range' 560SEC Coupé was capable of 0–100km/h (0–60mph) in 6.9sec and a top speed of 250km/h (155mph).

In September/October 1991, almost ten years to the day since the launch of the SEC Coupé, production was halted. An impressive 74,060 units were built, exceeding that of its SLC predecessors to the tune of more than 11,000 vehicles.

The revised C126.

The 5.6-litre M117 engine.

THE C 126 SERIES IN THE PRESS

***Auto, Motor und Sport*, Germany, issue no. 26/1981, on the C126 series:**

The feeling of space and the clear layout in the new Coupé are quite outstanding, especially in comparison with the direct predecessor, the SLC. No less impressive is the handling of the car, which weighs as much as 1,634 kilograms and is almost five metres long. The SEC handles like a dynamic mid-sized car and can be controlled most easily thanks to its precise power steering.

***Road & Track*, USA, April 1982, on the Mercedes-Benz 380 SEC:**

The new Mercedes Coupé is a stylish personal car that does so many things so very well. It has much of the performance and road manner of a lusty GT car, the elegance and plushness of a limousine, and the prestige of the three-pointed star (missing from the hood as an upright ornament, but found there as an emblem). Critics may question the price, but the excellence is indisputable.

***Road & Track*, USA, September 1985, after a speed test with the 500 SEC:**

You've got to be fairly strong to keep this throttle glued to the floor all the time; it's pretty heavy. The car is incredibly quiet at maximum speed. It's very comfortable and the steering is dead positive, only needing a bit of correction coming into the quartering wind along the straight. The seats are firm but comfortable in the Germanic fashion. It feels like a large car, which it is, but nevertheless goes fairly quickly, and, again, the lack of noise is remarkable.

140 SERIES S-CLASS

The first drawings of what was to be the successor of the 126 began around 1983, only four years after the introduction of the second Sonderklasse. Daimler-Benz were hoping that the replacement would be introduced by around 1988, but this was not to be, mainly due to 'board differences' of opinion as to its size, but also in the manufacturing of the completely new range of engines.

By 1990 the 126 was struggling to compete with the likes of the BMW 7-Series and the 'new kid on the block', the Lexus LS400. Daimler-Benz had to accelerate its production, and it knew that the new series had to be bigger and better than anything on the market.

The 140 series was introduced at the Geneva Motor Show in March 1991 to a shocked public and press. Words such as 'whale' and 'behemoth' were bandied about. But although seemingly a hundred miles from the lithe, sleek lines of the 126, it wasn't a completely different look: the body design still incorporated the typical traditional Mercedes-Benz stylistic elements, and homogeneously followed on from that of the R129SL. The trademark radiator grille of the 140 was given a new stylistic interpretation while still retaining the traditional basic shape.

As with the previous two S-Class generations, the standard version was accompanied by a long-wheelbase variant, with an additional 10cm (4in) once again added to the area behind the front seats to increase legroom in the rear.

The Engine and Final Drive Management System

Initially made available with four engines, only the 5-litre V8 M119 had been seen previously on the R129 and the 124 500E, once again fuelled by the fully electronic LH Jetronic injection system from Bosch.

Early renderings from 1983 of the potential 140 S-Class.

BELOW LEFT: **Designated the 'integrated radiator', it had a much narrower chrome frame around the radiator shell but was set in to sit flush with the shape of the bonnet – and for the first time on a saloon, it was not possible to fit the star on the grille itself, so it sat atop the bonnet, seated a little way back from the edge.**

The other three engines were newly developed. The 4.2-litre 4-valve V8 was based on the 4.2-litre 2-valve engine, and the 6-cylinder inline engine with 3.2-litre displacement was based on the 3-litre 4-valve unit introduced two years earlier. Because the engines did not accurately reflect the displacement, as had always been the case in the past, for the sake of consistency the models were designated as 300 SE/SEL and 400 SE/SEL.

From June 1993 the first 12-cylinder engine that Mercedes-Benz had made for a production passenger car was introduced. The M120 had a displacement of 6 litres. With a rated power output of 300kW (408bhp) and a peak torque of 580 Nm, it was also the most powerful Mercedes-Benz car engine of its day.

With all new engines, a high priority was placed on minimizing exhaust emissions and reducing fuel consumption – so as with the other engines, the 12-cylinder was also equipped with 4-valve technology, variable intake camshaft, and an electronic injection system with hot-wire air mass sensor. The new, fully electronic ignition system calculated the optimum ignition point from 300 ignition maps, tuned for each cylinder individually and to the knock limit in each case. The M120 was the only 12-cylinder engine in the world to feature this cylinder-selective anti-knock control, without which it would not have been possible to achieve the high compression ratio of 10:1, necessary for optimum fuel consumption.

The engine and final drive management system were unique in that for the first time all control modules were

The M120 was the first ever V12 production engine for Mercedes-Benz.

active live and communicated with one another continually – everything from cold-start engine management to how the environment dictated handling and stability of the entire suspension system.

Setting New Standards

Not only did the developers of the new S-Class lower fuel consumption and improve environmental compatibility with responsible exhaust emission advancements, the 140 S-Class was a pioneer of environmentally responsible manufacturing. Apart from being a completely CFC (chlorofluorocarbons) free vehicle, it set new standards in recyclability. Not only were the plastic parts recyclable in themselves, they were manufactured from re-granulated, recycled plastics.

Comfort and safety levels had been raised again from that of the 126. The 140 range benefited from a completely new double-wishbone front axle, and a subframe-mounted front suspension system. Also, alongside the multilink independent rear suspension set-up as had been used on other models, tyre noise and vibrations transmitted to the passenger compartment were kept to a level never realized before.

In terms of 'active safety', this new suspension system enabled an exceptionally good straight-line stability even on uneven road surfaces, and despite its size the 140 had an extremely low crosswind sensitivity, largely unaffected even by the size of payload.

The brake system for the 8- and 12-cylinder models was a major innovation.

More force was applied to the rear wheels, which reduced brake fade as well as reducing wear to the front brakes; however, it also minimized the pitching and diving of the vehicle on acceleration and braking. Speed-sensitive steering power assistance was fitted as standard to the 8- and 12-cylinder variants, which greatly reduced the steering effort required by the driver at low speeds, but also added 'feel' at higher speed.

The new body structure contained numerous advances in 'passive safety' in all types of accidents, including several external improvements to reduce impact hazards to pedestrians and cyclists.

For ultimate levels of comfort befitting an S-Class Mercedes, and for the first time ever, the 140 benefited from double-glazed side windows: these primarily cut down the likelihood of them misting and/or icing up, but also offered vastly improved soundproofing.

Further Design Details

Two further design details were added: first, electronically controlled folding exterior mirrors, which gave a

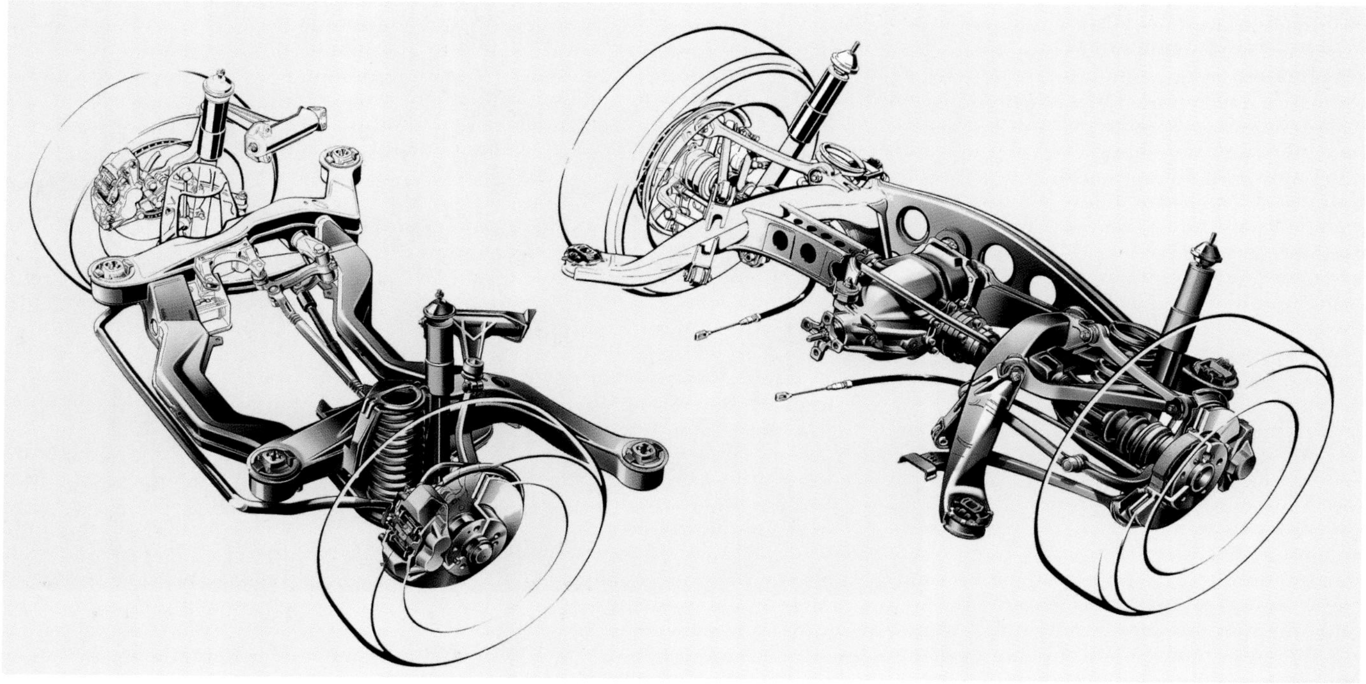

The multilink suspension was located in both front and rear subframe units.

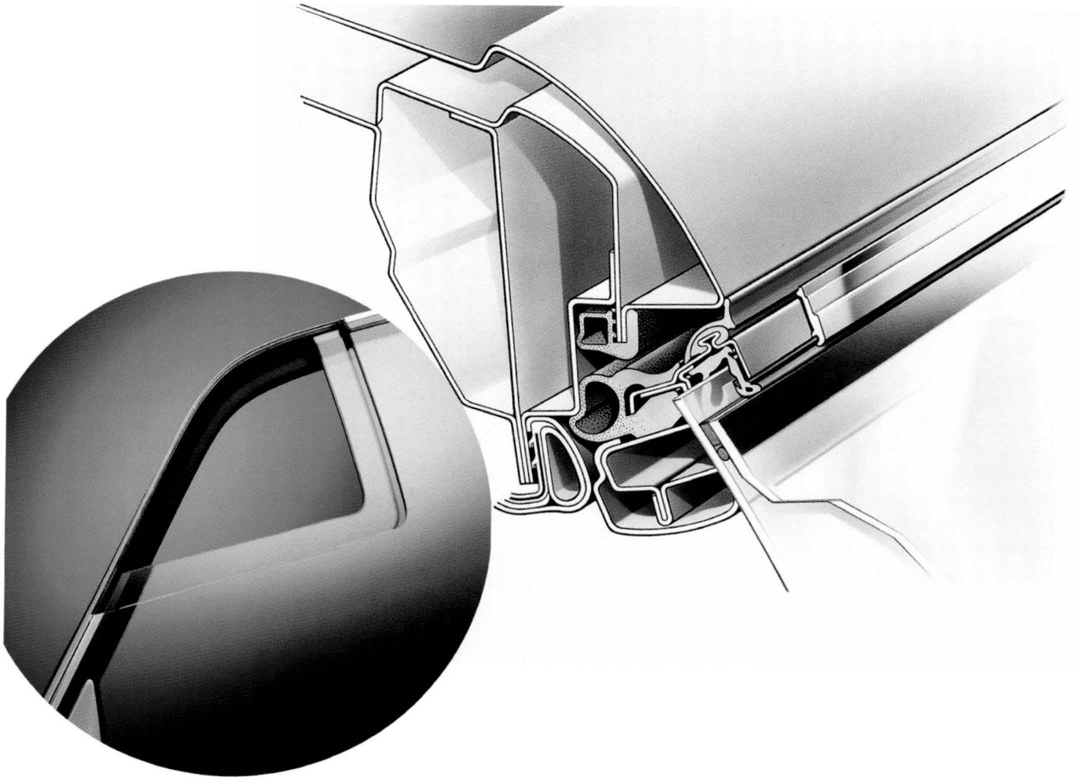

For the first time in any automobile the 140 had double glazing.

little extra space when manoeuvring in tight spaces, but also kept them out of the way of traffic while parked. Secondly, 'reversing guide rods' on the rear wings assisted the driver to judge distances to obstacles when reversing. Two seconds after selecting reverse gear, these pneumatically operated, 65mm-long chrome rods automatically extended vertically, returning eight seconds after a new gear had been selected.

Additional comfort features were as follows:

- Automatic rain-sensing wiper
- Automatic anti-dazzle interior mirror, and memory seats and steering wheel
- Orthopaedic seats, an expensive factory option, but composed of several air cushions in the seat that the user is able to inflate and deflate at will to find the perfect driving position
- Dual-zone air conditioning
- Heated and reclining rear seats (introduced with Mercedes-Benz W126, S-Class W126 sedans)
- A climate system that can be configured to operate for 20min with the engine off
- Automatic boot-lid closure
- Automatic door closure

Models Offered

The 140 was offered from the beginning with four engine types: the 500 with a 5-litre V8 engine; a 420 with a 4.2-litre V8 engine; the 320 with its 3.2-litre straight 6; and lastly the flagship 600, with the very first production version V12 6-litre engine. All these engines had the new 4-valve per cylinder heads.

At the Paris Motor Show, in October 1992, two 'entry-level' models also appeared: the 350SD (diesel) with 150bhp, and the 300SE 2.8-litre. In 1994, the Coupé also received the new V8 engine of the 420.

Stylistic Revision

A facelift three years after the première brought a subtle stylistic revision. The new variant was presented at the Geneva Motor Show in March 1994. The model nomenclature had followed a new pattern for around a year, the model designations having changed in June 1993, with the 'S' placed before the three-digit number.

In May 1995, the old rear parking assistance system with two small retractable antennae gave way to the new Park-

Rear view of the 1994 facelift.

Front view of the 1994 facelift.

tronic system, in which ultrasonic sensors communicated the distance from obstacles. In September of the same year, the four-speed automatic transmission gave way to the new five-speed automatic transmission for the V8 and V12, and the ESP appeared as an option; but both the saloons and the Coupé were fitted with ASR and traction control as standard.

For all this equipment, the W140 is often considered to be the last Mercedes 'over-equipped', a characteristic that caused delays and was said to have cost Daimler a one billion dollars overspend and resulted in the departure of Daimler-Benz chief engineer Wolfgang Peter. For customers, the W140 was 25 per cent more expensive than the W126.

Up to the end of production a total of 406,717 saloons of the model series 140 were manufactured at the Sindelfingen plant, some 28,101 units of which had a diesel engine.

In January 1992, the C140 (Coupé) was called upon to succeed the famous 126SEC. It made its appearance with two engines: the V8 5-litre and the V12 6-litre.

THE M120 V12

To power what many referred to as the best saloon in the world, and of course to compete with other manufacturers such as BMW, Mercedes-Benz decided it was time to build a V12.

Daimler had toyed with the idea of a V12 engine as far back as the 1960s, when the W100 (600) was in production. One initial plan for the W100 was to include a 5.0-litre V8 and call it a 500S, alongside a massive 380bhp 7.5-litre V12 calling it a 750S in the W100 model. However, with the development of the M100 V8 engine, Mercedes-Benz management deemed the V12 no longer necessary.

In the 1970s, Daimler engineers also experimented on the development of transitioning a V8 90-degree configuration to a V12; however, it was beset with technical woes, most notably in that the 90-degree V angle created a great many problems concerning noise, vibration and harshness, uncharacteristic of any potential range-topping Mercedes-Benz.

They were back at it in the 1980s, this time working with a 60-degree V6 that they considered would do better at scaling up to 12 cylinders. It was seriously considered as an addition to the 126 S-class range. However, it was late in the day for the 126, so once again, management put their V12 plans on hold, albeit briefly.

Competition from BMW

In 1986 BMW released their all new, full-size luxury saloon, the E32 7-series – and for the first time it put Mercedes-Benz on the back foot: Daimler had to act at once or risk falling further behind. So they took delivery of one of the BMW V12 cars immediately, and their engineers reported that it was 'as competent a drive as any four-wheeled BMW that had ever come before it'. It also demonstrated that at a time when Mercedes' top powerplant in the USA was a 238bhp V8 whose origins dated back nearly twenty years, BMW's 296bhp sohc V12, and the car that featured it, had significantly overtaken Mercedes as the class leader when it came to luxury, space, refinement and power.

Daimler-Benz had been made aware of the forthcoming BMW V12 for quite a while before it was released, but for some reason – maybe considering the climate where engines were becoming smaller and more efficient – they didn't take the threat seriously. This was a mistake on two levels: the first was that they didn't have anything with which to counter the BMW threat, but more importantly, if they wanted it to be a part of the forthcoming 140 S-Class range, it would ultimately play a part in delaying its release. Thus the ageing 126 S-Class, although still selling well enough, would have to continue for at least another two to three years.

Architecture of the M120 V12

Work began in earnest on the M120 V12 in 1987.

Considering that 4-valve head technology destined for the next generation of the Mercedes V8 and straight-six engines was already under development, the decision was made to go with four camshafts and 4 valves per cylinder on the M120, too. Following the lead of BMW, who apparently

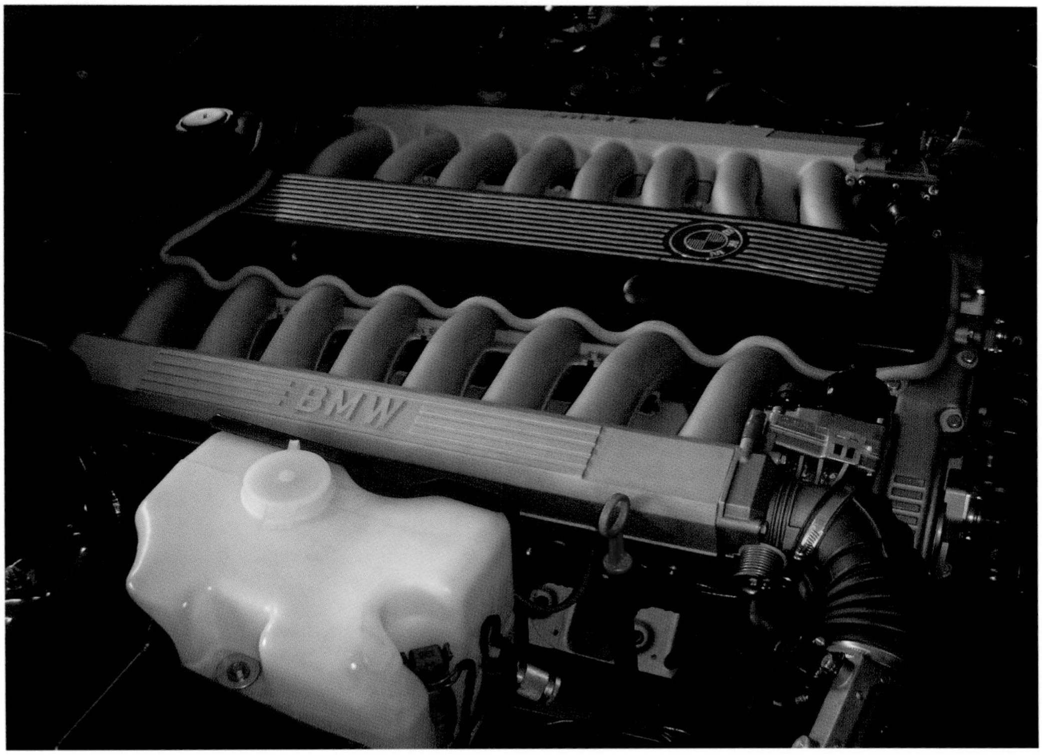

There were even rumours that BMW was also developing a V16, confirmed later as a prototype fitted to a 750iL.

grafted a pair of inline-sixes into a V configuration, Mercedes-Benz based the architecture of its V12 on much the same principle, using the block pattern of their M104 straight-six engines, but not its cast-iron make-up. For the M120 they used a silicon-rich aluminium with a high copper content similar to that used in the M117 engines; this also resulted in a significant weight reduction.

The resulting block was deeply skirted and allowed space for a seven-bearing forged-steel crankshaft, increasing its robustness. Pistons were also forged aluminium with an iron

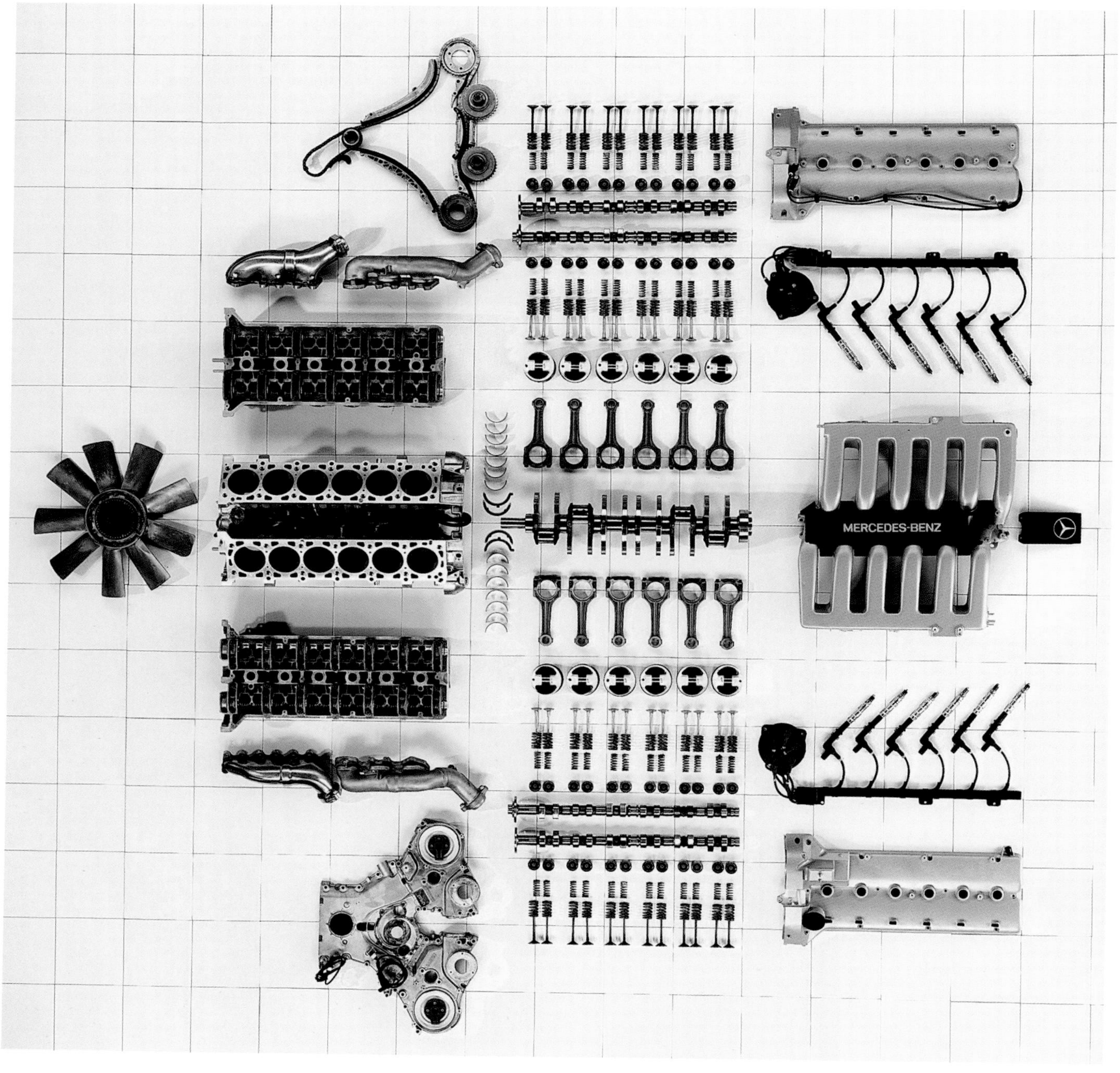

Exploded view of the parts in an M120 V12.

and zinc coating, and with the high silicon content of the block, the pistons reciprocated in linerless cylinders. Retaining the same bore spacings as the 3-litre M104, the V12 had the same 80.2mm bore, although the stroke was slightly increased from 88.5mm to 89mm, resulting in a displacement of 5987cc.

By using the same M104 block design, ingeniously engineers were able to use the head from the 24-valve M104 intact on the right side, and to cast a mirror version for the left side.

The entire valve-train operated via a single double-chain assembly connecting all four camshafts and the crankshaft, and it incorporated an ingenious variable valve timing system on the intake cams.

A multi-piece sump also included a 'windage tray', a device normally used on Formula 1 cars to prevent the oil foaming.

The intake manifold on top of the engine was not made up from individual components, but was cast and fitted as a single piece. It was so aesthetically pleasing that it was said by a member of the press to 'appear like the hands of a six-fingered man playing the clarinet'.

Bosch provided an updated version of their LH-Jetronic ECU software, which controlled a pair of knock sensors to protect the 10.0-compression engine from pre-detonation with lower-octane gasoline.

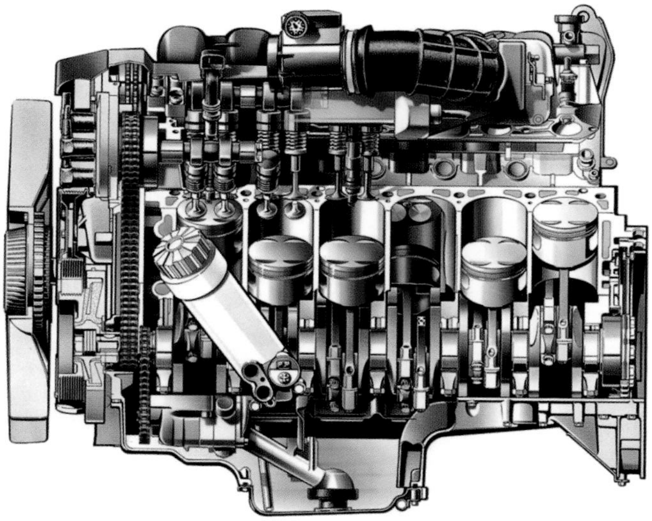

Side elevation technical drawing of the M120.

Front elevation of the M120.

Performance

Initially the first 600SE and SEL model 140s rolled off the production line with the M120 producing 402bhp at 5,200rpm, along with an equally impressive 428lb ft of torque at 3,800rpm. The only automobiles to come anywhere near these numbers were the likes of Ferrari and Lamborghini, and even though they could achieve similar power on paper, these engines only achieved their power at very high revs and at a far higher decibel level.

Although the 140 S-Class was undeniably tall, it returned a very sporting coefficient drag of 0.31Cd, and the M120, even in the SEL version, pulled like the proverbial locomotive, albeit a very quick locomotive.

On press testing, the heavy-footed drivers at *Car and Driver* were able to propel the big Benz from 0 to 100km/h (60mph) in just 5.7sec: in 1992 this was supercar speed. In comparison to the BMW E32 750iL, the best that *Car and Driver* could achieve of the same vintage was a 0–100km/h (60mph) of 7.8sec. Still, despite the potential for a much higher top speed, the engineers at Mercedes-Benz electronically limited the top end of all its V12 models to 250km/h (155mph). They also stated, 'For a car as large as the 600SEL, the sense of intimacy behind the wheel is unparalleled.' It not only went fast, but handled surprisingly well for its mass, achieving a respectable 0.79g on the skid-pad test with 235/60ZR16 tyres.

Adjustments to emissions controls from late 1993 saw the M120 slightly downrated to 389bhp, and from 1996 a few other refinements – such as implementing the Bosch Motronic combined fuel-injection and ignition ECU, along with converting the ignition system to coil-on-plug technology – improved the power band.

The one-piece intake manifold installed in the W140.

The same engine was put into the AMG CLK.

A version of the M120 in the Pagani Zonda.

The M120 went on to be used to power several high-end Mercedes-Benz automobiles, including the CLK GTR in road-going and race-track guise. Its displacement went from the original 6 litres to 6.9 and 7.3 litres.

The M120 Makes its Mark

The M120 became the standard power plant for the hyper-exotic Pagani Zonda, albeit producing a massive 800bhp from its 6 litres. It remained in production until 2013, long after Mercedes-Benz had stopped using the 4-valve V12 in its passenger car in favour of its 3-valve, 5.6-litre, M137 V12, which arrived with an all-new S-Class in 1999.

The M120 saloons and Coupés truly made their mark on the automotive landscape. As engineering powerhouses, they wowed their fans. They were a billion-dollar investment for a massive global company that was delayed by the V12 engine programme, and ultimately met with somewhat underwhelming sales; however, the programmes changed the way Mercedes-Benz developed road cars. Within a few years, the attitude that the best engineering and design trumped all other factors, gave way to a more pragmatic tone that saw the company responding to the market, rather than setting it.

V12 M120 Saloon Engine Specifications 1992–2001

Engine type	M120 E60/120.980 (from June 1995: E60/120.982)
Number of cylinders	12/60 degrees V; light alloy block
Bore × stroke	89.0 × 80.2mm
Total displacement	5987cc
Compression ratio	10.0
Rated output	394bhp @ 5,200rpm
Rated torque	570Nm @ 3,800rpm
Number of valves	2 intake, 1 exhaust
Fuel system	LH-Jetronic from June 1995
Cooling	water cooling/pump; 18.5ltr water

140 SERIES S-CLASS COUPÉS, 1992–1998

Considering most Mercedes cars start development around six years before their release, one of the hardest things

Brain-storming ideas for the C140.

BELOW: **Pre-Olivier Boulay design, dated October 1985.**

about introducing a new car is predicting the 'society' into which it will have to fit.

The saloon versions of the 140 had a hard time of it, as its very existence, in some people's eyes, was as close to the seven deadly sins as modern society could get. In its 6-litre V12 form it became the epitome of capitalist excess in a world that was fast becoming conscious of environmental issues.

Even though everything had been done to minimize the physical excessiveness of the car by making it as ecologically responsible as it could be, it still had an image problem. If the saloon was a 'necessity' in which the plutocracy had to waft about, the Coupé was just a toy. Greenpeace mounted a protest on the roof of the Sindelfingen factory in 1995 against just this car, and it worked: the C140 really sounded the death knell for the bloated, overtly excessive automobile, and all subsequent Coupés became a shadow of their former selves.

The world première of the C140 took place at the Detroit Autorama in 1992; the première in Europe was two months later at the Geneva Motor Show. The car was initially released as the 500SEC with the 5-litre V8, and the 600SEC with the new 6-litre V12 as fitted to the saloon versions. In technical terms they were based upon the Saloon 140; however, in exterior styling they were more independent. The interior was also completely redesigned, and only the dashboard of the Saloon models was retained.

The C140 followed its own design ideas, although it was based on the 140 saloons.

The C140 interior (top) was markedly different to the Saloon 140 (bottom).

Like the saloon versions, the Coupé came with diamond-cut alloy wheels, double glazing, 'close-assist' doors and boot lid, dual-zone climate control, and full Napa soft-feel leather as standard.

Unusually for Mercedes, the options list was very short, no matter which engine you went for. Orthopaedic front seats with inflatable cushions were among the more pricey options, while the V12 version had several features as standard that were extra on the smaller-engined versions, including stability control; in later years it became the first Mercedes to have satellite navigation as standard, followed by a 'linguatronic' voice-control system. But for

The sculptured rear seating of the Coupé followed design cues from the C126.

The original C140 (top) compared to the new CL140 (bottom).

the first time in Mercedes history it came with a radio as standard.

The start price of the 500SEC was 156,000DM, but the 600SEC was around 65,000DM more; but from 1994, a 4.2-litre V8 was introduced at only 48,000DM.

Parallel to the other Mercedes passenger-car types, new type designations were introduced with the S-Class Coupés in June 1993; the 600SEC became the S600 Coupé. The type label on the deck lid now only documented the displacement and the class to which the car belonged, but no longer designated body style, as this was visible anyway.

THE CL600 COUPÉ BREAK CONCEPT

Back in 1994 Zagato took a C140 Mercedes-Benz CL600 and modified it as a 'shooting or golfing break'. Little is known of this vehicle, however, it was unveiled at the 1995 Geneva Motor Show. Zagato simply added a rear cell to the large V12 Coupé, creating a hatchback. At the time it was well received; however, nothing more is known of its existence to date.

The Zagato version of the CL140.

The CL Coupé

In June 1996 the type designations for the Coupés were changed once again to CL ('Large Coupé'). The CL Coupés were also slightly modified in terms of style: externally visible were the revised bumpers, with the integrated sensors for the ultrasonic parking aid, 'Parktronic' being part of the standard delivery programme. Through this parking aid the back-up markers were no longer needed in the rear wings. Other remarkable novelties were xenon headlights with dynamic headlight-range adjustment, a Tempomat with speed limiter, standard side bags, as well as a seat identification system for the front passenger seat.

Assembly of the 140 Coupé CL models ceased in September 1998, almost six years after the commencement of standard production. With a total of 26,022 units produced at the Sindelfingen plant, it wasn't one of their best-selling cars, selling only a third of the total number of 126 Coupés sold.

The change of name was not an end in itself, but it would show that the Coupé 'Large' was now a standalone model in the range: as the CL it would take its styling cues from the S-Class and the E-Class range, but it would become the 'daddy' of what would be a whole family of Coupé cars for Mercedes-Benz in the near future.

What unites all these Coupés, in addition to their styling, is the fact that they always have the latest automotive engineering on board, and many technical innovations often make their debut both in S-Class Saloons and Coupés before being widely used in other models.

S-CLASS COUPÉ LARGE (CL)

The 215 Series CL-Class Coupés, 1999–2006

The end of the 1990s brought with it a difficult time financially for Daimler AG, and consequently several challenging changes. One of them was to 'Give the customers more of what they wanted', starting with a wider range of model choice but also a 'feeling of responsibility'. The overt extravagance of the late 1980s and the early 1990s had gone, and subtlety and refinement was more the name of the game.

Side-by-side comparison of the outgoing C140 (right) and the new C215 (left).

At the Geneva Motor Show in March 1999, the Mercedes-Benz C215 series – beginning with the CL500 – celebrated its world première. Although the CL Coupé was still derived from the platform of the 1999 W220 S-Class, it differed in that it followed the styling cues of the second series W210 E-Class saloons. Daimler had learned its lesson with the bulkiness of its predecessor the CL140, and the 215 was presented shorter by 7.2cm (2.8in) and less wide by 5.5cm (2.2in). The wheelbase was also shortened by 6cm (2.4in) and the height by 5.4cm (2.1in). Its elegant styling produced a mere aerodynamic value of 0.28Cd.

The stylistic cues of the CL140 remained, however, with its strong line, long sloping squat bonnet, the dynamic curvature of the roof line, and the distinctive rear end. Its full-length side windows and lack of B posts gave the body the same airy look of both its 126 and 140 predecessors.

To further the distancing from the S-Class styling, the large Coupé sported the typical E-Class Mercedes front end with expressive twin headlamps as a reinterpretation of the familiar 'four-eyes face' first seen on the Coupé concept of 1993.

At its debut in March 1999 it was released with the 5-litre V8 M113, as in the W220 S-Class. The all-aluminium engine had 3 valves per cylinder, two intake and one exhaust, and the reasons for doing this was to reduce heat loss from burnt gases as well as keeping the catalytic converter at its optimum for longer, reducing polluting emissions when cold. Its double ignition with two spark plugs per cylinder reduced noise and allowed more complete combustion of the fuel mixture, and went a long way to producing the 306bhp at 5,600rpm and 460Nm torque from 2,700 to 4,500rpm.

Mated to the four-speed transmission, it was not the most powerful or sporty of engine combinations; however, it was meant as a pure grand tourer. It was also offered with an optional cylinder shut-off system to cut emissions in low load environments.

Mercedes-Benz did not skimp on driving assistance, and offered the following: ESP (anti-roll), ASR (traction control), ABS (anti-lock braking), EBD (brake distributor) and, although there was no LSD rear axle, ABC suspension (active body control). The ABC suspension system optimized stability by means of sensor signals and special hydraulic cylinders on the axles; it almost totally compensated for rolling and pitch motions of the body when starting off and when cornering and braking, and kept the car on an imperturbable course at all times.

The top-of-the-range position of this Coupé was confirmed by equipment such as the multi-function steering wheel, adjustable steering column, five-speed automatic with one-touch paddle gear shifting, Tempomat cruise control with variable speed control Speedtronic, automatic climate control with activated charcoal filter, electrically adjustable leather-covered seats with memory function, Mercedes-Benz Audio 30 radio, leather trim on the dashboard and doors, and fine wood trim.

The list of options included an electronic tyre-pressure control system, the dynamic navigation system DynAPS, the chip-card-controlled Keyless-Go driver authorization system, and active seat ventilation.

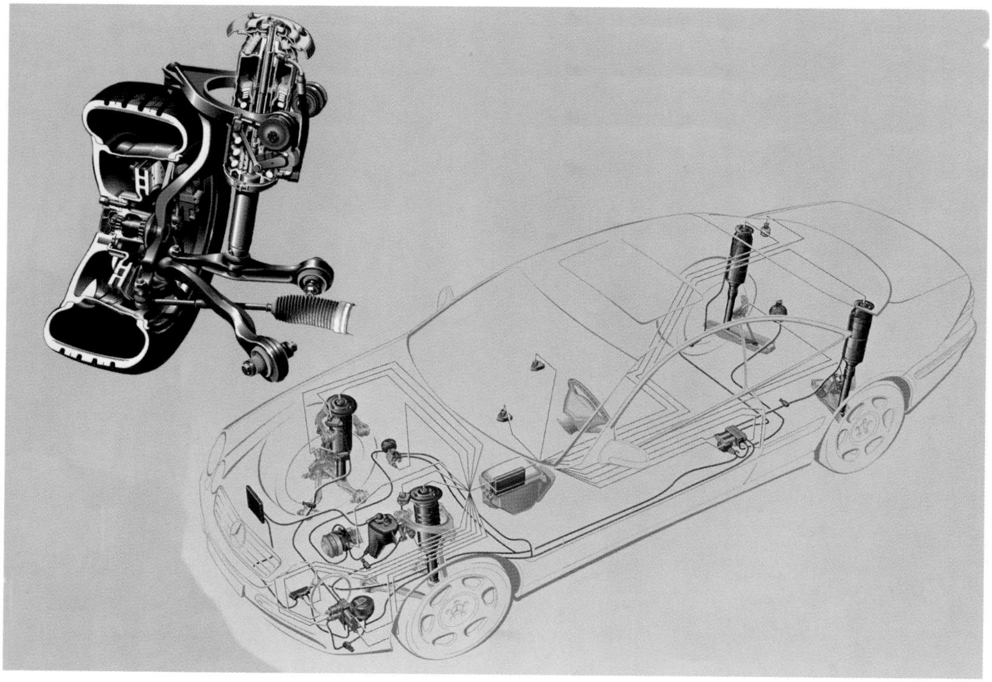

The new ABC suspension system in breakdown.

The V12 CL600 showing the M137 engine (inset).

The CL600 with 12-cylinder Engine

Sales in Europe and Japan started in the autumn of 1999, and in early 2000, the CL600 with 12-cylinder engine joined the line-up; it was offered with the 'COMAND' operating and display system, a car phone, a Bose sound system, and upholstery covered with exclusive Napa leather – and a roof lining made of soft ultrasuede underlined the special class of this car.

The CL600 boasted the newly developed, smooth-running M137 12-cylinder engine, which generated 270kW and a torque of 530Nm. It also had an advanced lightweight

Distronic sensor (top) and BiZenon HiD headlamps (bottom).

design, 3-valve technology, double ignition, an automatic cylinder shut-off system that reduced fuel consumption under part-load, six catalytic converters and eight oxygen sensors.

The C215 was the second car, after the W220 S-Class, with the DISTRONIC system; it was the first world-wide radar-assisted 'autonomous cruise control' system. It was also the first car in the world to be fitted with both low and high beam 'Bi-Xenon' HiD (high intensity discharge) headlamps.

The CL55 AMG F1 Limited Edition

A very special model was the CL55 AMG F1 Limited Edition, which became available from the autumn of 2000 in a limited edition of fifty-five units. It was fitted with a number of exclusive appointments, and also a bold price tag of 330,000DM (approximately 168,500 euros). It was based upon the CL55 AMG safety car used in Formula 1.

The F1 version was the world's first road-going car with internally ventilated brake discs made of fibre-reinforced ceramics. The ceramic brake discs were pressed into shape under high pressure at the Daimler plant in Esslingen-Mettingen near Stuttgart; they were made from carbon fibre, coal powder and resin before being baked at 1,000°C. Having cooled, the brake discs underwent brief machining before being treated with liquid silicon. The carbon matrix absorbed the silicon like a sponge, and reacted with the ceramic. In operation they gave a highly sensitive response, extreme thermal stability, continuous-load capability and a longer service life. In an emergency braking manoeuvre from top speed they gave a braking power of 1,475kW, or the equivalent of 2,000bhp.

The F1 Limited Edition showing the ceramic brakes (inset).

The F1 Limited Edition interior.

This CL55 AMG F1 Limited Edition was powered by a 5.5-litre M113 V8 engine, which produced 355bhp (265kW). The interior featured distinctively sporty front seats with optimized lateral support, an AMG sports steering wheel with perforated leather cover, carbon-fibre trim – and an 'F1 Limited Edition' logo with consecutive numbering on the centre console.

The M137 6.3 engine.

Having already introduced the 55AMG model, it was now to become the smaller brother of a new model. At the Frankfurt International Motor Show in 2001 the CL63AMG was introduced as the new top-of-the-range model. The advanced M137 6.3-litre engine was reminiscent of the 300SEL 6.3 of the past, but the new V12 of the CL63AMG developed 444bhp (326kW).

Face-Lifted Version of the Series C215 CL-Class

In the autumn of 2002, Mercedes-Benz unveiled a face-lifted version of the Series C215 CL-Class featuring revised body styling, an upgraded interior, and the latest state-of-the-art technology. Especially striking was the vehicle's restyled twin-headlamp face with a state-of-the-art clear glass look, as well as the revised front bumper, which yet further emphasized the strong appearance of the Coupé.

The outside mirror housings were modified and fitted with ambient lighting in the base: this illuminated the area around the side of the car automatically whenever the central locking was operated by remote control or the door opened. This feature enhanced the safety and comfort of passengers when entering and leaving the vehicle. The rear-light clusters were given a glossy look to match that of the headlamps.

The facelift also included an enhanced 'active body control' (ABC). This unique system continuously measured the current gross weight of the vehicle, and included this value when computing the active suspension control, and adjusted the springing and damping at lightning speed to suit the current driving situation; it also minimized the movement of the body when starting off, cornering and braking.

The CL Coupé had boasted an exemplary standard of occupant safety since the start of production of the Series 215 in autumn 1999; however, in the face-lifted CL-Class, Mercedes-Benz augmented this passive safety equipment with a far more advanced and personalised system. Additional sensors in the front end of the body detected the severity of any impending impact in milliseconds, which allowed the deployment of the front passenger airbag to be controlled in two stages depending on the situation. Moreover, thanks to these sensors, the emergency belt tensioning retractors could be activated even sooner for

EXCLUSIVE WORLD FIRST: NATURAL STONE TRIM

From the spring of 2001, buyers of the C215 series were the first to be able to order natural stone trim for the interior. In a special patented process, wafer-thin granite panels (0.6–0.8mm thick) were produced before being specially formed and applied to the centre console, interior door cladding, steering-wheel rim and selector lever. This exclusive trim was made available by the individualized Designo programme.

These stone-based parts were made from high-grade south Norwegian Larvikite stone known as 'Labrador Blue Pearl', an extremely hard plutonic rock composed mainly of feldspar, which reflected incidental light, making some crystals appear light blue while creating a pearl-like shimmer on the surface. One of the greatest challenges in production was to avoid bending the natural stone when forming curved surfaces: the solution was protected by four patents.

First, a 0.6 to 0.8mm thin stone section was prepared with a diamond saw. These plates were fixed in place with an adhesive layer before their structure was broken up between two rotating rollers. This resulted in a layer that could be laid around tight edges, while the typical features of the stone remained intact – including the crystalline structure crucial for optical effect.

The 'Labrador Blue Pearl' stone interior items.

optimal protection of the occupants much quicker upon impact.

Another innovation was automatic weight classification of the front passengers by means of a special seat bolster sensor that not only reacted according to impact severity, but also in two stages according to the weight of the front passenger.

Additional sensors also controlled window bags and side airbags, high-performance emergency tensioning retractors, belt force limiters and automatic child seat recognition.

The headlamps gave a cleaner, clear glass look to the second series.

Multiple seat sensors responded according to the weight of the passenger.

From the autumn of 2002, the CL55 AMG Coupé was powered by a supercharged 5.5-litre, which increased the power to 500bhp (368kW); this powerplant accelerated the two-door vehicle from 0 to 100km/h in just 4.8 seconds. A five-speed automatic transmission with racing-car-style shift paddles on the steering wheel rounded off the sporty driving experience offered by the new CL 55 AMG.

The AMG CL65

To match the upgrade to the V8 CL55 AMG, the V12 versions also received a new engine in 2002 and although based on the M137, the M275 received a number of upgrades, including a better cooling system to accommodate the twin turbos that boosted output to 500bhp (368kW). The AMG CL65, which was introduced in the autumn of 2003, had its power boosted to 612bhp (450kW).

Power transfer was by means of the AMG Speedshift five-speed automatic transmission with paddle-style gear shift on the steering wheel. The high peak torque of 1,200Nm required limitation to 1,000Nm, and strengthening of various transmission components, such as newly developed clutch plates with high-quality metal coating and a modified shift and torque converter lock-up logic. Modified driveshafts and larger wheel carriers also accommodated the high power and torque. The M275 was the most powerful engine to date built by AMG.

The cars accelerated from standstill to 100km/h in 4.8sec and 4.4sec respectively, although both top speeds were electronically limited to 250km/h (155mph).

The CL65 AMG came as standard with ABC, with AMG-specific suspension struts and stiffer shock absorbers. Further measures to improve the performance of the suspension included totally new vehicle dynamics control systems such as ABS, BAS, ASR (acceleration skid control) and the electronic stability programme (ESP). In line with the high power on offer from the biturbo engine, the front axle was provided with a new, large-sized eight-piston composite braking system with cast-iron discs and aluminium pot size of 390 × 36mm. Contact with the road was ensured by 19in AMG double-spoke wheels with 245/40 ZR 19 (front) and 275/35 ZR 19 (rear) tyres.

The CL65 AMG received a chrome-plated 'V12 biturbo' plaque on the front wings indicating exceptional dynamics, while the two oval, chrome-plated twin tailpipes on the

AMG sport exhaust system lent a sporty look to the rear end.

The interior received rich fine-wood trim and three-tone 'Exclusive Napa' leather upholstery to complete the package. The electrically adjustable AMG sport seats had AMG-specific seat graphics and perforations, optimal lateral support, multi-contour function, memory and heated seats to enable the most comfortable ride, regardless of high-speed twisting roads or long motorway cruises.

The exquisite style was rounded off by the AMG instrument cluster with a 360km/h (224mph) scale, AMG ergonomic sport steering wheel with shift paddles, and chrome-plated stainless-steel door sills with the AMG logo.

ABOVE: **The new V12 biturbo.**

The rich interior of the CL65AMG.

PRODUCTION FIGURES

By February 2006, a total of 47,984 units of the exclusive two-door CL215 had left the assembly line in Sindelfingen, almost double that of the C140. The most successful variant was the CL500, of which 32,224 units were built, accounting for over two-thirds of total production.

Full production numbers are as follows:

CL500 (1998–2006):	32,224
CL600 (1998–2002):	6,348
CL600 (2002–-2005):	2,255
CL55AMG (2000–2002):	2,217
CL55AMG (2002–2005):	4,163
CL63AMG (2001):	26
CL65AMG (2003–2005):	777

216 SERIES CL-CLASS COUPÉS FIRST GENERTION, 2006–2010

In the autumn of 2006 Mercedes-Benz introduced the C216 series. Once again Mercedes-Benz went for unsurpassed exclusivity and charismatic design with the sort of cutting-edge technology that no other manufacturer worldwide could match.

Technological Advancements

As the two-door Coupé was the flagship Coupé, once again it brought with it innovation and technological advancements. For the first time the new 'Pre-Safe' system was introduced in both the S-Class and the C216 Coupé. The system was a vastly improved version of the 'brake assist plus' system (BAS Plus) used previously, and the only system of its kind in the world.

THE 215 SERIES AS SEEN BY THE PRESS

***Auto, Motor und Sport*, Germany, issue no. 23/1999, on the Mercedes-Benz CL600:**

The special fascination of the CL600 lies in the unique effortlessness of driving, and the new 5.8-litre V12 engine is a perfect match in this respect. The composure with which its 367bhp produces virtually every desired speed instantly but highly discreetly is awfully impressive, and besides, also answers the question as to such an engine's right to exist. The five-speed automatic, which interacts with the V12 in rarely encountered perfection, also deserves praise.

***Frankfurter Allgemeine Zeitung*, Germany, 5 October 1999, on the Mercedes-Benz CL600:**

The new CL, an impressive four-seater, is without doubt a high point in the brand's design history – with its four-eyed front, bonnet remodelled around the headlamps, side lines rising steeply towards the rear, and spoiler-like bootlid edge protruding over the triangular tail lights. It not only looks lighter and more dynamic than its predecessor, it really is.

***Road & Track*, USA, November 2000, on the Mercedes-Benz CL55 AMG:**

The CL55's progress proved effortless and serene, even at Autobahn pace, where one is obliged, after all, to keep to the fast lane and set a good AMG example.

The second version of Distronic is now called Distronic Plus. One of the main improvements over that of the Distronic is that it works down to a full emergency stop, whereas the original Distronic would disconnect automatically under a minimum speed 40km/h (25mph) or less for the driver to take over. It also allows Distronic Plus to be used in heavy traffic areas and stop-and-go situations. In general, it has also been improved to operate more reliably than the previous generation (for example, better tracking of obstacles/vehicles ahead when car is on a curving road). Distronic Plus now also incorporates a radar function for Parktronic that eliminates the sensors in the bumpers.

The unique BAS Plus automatic braking system provides visual and audible warnings if it detects that the vehicle is about to run into the vehicle in front, and automatically calculates the brake force required to prevent the crash. This brake boosting force is available the moment the driver steps on the brake pedal – however, the Pre-Safe system goes one step further: if the driver does not react to the BAS Plus warnings and there is a severe danger of an accident, in conjunction with the Distronic Plus the system triggers automatic partial braking and decelerates the CL at up to 0.4g, the equivalent of 4m per second, around 40 per cent of the maximum braking performance. It also provides the driver with a further clear prompt to act, on top of the visual and audible warnings. If the pilot immediately goes on to activate the brake, maximum braking force remains available. If it deduces that an impact is imminent, the Pre-Safe brake reduces the severity of the impact by pre-emptively deploying protective measures in the interior, ensuring that the airbags and seat belts are able to operate to optimum effect in the event of a crash, which in turn reduces the risk of injury for the occupants of the car.

Model Dimensions

Compared with the outgoing model, the new Mercedes-Benz top-of-the-range Coupé grew only slightly in all dimensions. At 5,065mm (199.4in) long, 1,871mm (73.7in) wide and 1,418mm (55.8in) high, the body was just 75mm (2.9in) longer, 14mm (0.55in) wider and 20mm (0.79in) higher than before, providing even more comfort and space in all four seats.

The Newly Developed V12 Engine

Initially the C216 was introduced as the CL500 and the CL600 V12 engine. The new 4-valve per cylinder V8 M273 powerplant was among the most advanced, powerful engines in its displacement class, delivering 388bhp (285kW) and generating a maximum torque of 530Nm from 2,800rpm. As

The slightly downward tapering C-pillar and SL-style open grille were still recognizable from the C126; however, the 'four eyes' look of the previous incarnation had gone.

Although lacking the styling cues of the W221 on which it was based, the familiar Coupé features – as always – brought tradition and modernity into harmony.

such, the newly developed engine outperformed the existing V8 unit by 26 per cent in terms of output, and 15 per cent in terms of torque, enabling the CL500 to accelerate from zero to 100km/h (60mph) almost a second faster than the C215 500, in just 5.4sec.

The M275 biturbo V12 engine under the bonnet of the new CL600 received numerous enhancements in refinement; compared with the predecessor model, output was increased by 17bhp (12kW) to 517bhp (380kW). The maximum torque, already on tap from 1,900rpm, was improved further by 30Nm to 830Nm, and remained constant up to 3,500rpm. The new CL 600 accelerated from 0 to 100km/h (60mph) in just 4.6sec.

Innovative Improvements

The improvement in power, refinement and acoustic characteristics made by the Mercedes-Benz engineers had made the CL216 by far the quietest car in its class. In September of 2006, a jury of 150 motoring journalists voted the new CL-Class the 'Top Car of 2007' in the 'Luxury' category, while readers of the German weekly newspaper *Bild am Sonntag* awarded it the 'Golden Steering Wheel'.

Once again Mercedes-Benz combined the standard-fit automatic transmission with the new Direct Select paddle-style gear shift, which allowed the driver to select the transmission settings 'P', 'N', 'R' and 'D' by flicking a lever on the steering column.

As well as the previously mentioned Pre-Safe system an even more sophisticated version of the 'Active Body Control' (ABC) suspension system was used in the C216 series, giving the Coupé unprecedented handling dynamics while offering an equally appreciable improvement in ride comfort.

The 'Intelligent Light System' made driving even safer in the dark. Together with bi-xenon headlamps it provided five different lighting functions that were activated to match driving and weather conditions: the new country-road mode illuminated the driver's-side edge of the road more widely and brightly than the existing low-beam headlamps. Motorway mode, which came on automatically when driving above 90km/h (56mph), delivered a uniform cone of light that illuminated the entire road width. In the centre of this cone the driver was able to see about 50m (160ft) further. The enhanced fog lamps were also new, which Mercedes-Benz used to provide better orientation in adverse weather conditions. Active light and cornering light functions were also part of the standard-fit Intelligent Light System on the CL-Class.

Stylish Interior

In true Coupé style the interior was also designed for stylish comfort and relaxation. Five colour combinations were available; automatic climate control, COMAND with car radio, and CD/DVD player as well as a glass sunroof were all part of the standard specification.

The standard specification for the interior of the flagship CL600 included dynamic multi-contour seats with massage function and seat ventilation, the hard-disc navigation system

COMAND APS, the Logic7 surround sound system with DVD changer, and the Keyless-Go access and drive authorization system. It also featured the exclusive 'Passion' leather appointments options, specially selected poplar wood, and an Alcantara roof liner with quilted seams. The same look and feel was also echoed in the seats with their 'Designo' styling, the chromed door-sill panels and floor mats with leather edging.

The newly developed integral seats in the CL-Class provide maximum individual seating comfort. All components of the seat-belt system are incorporated directly into the seat, forming an important component in the occupant protection system. Optional extras include luxury seats with active ventilation (standard in the CL600) that provide even more individual comfort, along with the further enhanced

ABOVE: **The easy hand controller for the sound and command system.**

The multi-contoured orthopaedic seat in the V12 was standard.

multi-contour seats with nine air cushions, and dynamic multi-contour seats with massage function (standard in the CL600).

Control System

A newly developed control system, which had already been successfully implemented in the W221 S-Class, refined driver–vehicle interaction even further. It provided convenient, rapid access to frequently used functions such as the car radio, DVD player, car phone or navigation system. The standard-fit automatic climate control with four independently adjustable temperature zones was also integrated into the new control system. The driver and front passenger could select temperature, air distribution and other settings either using the COMAND controller and menu-based control, or by means of an attractively styled switch array beneath the air vents.

AMG VERSIONS OF THE C216

The CL63AMG

Although both C216s were fast and refined, it was said that they lacked an emotional drive appeal; although fast and smooth, they were too refined for some, with their chassis biases towards the comfort side.

At the 2006 Paris Motor Show Mercedes-Benz presented the CL63AMG with the 6.3-litre V8 engine as its flagship model in the C216 series. It was joined the following year at the 2007 New York International Auto Show by the CL65AMG with the V12 engine.

THE AMG 6.3-LITRE V8 ENGINE

The heart of the CL500 V8 model was the 100 per cent AMG-developed AMG 6.3-litre V8 engine. With a displacement of 6208cc, this high-revving, naturally aspirated engine delivered an output of 525bhp (386kW) at 6,800rpm, and a maximum torque of 630Nm at 5,200rpm. Compared with the CL600, the CL63AMG had a slight advantage in horsepower, and even though it was nowhere near as torquey as the 5.5-litre twin-turbo V12, it was also around 100kg (220lb) lighter. The V8 AMG accelerated from a standing start to 100km/h (60mph) in 4.6sec; its maximum speed

The CL63AMG.

was electronically limited to 250km/h (155mph), although you could pay extra money to raise the limit to 300km/h (186mph).

The main advantage of the AMG engine was not all about performance, but the subjective feel quality it delivered compared with the non-AMG V8. Its eager and flexible character enabled it to pull away from as low as 1,000rpm and rev cleanly all the way to 7,200rpm, with a soundtrack turning from melodious bass to thundering wail. The tweaked V8 gave 80 per cent of its peak torque from

The 6.3-litre V8 engine.

around 2,000rpm upwards, giving a much more sporting feel overall.

AMG reprogrammed the 7G-Tronic gearbox and Active Body Control to offer three driving modes: 'comfort' is equivalent to the standard CL; 'sport' enables 30 per cent quicker gearshifts and stiffer suspensions; while 'manual' allows 50 per cent quicker gearshifts via paddles as well as the stiffest suspension setting. They also altered the throttle response of the engine. In sport and manual mode, the CL63 handles more sharply, and corners even flatter than the standard car, while it remains one of the most comfortable rides in the grand tourer segment.

AMG dash including the IWC clock (inset).

EXTERNAL APPEARANCE

Externally the CL63AMG gave a much better impression of the high-performance athlete, albeit in a bespoke suit. The extra equipment included the muscular AMG bumper with round fog lamps set in chrome rings, large air intakes and side vents, and of course the striking AMG version of the SL radiator grille, with two horizontal chrome louvres and numerous vertical slats in black. Other highlights that were included to differentiate the models were the two chrome twin tailpipes of the AMG sports exhaust system, and the '6.3 AMG' lettering on the front wings. This sporty and exclusive styling was continued in the interior.

AMG styling throughout.

THE INTERIOR

Standard accoutrements included Passion leather upholstery and multi-contour AMG sports seats, with their own cross-piping design and massage function. The AMG instrument cluster displayed the AMG main menu with the addition of a 'Racetimer' for track days. Another eye-catching feature in the interior was the exclusive analogue clock modelled on the design of the 'IWC-Ingénieur' series in the centre console. The overall picture was rounded off by AMG entry sills of brushed stainless steel.

The CL65AMG

Another equally exclusive AMG-tuned car joined the AMG model range in 2007. The new generation CL65AMG was the combination of a new chassis and old engine, but the engine was so perfect that Mercedes and AMG found no need to improve it further.

THE ENGINE

AMG's 6.0-litre twin-turbo V12 had started life in the last generation C215, and since then spread to a number of other big Mercedes-Benz. However, its roots can be traced back to the outgoing Mercedes 5.8-litre single overhead camshaft V12 that made its debut in 1999.

Alubeam paintwork made the body of the CL65AMG appear like molten metal.

Despite the rather outdated 3 valves per cylinder design, the addition of two turbochargers and structural strengthening resulted in 612bhp, with a boost in torque of 1,000Nm available from 2,000rpm all the way to 4,000rpm. This delivered a truly impressive driving experience, accelerating from 0 to 100km/h (60mph) in 4.4sec and reaching the 200km/h (120mph) mark in 13.3sec. Its maximum speed was an electronically limited 250km/h (155mph) – or once again, for an extra fee, this could be extended to 300km/h (186mph).

CHASSIS

The C216CL chassis was stronger and more agile than the C215. The power steering was uprated to give a heavier, more responsive feel at speed, and the brake pressure distribution changed to give better overall balance, with new double-frame sliding callipers offering maximum deceleration without fading.

Standard features included AMG body styling, 50.8cm AMG forged wheels, the unique AMG interior and highly advanced technology, such as AMG sports suspension, based on the Active Body Control system, and the anticipatory occupant protection system Pre-Safe.

THE 40TH ANNIVERSARY EDITION

The 40th Anniversary edition with AMG offered the exclusivity of the 'Alubeam' silver paint finish: this looked as if molten silver been poured over the vehicle's body, emphasizing the compelling lines of the large Coupé. This finish was made possible by the use of pigment particles measuring just 30 to 50 nanometres in size, and which were therefore incorporated into the surface of the paint even more evenly. As a result, the light was reflected much more intensely, and the lustre of the paintwork enhanced. To put this into perspective, conventional paintwork pigments measure between 100 and 300 nanometres in size; it had to be hand-painted at the Sindelfingen factory, making production a labour-intensive endeavour.

The CL65AMG '40th Anniversary' featured two-tone Exclusive Passion all-Napa-leather upholstery with the new AMG V12 diamond pattern, a colour-coordinated Alcantara roof lining and embossed V12 logos on the front head restraints.

BLIND SPOT ASSIST

From 2007, the CL-Class optionally came with the newly developed 'Blind Spot Assist' to guide the driver when changing lanes. The new assistance system from Mercedes-Benz employed six short-range radar sensors in the front and rear bumpers. These monitored the area to both sides and behind the vehicle, including the driver's blind spot, the area not covered by the outside mirrors. If the system detected another vehicle in the warning zone, a red warning symbol appeared in the glass of the outside mirror. This symbol told the driver that it might be dangerous to change lane. If, ignoring this information, the driver operated the direction indicator, the red symbol in the mirror glass would begin to flash, reinforced by an audible warning.

The Coupé All-Wheel Drive

From the summer of 2008, having already used the latest generation system in the W221 S-Class, Mercedes-Benz also offered all-wheel drive for its luxury CL-Class Coupé

ABOVE: **AMG 40th Anniversary V12.**

for the first time. The new CL500 4Matic provided even greater traction and handling stability in the wet, in snow or on ice. The 4Matic system was permanently active and therefore required no response time to come to the driver's aid in unfavourable weather and driving conditions. The heart of the all-wheel-drive system was a transfer case with a central differential, which was integrated into the seven-speed automatic transmission. From here, the drive torque was split between the front and rear axle at a ratio of 45:55.

Another new feature was the twin-plate clutch at the central differential. This produced a locking effect of around 50Nm between the front and rear axle, which allowed variable torque shift between the axles as the situation dictated.

The new 4Matic model in the CL-Class range was characterized by the same high-quality safety and comfort features as the luxury Coupé with rear-wheel drive.

AMG V12 logos and diamond-pattern Napa leather.

For the CL216, drive was split 45:55 front to rear on the 4Matic system.

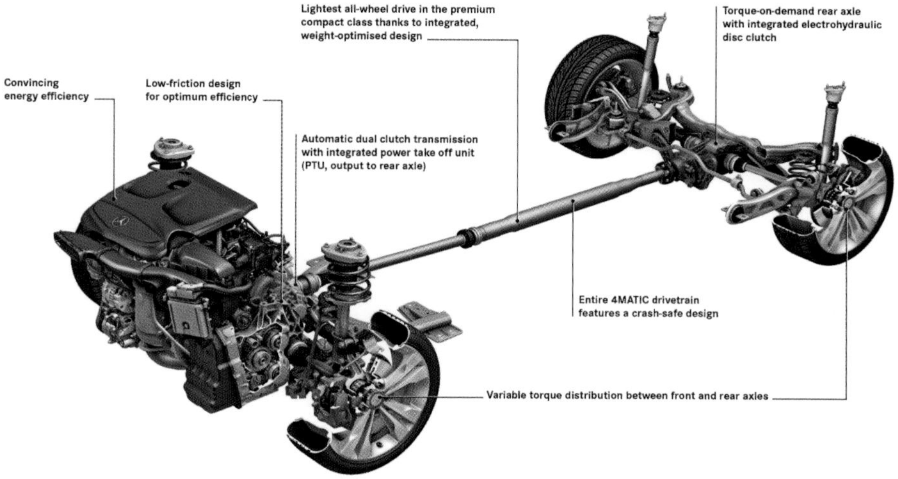

'TRADEMARK CENTENARY' EDITION

In 2009 Mercedes-Benz celebrated the one-hundredth birthday of the Mercedes star and the Benz emblem with a particularly exclusive edition of the CL Coupé. The exquisite equipment details included beautifully executed emblems of the original trademarks inset into the centre console. These were accurate reproductions of the emblems that Daimler-Motoren-Gesellschaft and Benz & Cie had registered as trademarks one hundred years before, forming the basis for the Mercedes star. With its exclusive equipment, the unique 'Trademark Centenary' edition underlined the special position held by large Coupés from Mercedes-Benz.

AMG SPORTS PACKAGE

Also in 2009, Mercedes-Benz introduced for the first time an AMG sports package for the CL500 and CL500 4Matic. This included a front skirt with large cooling air inlets, a rear apron with a distinctive black insert and permanently integrated rectangular exhaust tailpipe trims in polished stainless steel, AMG side sill panels, and 19in AMG five-spoke light-alloy wheels. The interior sported wood trim and a wood/leather steering wheel in black ash, velour floor mats

PRODUCTION FIGURES

Production of the first generation C216 ended in July 2010, having produced 23,139 units. Individual model units produced are as follows:

CL500:	14,550
CL600:	2,357
CL63AMG:	5,100
CL65AMG:	1,132

THE C216 SERIES IN THE PRESS

***Frankfurter Allgemeine Sonntagszeitung*, Germany, 3 September 2006:**

In a Mercedes Coupé it becomes obvious that Saloons are redundant. Rear seats are only there in case someone unexpectedly needs a lift – an event any Coupé driver would rather not think about. For the Coupé driver appreciates the serenity of automotive mobility, and desires to stand out among the crowd of everyday vehicles. His Coupé is a 'Sunday best' car for every day of the week.

***Autorevue*, Austria, issue 12/2006:**

In the CL, sensibility takes priority over actions. One drives, one hears the engine – but nothing more than an atmospherically enlivening fundamental, a note that changes key depending on the angle of the accelerator pedal. One is not even affected any longer by noise from the world outside. One is embedded in a control loop that creates an overall situation from the tiniest of movements. The manner, speed and force with which one steers, brakes or accelerates set in motion actions initiated or reinforced by the system that keeps the car on track, retards it powerfully or keeps it horizontal on cornering. A part of this is the driver's will. But in extremis, the car takes from one's own input only what it considers reasonable. And the first unexpected encounter with wet autumn leaves or early snow reminds one what an excellent idea this is.

***Road & Track*, USA, August 2007:**

Out on the open road, the CL600 stretches its legs and covers ground in a comfortable flash. Ride quality is excellent, no matter the surface, and the handling is quite impressive for a large, substantial Coupé. Winding country roads with little or no traffic are the ideal setting for this car, as you can exercise the V12 with complete confidence in the Mercedes multi-link suspension with Active Body Control, four-wheel disc brakes with ASS, and lots of other technology to keep you on an even keel.

with AMG lettering, as well as the sport pedal assembly of brushed stainless steel with rubber naps.

216 SERIES CL-CLASS COUPÉS, 2010–2014

The Second Generation C216

Mercedes-Benz was adamant that the CL-Class would remain exclusive, and exclusive it was: in the USA only the G-Class and the two-seat SLS AMG sold in smaller quantities, and in fact, annual CL-Class sales equalled that of the Ford pick-up sales for one day in the USA. Mercedes-Benz had the idea that that degree of distinction would be alluring to CL-Class buyers, and once again decided to 'upgrade' the C216.

The facelifted C216 was initially unveiled at the 2010 Goodwood Festival of Speed, and a little later at the 2010 Paris Motor Show. However, it didn't go on general sale until September 2010, and the North American version only arrived at Mercedes-Benz dealerships in November 2010 as the 2011 model year vehicle.

UPGRADES IN APPEARANCE AND TECHNOLOGY

The changes made on the exterior were subtle, revised wings, while the bonnet and a new grille pulled all the body's curves into tauter, straighter lines for a more aggressive

look. New bi-xenon headlights with LED technology, LED fog lamps and new exhaust pipes added to the upgrades. On the interior the upgrades included a new range of interior wood trim. However, by far the majority of upgrades involved electronically based driver aids; these included Adaptive High-beam Assist, Attention Assist, Active Blind Spot Assist and Active Lane Keeping Assist.

The new C216 was the first series production car with night vision-guided pedestrian spotlighting; the NVAP (Night View Assist Plus) with spotlight function was able to flash at any pedestrians it detected in order to warn both the driver and the pedestrians. The flashing light was directed in such a way that vehicles in front and oncoming traffic were not dazzled.

Pre-Safe brake upgrades now activated maximum braking pressure about a half second before what it recognized as an unavoidable collision. Direct-Steer and Active Body Control (ABC) now came with electronic crosswind stabilization, and were standard equipment on all rear-wheel-drive C216s. Airmatic air suspension with the continuously Adaptive Damping System Plus was also standard on the home market and for the US market CL550 4MATIC, but not for the CL600 and AMG.

INTERIOR UPGRADES

On the interior the new C216 received COMAND with SPLITVIEW dual view display and a Comand APS navigation system that replaced the DVD with 40Gb hard-drive map system. Other interior upgrades included the following:

- Nine airbags as standard
- ESP Dynamic Cornering Assist

ABOVE: **The front-end difference can be clearly seen from (top) Generation 1 to (bottom) Generation 2.**

Generation 1 (left) and Generation 2 (right) shape comparisons.

- Traffic Sign Assist with Speed Limit Assist
- Attention Assist (as standard)
- Neck-Pro crash-responsive head restraints
- Back-up camera
- Electric parking brake with emergency braking function

THE NEW M278 ENGINE

The most significant changes for the second generation C216 were under the bonnet. Mercedes saw fit to follow the trend of downsizing turbocharged motors in a bid to cut carbon-dioxide emission drastically, and to this end a completely new engine, codenamed the M278, had been fitted under the bonnet of the CL500. It had been downsized from 5461cc of the old M273 to 4663cc; the only thing that revealed this was just behind the front wheel arches, a 'V8 Biturbo' badge. Apart from the twin turbo, other key improvements were variable twin camshafts and direct fuel injection. Low-friction pistons, on-demand oil and coolant pumps, on-demand alternator and auto stop-start also helped to make it more efficient. Overall the new engine was 22 per cent more efficient than the old M273, a notable improvement considering the rest of the car was basically unchanged.

The new M278 engine was considerably more powerful than its predecessor; it managed to produce 435bhp instead of the previous 388bhp, the new biturbo motor produced 45 per cent more torque than the old V8, and more importantly, much earlier, at between 1,800 and 3,500rpm – the old engine needed 2,800rpm. 0–60mph was reached in 4.7sec, half a second quicker than before. Rolling acceleration was even more impressive, as it was almost instantaneous, without the need to gather engine revs.

AMG Versions of the CL63 and the CL65

Less than a month after the presentation of the restyled CL, Mercedes-Benz also announced the new AMG versions of the CL63 and the CL65.

ABOVE: **COMAND GPS with split-view dual display in the slightly revised interior.**

The new M278 cutaway and (inset) complete.

CL63AMG UPDATES

For the CL63AMG, the old M156 6.2-litre V8 was now replaced with a twin-turbocharged 5.5-litre V8 engine based on the new M278. The new engine delivered a mere 11bhp more than its predecessor. However, it was cleaner and more efficient than the original. It was also coupled to a more advanced AMG MCT seven-speed transmission, allowing 0–100km/h (60mph) in 4.4sec; top speed was limited to 250km/h (155mph).

Mercedes Benz also offered a 'Performance Package', which gave a claimed 0–100km/h in 4.3sec, but also a top speed limited to 300km/h (190mph), almost on a par with the last Generation I CL65AMG. With the better performance came better efficiency, mainly due to the integrating of the turbochargers into the exhaust manifolds, which kept down lag and increased efficiency to such an extent that Mercedes did away with the blow-off valve, relying entirely on a vacuum-operated wastegate to manage pressure. The result was a claimed reduction in CO_2 emissions of 30g per kilometre, and 27 per cent better fuel economy. Based on EPA numbers for the previous model, that figure equates to CO_2 emissions of 1.14lb of CO_2 per mile, down from 1.46lb per mile. More importantly to most consumers, that meant almost 30 per cent better fuel economy overall.

All the new engine functions were executed and controlled by a particularly efficient Bosch MED 17.7.3. control unit. The state-of-the-art engine computer not only controlled the direct fuel injection, eight ignition-coil packs, charge pressure, camshaft adjustment and variable oil supply, it also communicated with all the other onboard control units to ensure the engine worked at its optimum settings at all engine speeds and under all load conditions.

In a world where everyone was becoming increasingly aware of their carbon footprint, it made sense that the purchase decisions people made should take into consideration the effect it would have on the environment – so all engines in the C216 range, as well as other models, were offered with the BlueEfficiency package.

The CL63AMG also came with higher-performance brakes, suspension, wheels and tyres. Options include the Driver Assist package, Premium 2 package, forged 20in wheels, carbon-fibre cabin trim, AMG illuminated door sills, and a heated wood and leather steering wheel.

THE CL65AMG UPDATES

The CL65AMG's updates were not quite as involved. The 6.0-litre V12 had a new set of turbos that managed to push power

THE BLUEEFFICIENCY PACKAGE

The BlueEfficiency trademark was a way to show that the company was aware of the purchase decisions people make, and how they are actively taking steps to reduce the pollutants produced by their vehicles. The BlueEfficiency package was as follows:

- A diesel oxidation system reduced the amounts of carbon monoxide and hydrocarbon emissions
- Advanced catalytic converters began the initial elimination of oxides of nitrogen
- A special filter traps soot particles and stores them before burning them when the filter fills
- The ECO start/stop technology turns the motor off for a brief moment when the vehicle stops, lowering power consumption, especially during urban stop/start traffic
- The alternator is one of the key components of the BlueEfficiency system. Each time a car brakes, the vehicle converts the kinetic energy into heat, which is normally wasted; however, with the BlueEfficiency system, the alternator gathers that energy and converts it into electrical energy. This helps to save fuel at around 0.1ltr per 100km on paper, and up to 0.2ltr per 100km when driving in urban environments where stopping and starting is more common
- The sensors in the electrical system actively check voltage and temperature levels to contribute to more effective storage
- Engineers adjusted the tyre profiles and compounds for optimal rolling resistance, requiring lower energy while driving to reduce gas usage

from 604bhp in the last model to 621bhp, mostly achieved by an additional 22psi of boost. Torque remained limited to 738lb ft, even though the engine was capable of producing 885lb ft, because neither the chassis nor drivetrain could handle it; the CL65AMG also continued to use the speed-shift five-speed automatic transmission because the seven-speed dual-clutch transmission couldn't handle the power.

Similar refinements to that of the CL63 engine – such as the alternator only charging on the overrun – helped to increase its fuel economy by about 15 per cent, and CO_2 emissions dropped by 3.5 per cent.

UPDATES FOR THE CL63 AND THE CL65

Both cars also received extras as standard such as 'direct steer', a lighter, more direct steering system; 'torque vectoring brake', which could automatically brake the inside rear wheel to kill understeer; and automatic crosswind stabilization. The AMG cars also picked up the following CL-Class features: Active Lane Keeping Assist, Active Blind Spot Assist, Night View and Drowsiness Detection systems, along with Active Body Control.

Both AMG models were given slightly revised front and rear elevations, the CL65AMG being distinguished by chrome accents on the front splitter and rear diffuser. The updates also included new LED daytime running lights, new tail-lights, the appropriate 'V8 biturbo' and 'V12 biturbo' badging, and an AMG performance exhaust with unique chrome tips.

Inside, each of the cars was updated with leather AMG sport seats, both of which were heated and ventilated, a leather-wrapped AMG steering wheel, and a race timer function for recording lap times. To distinguish the CL65AMG as the flagship, it received exclusive wood trim and diamond-patterned, top-quality leather on the seats, doors and other trim. Mercedes-Benz also offered the 'Designo' customization feature for those who wanted something different.

The CL Grand Edition: The Epitome of the Luxury Coupés

The S-Class Coupé had been around indirectly since the 300S W188 of 1952, and not one to miss a landmark, Mercedes-Benz released the celebratory CL Grand Edition. Irrespective of which base model was chosen, the CL Grand Edition was available for a package price of 4,850 euros (excluding tax). The complex Designo paintwork alone was priced at an additional 1,500 euros.

In order to emphasize the hand-finished character of the CL Class Grand Editions, Mercedes-Benz furnished them with some of the finest ingredients from the exquisite Designo range; this included a choice of three body colours: platinum black metallic, mocha black metallic, and magno

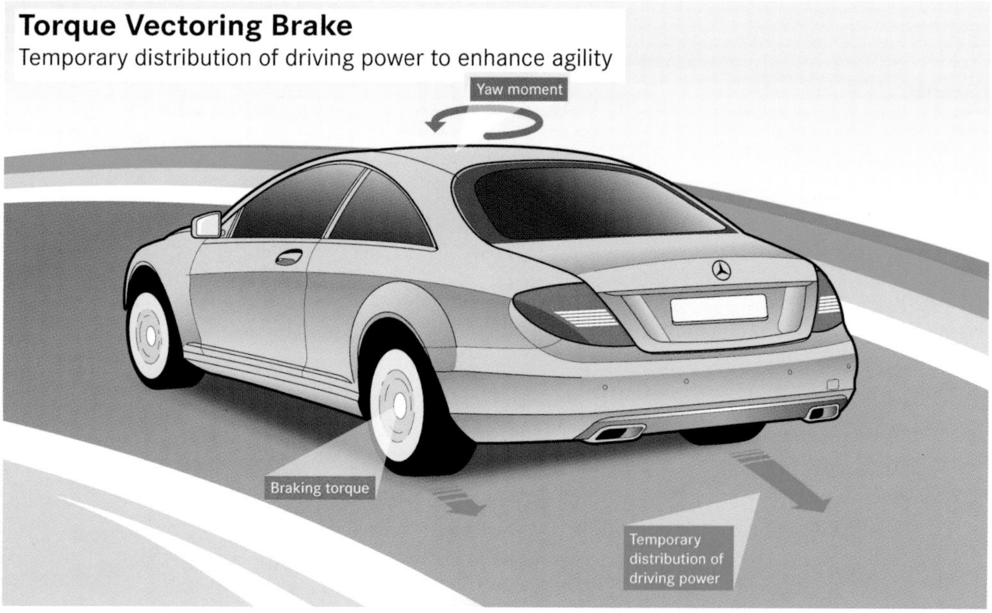

Torque-vectoring diagram.

Active Body Control (ABC).

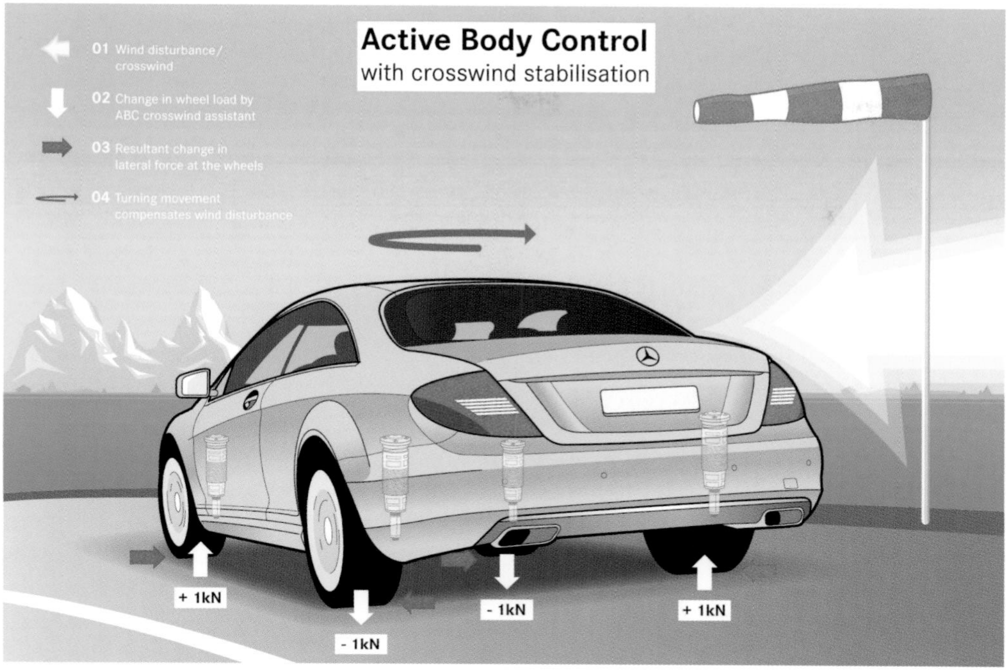

BELOW LEFT: **New C216 badging.**

BELOW RIGHT: **The Grand Edition interior.**

cashmere white. There was also a choice of three high-quality Designo leather interiors, namely aniline Armagnac, aniline deep black, and aniline porcelain, with interior wood trim appointments including black ash and high-gloss burr walnut.

To give a sporty touch to the Coupé, Mercedes equipped the vehicle with the AMG pack: this provided a more aggressive front bumper, and 20in alloy wheels in a choice of five-spoke or filigree ten-spoke designs. A Grand Edition badge provided a discreet indication of the CL Coupé's exclusive edition status.

The CL Grand Edition came with all the trappings of the regular C216 range. The active suspension system Active Body Control (ABC) with crosswind stabilization, safety systems such as the drowsiness detection system Attention Assist, Pre-Safe automatic emergency braking, and the optional Active Blind Spot Assist, Active Lane Keeping Assist and Adaptive High-beam Assist systems.

The same was true of the engine range: both the V8 biturbo and the V12 were offered with the BlueEfficiency package to ensure that the CL remained firmly planted not only as the flagship Mercedes-Benz, but also as the most ecologically responsible automobile to date.

THE 217 SERIES S-CLASS COUPÉS, 2014–2018

The Coupé model designation had been somewhat blurred over the previous fifteen years, especially with the inclusion of the E-Class and the C-Class Coupé, so with the introduction of the next CL-class Coupé, the C217, the Stuttgart company decided to return to their roots and bring back the nomenclature 'S-Class Coupé'. Ola Källenius, member of the Divisional Board of Mercedes-Benz cars responsible for marketing and sales said: 'The large Coupé has always been, and must always be, the supreme pinnacle of our model range, and that's why it is now called the "S-Class" again.'

Gorden Wagener, Vice President of Design at Daimler AG, added:

> The concept of the S-Class Coupé combines tradition and emotion, and is a symbol for the embodiment of our design style of sensual clarity. The perfected design with self-assured style, and the highly exclusive appointments, make the Coupé a true design icon and an expression of modern luxury.
>
> Design needs the sublime! Because design is the best brand ambassador. At the centre of our work is sensual clarity as an expression of modern luxury, because this is precisely what gets to the heart of our brand philosophy – the bipolarity of intelligence and emotion.

Just a few months after the updated W222 S-Class Saloon made its debut in China, Mercedes-Benz finally unveiled the highly anticipated replacement to the C216 at the 2014 Geneva Motor show. For the first time the C217 S-Class Coupé was offered with a cabriolet version (A217). As was expected, both received the revisions that were available for the S-Class saloon. The range also included revised AMG models.

With the return of the 'S' reclassification, much was done to 'bring back' the design ethos that many thought had been lost with the introduction of other Coupé models.

Once again the positively arched profile of the S-Class Coupé had to embody the sensual clarity that came with the C126; the elegant sculpted lines formed a perfect symbiosis of classic design infused with the modern-progressive design idiom.

External Appearance

Externally the creative interaction of various design elements gave the S-Class Coupé a superior and self-assured front: in the middle is the three-dimensional and further

The return of the S-Class name.

evolved diamond-patterned radiator grille, as always framing the central Mercedes star; however, this time it had returned to the single chrome blade look of the W198.

Both C and A models received new front and rear bumpers, the former featuring a chrome-plated front splitter and sizeable air inlets – although as you might expect with the 'AMG-line styling package', the front apron became more conspicuous with the addition of two chrome-plated fins inside the inlets. The rear saw a more standard, prestigious 'V12 look' thanks to the chrome-plated twin tailpipe trims that replaced the dual outlets on the C216 model.

Advances in Engine Efficiency

The C217 Coupé was initially available with a 455bhp (335kW), 4663cc V8 biturbo engine with the spray-guided combustion system with third-generation direct injection known as BlueDirect. It came with the 4Matic all-wheel-drive system as standard, although there was an optional rear-wheel-drive variant.

It was capable of 0 to 100km/h (60mph) in an impressive 4.6sec, and went on to reach a top speed of 250km/h (155mph), which, as always, was electronically governed.

The advances in efficiency compared with the previous model were evident: the CL500 4Matic model of 2008 had a much lower maximum output of 388bhp (285kW), and even though it provided far less torque (530Nm), it consumed far more fuel at 12.1ltr/100km (23.3mpg).

Improved Assistance Systems

Like the W220 S-Class saloon, the new Coupé was available with numerous new assistance systems that made driving safer and even more comfortable. The 'intelligent

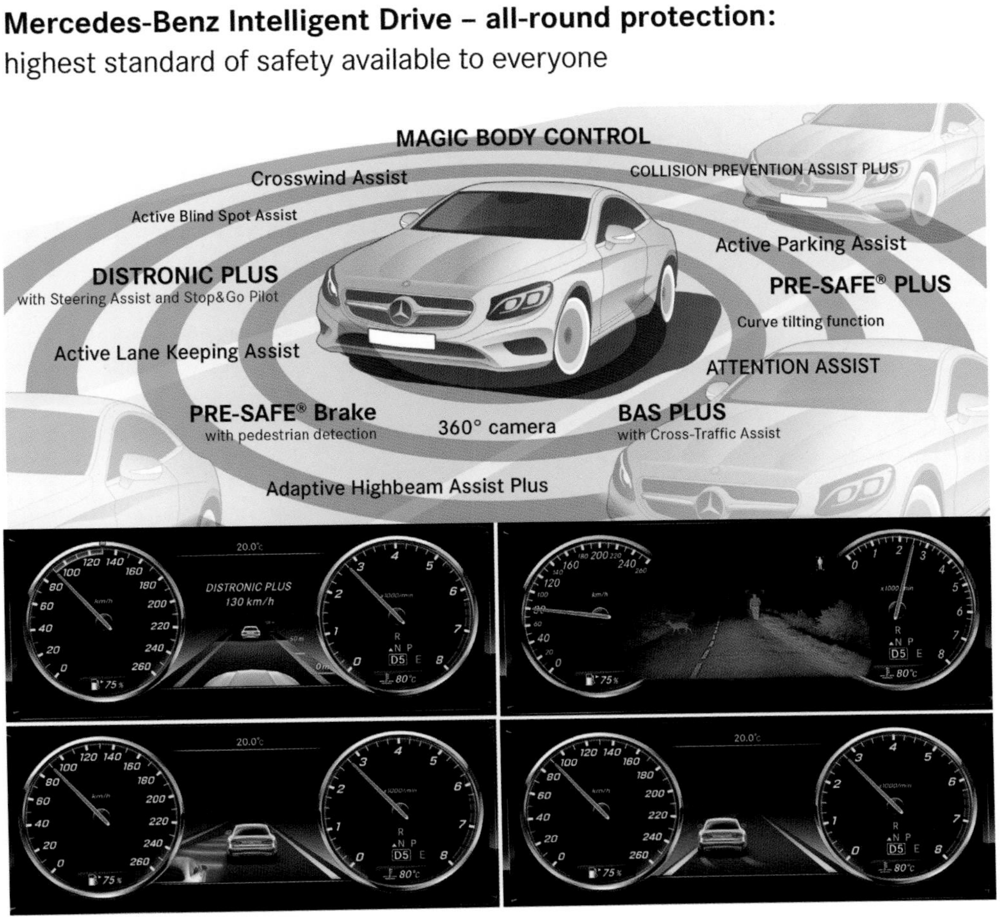

All-round intelligent drive assistance.

drive' systems included Pre-Safe Brake with pedestrian detection, and Pre-Safe Plus, which was able to recognize an imminent rear-end collision when stationary and warn following traffic by flashing the rear hazard warning lights at a high frequency.

If the danger of collision persisted, the system can 'lock' the brakes of the stationary vehicle prior to a rear-end collision, and activate the Pre-Safe belt tensioners immediately before impact. This action minimizes the risk of whiplash injury by reducing the forward jolt caused by the impact, and ensuring that the occupants are in the best possible position.

Also available were Distronic Plus with Steer Assist, and Stop and Go Pilot, Brake Assist BAS Plus with Cross-Traffic Assist, Active Lane Keeping Assist, Adaptive High-beam Assist Plus and Night View Assist Plus. In addition to a distance and collision warning function in conjunction with Adaptive Brake Assist, which offers collision protection from speeds as low as 7km/h (4mph), the Collision Prevention Assist Plus system installed in even the standard vehicle features an additional function: when a danger of collision persists and the driver fails to respond, the system is able to carry out autonomous braking at speeds of up to more than 100km/h (60mph), thereby reducing the severity of collisions with slower or stopping vehicles. At speeds of up to around 50km/h (30mph) the system also brakes in response to stationary vehicles, and can prevent rear-end collisions at up to around 40km/h (25mph).

World-Beating Aerodynamics

Good flow characteristics played a decisive role in ensuring low fuel consumption under everyday conditions; however, a low interior noise level was also a declared objective when developing the new S-Class Coupé, and to this end extensive aerodynamic development work on the C217 was undertaken.

Engineers managed to keep the Cd value for the S500 4Matic Coupé with standard-fit 18in wheels at an impressive 0.27Cd, similar to that of the C216. They achieved this by sealing bodyshell shut-line gaps and the door perimeter rubber sealing; even the gaps around the headlights were configured to reduce wind noise and manage air flow. Wheel spoilers were added to produce an optimum flow ahead of the front wheels. The front and rear axle lift, and the balance between the two, were configured by shaping and lowering the front of the vehicle in a way that optimized efficient air flow, but also by adding large areas of cladding on the underside of the vehicle as well as over the rear axle.

As a part of the aerodynamic enhancements, much consideration was given to body flow safety in an inclement weather period: dirt-laden water that impacted the windscreen, the side windows and the exterior mirrors was deflected by channelling it over the roof along suitably designed water runnels with continuously decreasing step height and an optimized roof-trim strip along the A-pillar. This meant that the areas of the side windows affording a view of the exterior mirrors were kept free of water drops. The rear window remained free of dirt even up to a speed of approximately 160km/h (99mph).

Aeroacoustics System

As people are particularly disturbed by fluctuating auditory impressions, Daimler employed specially trained aeroacoustics experts to optimize interior acoustics. In addition to the sound level in the interior, psychoacoustic variables such as sound sharpness and articulation quality (speech intelligibility when there are various forms of background noise) were taken into account.

The excellent aeroacoustics performance was not just down to the Coupé form: optimization measures on the bodyshell were also implemented to reduce high-frequency wind noise, with the focus on special sealing for the windows and door handles as well as lightweight doors that help to reduce low-frequency wind noise. This much-improved insulation enhanced acoustic comfort in the easily audible medium-frequency range that was known to cause fatigue; as a result, even when travelling at high speed, it was just as easily possible to enjoy music and hands-free phone use as it was to talk to other passengers; articulation quality, such as speech intelligibility, was central to their test 'Index system'.

Interior Appointments

Numerous optional extras were available to make the interior of the S-Class Coupé exceptionally luxurious and comfortable. For example, the Air-Balance package included 'fragrancing' and 'ionization', plus additional air cleaning by means of activated charcoal filters.

If the vehicle was equipped with the optional Seat Comfort package, the front seats featured the energizing massage function based on the hot-stone principle; armrest heating was also a component of the Warmth Comfort package.

In cooperation with high-end audio specialist Burmester, two especially high-value audio systems were developed: the Burmester surround sound system and the Burmester High End 3D surround sound system.

Standard features included an electro-mechanical locking system, an almost silent power-closing of doors and boot lid, remote boot-lid release and closing, the Keyless-Go start function package, which included handle recess lighting, and the Keyless-Go access and drive authorization system. There was also hands-free access for the boot, where the driver merely has to wave a foot briefly under the rear bumper to open or close the lid.

Improved Visibility Systems

The new S-Class Coupé required no bulbs whatsoever. Over 450 LEDs were responsible for illuminating the road, the vehicle, the interior and the luggage compartment. However, its multi-level functionality was another innovation: out of consideration for any road users behind, the intensity of the brake lights was reduced at night or while waiting at traffic lights.

Visibility was enhanced by Adaptive High-beam Assist Plus, which allowed the high-beam headlamps to be kept on permanently while driving by masking out any other road users detected in the beams' cones of light. If the camera-based system registers either oncoming traffic or vehicles ahead, it will adapt the light distribution according to the traffic situation when the high beam is switched on.

A third generation of 'Night View Assist Plus with a spotlight function' was available also if a pedestrian or indeed a large animal was detected in potentially hazardous positions in front of the vehicle. It could issue a warning in particularly relevant situations (darkness, unlit roads at speeds exceeding 60km/h) by automatically switching from the speedometer to a brilliant night view image in the instrument cluster display. This attracts the driver's attention to the danger, and the person at the road edge is warned at the same time, as a spotlight would repeatedly flash. Animals are intentionally not flashed, as their reaction to light impulses is unpredictable.

An additional (long-distance) infrared sensor in the radiator grille helped to enhance night-vision technology. Pedestrians could be detected at up to 160 metres (525ft), and animals such as deer, horses or cows at up to 100 metres (330ft). Two separate light sources in the headlamps illuminate the road ahead of the vehicle with invisible infrared light. A (short-range) infrared camera behind the windscreen near the rear-view mirror generated a brilliant greyscale image in the instrument cluster display.

Intelligent 450 LEDs throughout the lighting system.

The washer fluid metering system was integral with the whole blade.

A system called 'Magic Vision Control' kept the windscreen clean without the sudden splash of water that usually briefly impairs the driver's field of view in the case of conventional windscreen washing systems. With Magic Vision Control, the fluid was supplied to the windscreen by means of guide tubes integrated on both sides of the wiper blade with tiny spraying holes. It operated based on the vehicle speed and taking into account the outside temperature. The contact surface of the wiper blades on the windscreen was electrically heated as standard to prevent the wiper blades from getting stuck in snow.

Active Curve Tilting Technology

The curve tilting function in the new S-Class Coupé was a world first for series production automobiles. This technology was designed to counter the effects of centrifugal force when turning into corners: it angled the car into curves, providing an additional 2.5 degrees of roll towards the inside of the turn in order to lessen the lateral acceleration experienced by the driver and passengers of the car. The feature worked alongside the Active Body Control (ABC) suspension to make sure that the occupants of the car were comfortably seated even when the car was going round a tight curve on the road.

As an example, picture a motorcycle racer who is going into a bend: you will notice that when this occurs, the driver shifts his body the opposite way to the inclination of the motorcycle to maintain his balance and prevent the motorcycle from careering off the track. Instead of providing an enhanced balance to the car, the feature is designed to provide a convenient or better driving experience to its occupants. As Mercedes has put it, the technology aims to 'provide greater driving pleasure and comfort to customers'.

The active curve tilting feature can be activated from the ABC menu of the 2015 Mercedes S-Class Coupé. It functions at speeds between 30 and 180km/h (20 and 110mph), and it recognizes bends with the help of the stereo camera behind the windscreen, which registers the curve in the road surface up to 15 metres (50ft) ahead and using the ABC suspension's lateral acceleration sensor.

With the curve tilting function, the base points of the steel springs integrated into the ABC suspension struts are raised by plunger cylinders on one side of the vehicle and lowered on the other, depending on the bend being negotiated. This allows the vehicle to incline automatically and continuously in fractions of a second on bends – depending on the road angle and vehicle speed. The effect is felt much more since the vehicle would normally tilt outwards.

The active curve tilting function.

THE S63AMG COUPÉ

The AMG 5.5-litre was introduced later in the year, and like all AMG V8 and V12 engines, the 8-cylinder biturbo engine for the S63AMG Coupé was assembled by hand at the AMG engine shop in Affalterbach, based on the 'one man, one engine' philosophy – an AMG engine plate bore the engine technician's signature. Its V8 biturbo engine boasted an output of 585bhp (430kW) and 900Nm of torque, and was also offered as a 4Matic all-wheel version.

The exclusively produced AMG Speedshift MCT seven-speed sports transmission combined perfectly with the V8 biturbo engine. There were three modes to choose from: 'C' (controlled efficiency), 'S' (sport) and 'M' (manual). The ECO start/stop function was fitted as standard.

The S63AMG.

AMG Lightweight Performance Strategy

The S63AMG Coupé was the latest model to benefit from the systematic implementation of the AMG Lightweight Performance strategy. Lightweight construction reduced the vehicle weight by 65kg (143lb); this weight saving was achieved largely thanks to the following measures: the entire outer skin and the front end of the body were constructed from high strength aluminium, a lightweight lithium-ion battery was used, also AMG forged light-alloy wheels, and for the first time AMG offered a weight-optimized, fade-resistant AMG high-performance composite brake system.

The 20 per cent lighter design ensured a lower unsprung mass as well as enhanced driving dynamics, agility and ride comfort. The reduced weight improved driving dynamics and cut fuel consumption, while the low power-to-weight ratio of 3.41kg/bhp resulted in effortlessly superior performance: the S63AMG Coupé accelerated from 0 to 100km/h (60mph) in 3.9 to 4.3sec, depending on model variant, and went on to reach an electronically limited top speed of 250km/h (155mph).

Aerodynamic Elements

The S63AMG Coupé also boasted exciting aerodynamic elements to emphasize its sporty performance. The front end was dominated by the three-dimensional AMG 'twin-blade' radiator grille in silver chrome. The distinctive AMG lettering on the side between the louvres left no doubt: this was a high-performance model from Affalterbach. It is distinguished by the following features: a three-dimensional air-ducting element, painted in the body colour, spans the entire width of the front apron and displays the stylized 'A' that is a hallmark of AMG vehicles. Large black details surround the outer cooling air intakes, and the front splitter in silver chrome optimizes the flow of air to the cooling modules. A familiar sight in motor sport, it reduces front-axle lift and optimizes the vehicle's aerodynamic balance. Keeping the A-wing and front splitter separate makes the car appear closer to the road. A similar effect is created by the AMG side sill panels.

All the cooling air grilles have a high-gloss black paint finish, with three-dimensional inserts in silver chrome. Together with the lower feature line, these inserts give the impression that the S63AMG Coupé is moving even when it is stationary.

At the rear, the high-gloss black diffuser inserts catch the eye straightaway. The lower trim element in silver chrome is reminiscent of the A-wing at the front, and provides an effective contrast. The two chromed twin tailpipes of the AMG sports exhaust system with sports flaps are perfectly integrated into the diffuser insert. Stylized, vertical air outlets in the rear apron assume the role of a defined spoiler lip and optimize aerodynamics. The 'S63AMG' model designation in a new, contemporary typography below the tail lamps adds the perfect finishing touch to the rear-end design.

The Interior

The instrument panel makes a seamless transition into the doors in a wrap-around design, combining high quality with a sporty, exclusive design idiom.

The newly developed AMG sports seats with electrical adjustment, memory function and seat heating offer the driver and front passenger optimum lateral support. Fine Napa leather in AMG V8 design with piping and AMG badges on all four seat backrests, together with the embossed AMG emblem on the armrest of the front centre console, create an exquisite atmosphere on board.

Fine Napa leather with AMG chequer pattern.

Rear seating of the S63 Coupé.

The new three-spoke AMG sports steering wheel, with its distinctively contoured rim and perforated leather in the grip area, allows perfect vehicle control. New aluminium shift paddles shorten the reaction time when changing gear, and enhance dynamism. Another feature displaying the hallmark AMG look is the high-resolution TFT colour display, as an AMG instrument cluster with two animated round dials. In addition to the specific lettering and the needles in red/silver, further distinctive design features include the AMG start-up display, the AMG logo in the speedometer with 330km/h (205mph) scale on the left, and the 'V8 Biturbo' lettering in the rev counter on the right.

S63AMG COUPÉ 'EDITION I'

One year after the market launch of the S63AMG Coupé, an exclusive model, the AMG Coupé 'Edition I' package was made available.

The Edition I features special LED high-performance headlamps, each with forty-seven Swarovski crystals: seventeen angular crystals form the flare-shaped daytime running lamps, while thirty round-shaped crystals make up the turn indicator lamps. This gives the S-Class Coupé a uniquely striking appearance, while the 'Exclusive Interior package' adds an even more exquisite ambience on the inside.

Swarovski crystals around the headlamps.

Bengal red/black interior special to the Edition 1.

Prices for all C217 models

S500 4Matic	125,961.50€
S500 4Matic 'Edition 1'	140,193.90€
S63AMG 4Matic	170,586.50€
S63AMG 4Matic 'Edition 1'	181,326.25€

The AMG sports seats are upholstered in Designo Exclusive Napa leather in crystal grey/black or Bengal red/black, with contrasting top-stitching and piping. In keeping with this colour scheme, the upper section of the dashboard, the front and rear centre armrests and the door linings are trimmed in Napa leather with contrasting top-stitching, while the roof liner and the sunscreens are in Dinamica microfibre.

Further features of the 'Edition 1' include AMG Exclusive floor mats with Napa leather edging, door sill panels with illuminated AMG lettering, and a high-gloss black poplar wood trim. The AMG sports steering wheel has 'Edition 1' lettering.

THE FACELIFT C217 2017

Just a few months after the updated W222 S-Class Saloon made its debut in China, Mercedes-Benz unveiled the Generation 2 C217 S-Class Coupé and the A217 S-Class Cabriolet – and not surprisingly, both came in line with revisions made to the saloon.

The Exterior

On the exterior, new front and rear bumpers were immediately noticeable, with the former featuring a chrome-plated front splitter and considerably larger air inlets.

Only on the AMG did the front bumper apron receive the addition of two chrome-plated fins within the inlets. Other changes included new side skirts and optional 20in AMG ten-spoke alloy wheels, with either AMG wheel-arch flares painted in either titanium grey with a high-sheen finish, or high-gloss black with a high-sheen finish.

The rear styling was given a more 'V12 look' thanks to the chrome-plated twin tailpipe trims, which replaced the dual outlets on the pre-facelift model.

The 2017 facelift version of the C217.

One of the most obvious revisions was the change from LED rear lighting to the new OLED (organic light-emitting diode). Thirty-three individually controllable OLED cells across three rows were printed on a glass plate to make the light emitted appear as if it were fluid. As infinitely controllable units they were also illuminated at different levels of intensity for brake lamps and turn signal indicators, depending on the driving conditions and ambient brightness. They also 'danced' in response to the locking and unlocking of the doors.

The Interior

The interior featured several electronic upgrades, and a completely new steering wheel with touch-control buttons. However, carried over from the Generation One C217 was the optional 'Energizing comfort control', which used climate control, fragrancing, seats, lighting and media to ensure that you were the pilot and that the passengers were always comfortable. The six programs included Freshness, Warmth, Vitality, Joy and Comfort, all of which ran for ten minutes.

On the driving front, both the Coupé and cabriolet received an improved Magic Body Control. Coupled with the 'Airmatic' air suspension, which featured an infinitely variable damping control, it would pre-empt the suspension to deal with bumps sighted further up the road, even up to speeds of 180km/h (112mph).

A New Range of Engines

A whole new range of engines was introduced. The new M177 4.0 V8 biturbo replaced the old M157 5.5 V8 biturbo in the AMG S63 4Matic+. The all-wheel-drive system was standard in the AMG S63, with an additional drift mode feature.

The S550 was renamed the S560, and used a detuned version of the same engine, called the M176 and providing 469bhp. It came with cylinder deactivation technology to save fuel, and was mated to a nine-speed 9G-Tronic automatic transmission.

A new Europe-only base model, the S450 4Matic, was powered by a 3.0-litre biturbo V6 engine with 367bhp and 500Nm of torque; it also received the new 9G-Tronic transmission. The S65 was the only C217 to keep the 7G-Tronic.

AMG versions remained available in S63 4Matic+ and S65 guises. The former was powered by the M177 4.0-litre biturbo V8 engine with 612bhp and 900Nm of torque, while the latter had a more potent 6.0-litre biturbo V12 with 630bhp and 1,000Nm of torque.

Only left-hand-drive versions of the S63 Coupé came with the AMG Performance 4Matic+ all-wheel-drive system, with rear-wheel drive being standard on right-hand-drive versions.

Performance

Regarding performance, the S63 4Matic+ accomplished the 0–100km/h sprint in 3.5sec. The V12-powered S65s will do the same slightly more slowly, in 4.1sec, with top speed limited to 250km/h (155mph) as standard, with a 300km/h (190mph) option available.

The S65 Coupé received the exclusive AMG Active Ride control that continuously monitors and adjusts the car's suspension to deal with bumps ahead of time. It is also adjustable depending on driving situations, rising by up to 40mm (1.6in) for better ground clearance, and lowering by up to 15mm (0.6in) to reduce drag.

Other AMG items included speed-sensitive steering and the high-performance compound ceramic braking system, as well as the AMG Dynamic Select, which adjusted the engine, transmission, suspension, steering, ESP and all-wheel-drive systems according to the selected driving mode.

Further Updates in Appearance

Externally, the AMG versions of the Coupé feature the AMG Pan-American radiator grille with its vertical chrome bars as a nod to the W113 Coupé, as well as a 'hovering jet wing' in the front apron. The bumper face also received large air inlets and a front splitter to help reduce lift on the front axle.

Inside, compared with the standard versions, there are only a number of AMG additions, amongst which are AMG power sports seats, an IWC design analogue clock, the AMG performance steering wheel, and the AMG 'Track Pace', which allows the pilot to record vehicle data and lap times.

THE FUTURE

The C217 has continued to date (2020). However, there is already talk that it may possibly be the last S-Class Coupé that Daimler will build. The C218 or CLS is a four-door version that uses the E-Class W212 for its base.

ABOVE: **The new M177 engine in the S63 AMG.**

All AMG versions received the 'Pan-American' front grille.

CHAPTER FIVE

THE SUPER COUPÉ

THE 2003 SLR MCLAREN (C199)

When the car was developed, Mercedes-Benz owned 40 per cent of the McLaren Group, and the car was produced by the two companies in association. It was exclusively built in the English town of Woking in Surrey, near London, under the auspices of Gordon Murray.

The SLR 'Sport Leicht Rennsport' (Sport Light Racing) was to be a celebration of the Silver Arrows racing team as well as a homage to the Mercedes-Benz 300SLR – also known as the 'Uhlenhaut Coupé' previously mentioned – and as such became a thrilling fusion of tradition and innovation.

The development of the SLR was never smooth because the requirements of Stuttgart often conflicted with the vision of Gordon Murray: the former wanted more luxury and quality, the latter wanted lightness and pureness. Of course, Mercedes as the client won the argument; however, this resulted in the kerb weight of the SLR increasing from the original target of 1,400kg (3,090lb) to the production car's 1,693kg (3,733lb) – only 187kg (412lb) lighter than the standard SL.

There is a consistent theory that to handle well, a car must have a slight rear-biased weight distribution to sharpen steering and improve traction. Murray worked tirelessly to create as near perfect a balanced car as possible. Mercedes-Benz initially offered their V12 engine; however, he chose their more compact V8. It weighed around 70kg (155lb) less than the V12, and by placing it aft of the front wheels he managed to achieve a 49:51 weight distribution front-to-rear.

The complete SLR bodyshell benefited from race-car technology, and everything from the chassis to the boot lid of the SLR was made from corrosion-resistant carbon-fibre composite; this made it around 30 per cent lighter than the conventional steel structure of a comparable front-/mid-engine vehicle. It also offered the passengers an extremely rigid and hence extremely safe survival space in the event of a frontal, side or rear collision.

At the McLaren factory in Woking UK.

The new Gran Turismo adopted its distinctive gullwing doors from the 1955 'Uhlenhaut Coupé'; however, in their modern interpretation they were attached to the front

The SLR and the Uhlenhaut Coupé.

BELOW RIGHT: **Although this is a roadster, the interior was well appointed for a sport's supercar.**

roof pillars rather than the roof, and pivoted forwards and upwards in a wide arc. This was necessary to make it easier for the driver and passenger to get into and out of the vehicle.

The Interior

An eye-catching feature in the interior was the high quality, aluminium-trimmed centre console. The radio and navigation system were housed in the centre console, beneath a push-to-open cover. One of the switch modules in the centre console was designed to operate the airbrake on the boot lid, which automatically extended from 95km/h (59mph), enhancing downforce. When slowing down, it extended vertically into the air to ensure optimum deceleration. The SLR driver could also change the position of the airbrake manually if required.

Clearly visible, circular instruments were arranged in two tubular surrounds in front of the driver. Large dials featured lettering specially developed for the SLR McLaren. In the cockpit, aluminium and carbon fibre contrasted with soft 'Silver Arrow' leather, developed for the new, high-performance sports car in twenty different shades – including the distinctive red that was used as a highlight colour in the legendary 1950s SL and SLR sports cars.

The interior also benefited from the cutting-edge safety used in every other Mercedes of the time to protect the passengers. The SLR safety retention system included multiple airbags (including knee-bags), belt tensioners and belt-force limiters.

Performance

In view of the SLR McLaren's impressive sub-300km/h (190mph) performance capabilities, aerodynamics were of the utmost importance; not necessarily by achieving the lowest possible Cd value, but by optimising road-holding abilities to ensure safe and stable handling at high speed, and guaranteeing the body did not produce lift. As a result, the underbody area featured a virtually smooth surface – even the distinctive exhaust pipes situated on each side of the vehicle were the result of this high-performance sports car's special underbody concept, as a conventional exhaust gas system would have impaired the smooth line of the underbody and the diffuser design. Special air baffles for the rear wheels, front diffusers in front of the front wheels, and a six-channel diffuser (airbrake) at the rear contributed to its stability.

Engine and Transmission

The 8-cylinder engine was modified from the SL55AMG's, and was the first to be completely developed by Mercedes-Benz AMG. First, it was converted to a dry oil sump system in order to lower its centre of gravity as well as to ensure effective lubrication under high cornering force. Second, the SLR had the IHI-built Lysholm-type supercharger that featured Teflon-coated compressor screws and was driven at more than 23,000rpm at an engine speed of 6,500rpm. At this speed, the blower displaced 1,850kg of induction air per hour, and generated up to 12psi of boost pressure; it was also equipped with an electro-magnetic clutch that was used to switch it on and off, depending on rpm and load. A water-to-air intercooler was also used, and along with other enhancements to intake, exhaust and cooling, lower friction and lighter moving parts, it resulted in 626bhp (460kW) at 6,500rpm.

The SLR powerplant also delivered over 600Nm of torque from as low as 1,500rpm; the peak torque of 780Nm was available from 3,250rpm and remained constant across a broad engine speed range right up to 5,000rpm. Acceleration from 0 to 100km/h (60mph) took 3.8sec. The top speed was 334km/h (208mph).

As was the usual practice at Mercedes-Benz AMG, each SLR engine was assembled by hand. One AMG engineer was responsible for the complete assembly of each powerplant – installing the crankshaft in the engine block, fitting the camshafts and the supercharger, right down to the wiring.

The high-performance engine drew its fuel from two connected aluminium tanks with a capacity of close to 98ltr

The V12 engine in place.

(21gal); they were installed low down on the left and right of the rear axle to keep the centre of gravity as low as possible in the interests of dynamic handling. A secondary air injection and dual ignition system kept the exhaust emissions low to guarantee compliance with EU4.

TRANSMISSION

There were hopes that AMG's newest 7G-Tronic seven-speed automatic would be available, but unfortunately it was decided it was not strong enough to cope with the SLR engine, so they resorted to the time-tested five-speed automatic transmission, as it was also designed for high performance and extremely high torque capabilities.

The paddle-style gear shift that was specially developed by Mercedes-Benz AMG for particularly sporty driving was also implemented, as it offered even more functions in the new SLR. The driver could decide whether to leave the gear changes to the automatic transmission, or to change gear manually by using a rotary switch in the centre console that offered a choice of three settings: 'manual', 'comfort' and 'sport'. In 'manual' mode the five gears could be changed using the buttons on the steering wheel, or by using the steering wheel-mounted paddle levers. On top of this, with a particularly sporty driving style the driver could choose between three shift stages: 'sport', 'super sport' and 'race', which enabled the automatic transmission shift processes to become progressively shorter.

To reduce vibration, the engine and transmission were not bolted directly to the carbon-fibre shell, but instead were mounted to an aluminium cradle, along with the front suspension, and then bolted to the shell. At the rear, however, the suspension parts, along with the rear axle, were bolted to the integral metal link points on the monocoque.

Suspension and Brakes

Both front and rear double-wishbone suspension parts were forged aluminium. The lower wishbone arms were positioned so that the wheels had a negative camber on spring compression and when cornering at speed, ensuring optimum road holding. At the same time the axle technology prevented pitching at the front of the vehicle on heavy braking and at the rear when accelerating – but unlike that of the SL55AMG, it just employed conventional springs and shock absorbers, and there was no adaptive damping and Active Body Control (ABC).

SLR C199 Specifications 2003–2010

Model	C199
Production	2003–2010
Units produced	1,150
Wheelbase	2,700mm (106in)
Front track	1,638mm (64.5in)
Rear track	1,570mm (62in)
Length	4,656mm (183in)
Width	1,908mm (75in)
Height	1,280mm (50in)
Vehicle weight	1,550kg (3,418lb)
Engine type	M155SLR V8
Displacement	5439cc
Maximum speed	333km/h (207mph)
Acceleration	0–100km/h (60mph) in 3.8sec
Maximum output	617bhp at 6,500rpm

The highly robust, carbon fibre-reinforced ceramic brake discs, Sensotronic Brake Control (SBC) and the airbrake at the rear ensured the SLR McLaren was ready for high performance on both the racetrack and on the road. 18in light-alloy wheels were part of the standard equipment, although special five-spoke wheels were also available on request at no extra cost. Customers could also choose 19in turbine-look wheels, which emphatically underlined the dynamic character of the Gran Turismo. An electronic system monitored the tyre pressure.

THE SLR 722 EDITION

In 2006, the Mercedes-Benz SLR McLaren 722 Edition was developed at the headquarters of the Formula 1 constructor McLaren. The '722' referred to the victory by Stirling Moss and his co-driver Denis Jenkinson in a Mercedes-Benz 300 SLR, with the starting number 722 (indicating a start time of 7:22 a.m.) at the Mille Miglia in 1955. It was a limited edition of only 150 units, all of which sold immediately on its announcement.

The new model featured more than 300 modified components; the super sports car also served up a boost in output, more dynamic chassis tuning, improved aerodynamics and distinctly sporty interior appointments.

The SLR 722 Special Edition.

On top of this, the stiffer spring rates and shock-absorber characteristics of the chassis gave the SLR 722 Edition its increased directional stability, and in conjunction with the forged aluminium 19in wheels, which evidently allowed larger brake discs to be fitted, noticeably further enhanced dynamic handling.

Aerodynamic improvements such as a spoiler lip at the rear and wheel spoilers made for a smoother airflow and optimized road feel. The angle at which the airbrake extended was also adjusted. The special model was 44kg (97lb) lighter than the standard SLR.

Discrete touches such as the uninterrupted view of the red-painted brake callipers and brake discs, or the 722 insignia embossed on the head restraints, subtly set the special model apart from the SLR in visual terms.

The AMG supercharged V8 was reprogrammed to boost output from 626bhp to 650bhp, while maximum torque

The 722 was to commemorate the 300SLR of Stirling Moss.

The sportier interior of the 722.

increased from 780Nm to 818Nm. Weight was also reduced by 44kg (97lb) by removing sound-deadening materials, using aluminium shock absorbers, lighter magnesium alloy wheels and lighter fuel tanks.

Top speed was now 336km/h (209mph), while 0–100km/h (60mph) was achieved in 3.5sec, which was enough to defend its title as the world's fastest front-engined grand tourer.

When the SLR was first announced, Mercedes said that total production would be limited to 3,500 units; however, by the end of 2007 only 1,400 units had been sold, so on 4 April 2008, Mercedes announced, after only six years, that it would discontinue production of the SLR. The last of the Coupés rolled off the production line at the end of 2009.

Total sales were 615 units in 2005, 261 units in 2006, and 275 units in 2007, falling well below Mercedes-McLaren's goal of selling 500 units annually. A total of 2,157 cars were produced.

SLR 722 Edition Specifications 2006–2009

Model	C199
Production	2009
Units produced	150
Wheelbase	2,700mm (106in)
Front track	1,638mm (64.5in)
Rear track	1,569mm (62in)
Length	4,656mm 183in)
Width	1,908mm (75in)
Height	1,261mm (50in)
Vehicle weight	1,550kg (3,418lb)
Engine type	M155 SLR V8
Displacement	5500cc
Maximum speed	335km/h (208mph)
Acceleration	0–100km/h (60mph) in 3.6sec
Maximum Output	650bhp at 6,500/min

THE 2009 SLS AMG (197) COUPÉ

Although quite spectacular, the collaboration with McLaren was not the most successful either in terms of their relationship, or ultimately in the sales of the SLR. Daimler was never a company to rest on their laurels, and had already returned to their 'performance arm' AMG to set about a complete redesign.

The brief from Daimler Chief of Design Gordon Wagener was to draw inspiration from the past, but not to make any attempts at a 'neo-retro' design just for the sake of it. They wanted to return to the inspiration found in the W198 300SL, but first it was imperative to determine and recreate features found in any modern 'super-sports car'.

The Mercedes-Benz SLS AMG, the first independently developed sportscar by AMG, was introduced at the Frankfurt Motor Show (IAA) in September 2009, to be made available in mid-November for the princely sum of 149,000 euros + taxes.

The similarities to the W198 were immediately apparent, with the long flowing downward bonnet, culminating in the open-mouthed front grille with the 'Mercedes star' flanked by a single chrome horizontal bar, and the grilled side air vents

Early design renderings for the SLS.

The gullwing doors were a nod to the W198.

behind the front wheel with chrome flashes. Especially evident was the return to the full roof-hinged 'butterfly' or 'gullwing' door, with the added 'nod' to the 300SL's low-line door handles.

Engine and Transmission

Underneath the long bonnet was the unique AMG-designed M159 twin overhead camshaft V8 engine. Although its cubic capacity was 6208cc, it was labelled as the 6.3, to commemorate the famous M100. It developed 571bhp (420kW) with a torque of 650Nm at around 4,750rpm, and could complete 0–100km/h (60mph) in just 3.8sec. Placed aft of the front wheels, it contributed to an overall balance of 47/53 per cent. The adoption of a dry sump lubrication system also allowed for a much lower position of the engine in the vehicle, to optimize the lowest centre of gravity possible.

Forged pistons, reinforced bearings and an optimized crankcase structure all compensated for the increased engine load associated with the increase in power, as well as improved lubrication thanks to an electronically controlled high-performance oil pump, which operated on demand; it also optimized durability.

Despite these increased load capabilities, the M159 engine had also been optimized for weight, reaching a mere 206kg (454lb) and a power/weight ratio of 0.36kg/bhp. This made the 6.3-litre AMG V8 engine by far the most powerful of all its engines.

TRANSMISSION

The AMG M159 responded very quickly to movements of the accelerator pedal, demonstrating flexibility across the entire rpm range. It delivered its power to the rear axle via a dual-clutch transmission permanently connected to the engine housing via a torque tube. A carbon shaft rotated at engine speed inside the torque tube. The all-new, AMG Speedshift DCT, seven-speed sports transmission enabled fast gear changes (up to 100 milliseconds) without loss of traction force.

The driver was able to choose from four driving modes: C ('controlled efficiency'), S ('sport'), S + ('sport plus') and M ('manual'), not forgetting the 'race start' function. In sport, sport plus and manual modes, the automatic double clutch is permanently active and controlled via the AMG Drive Unit torque regulator. Optimal traction is guaranteed by locking the mechanical diff, integrated in the compact transmission housing.

Chassis and Frame Design

For the first time ever, Mercedes-Benz and AMG presented an automobile whose complete chassis (excluding

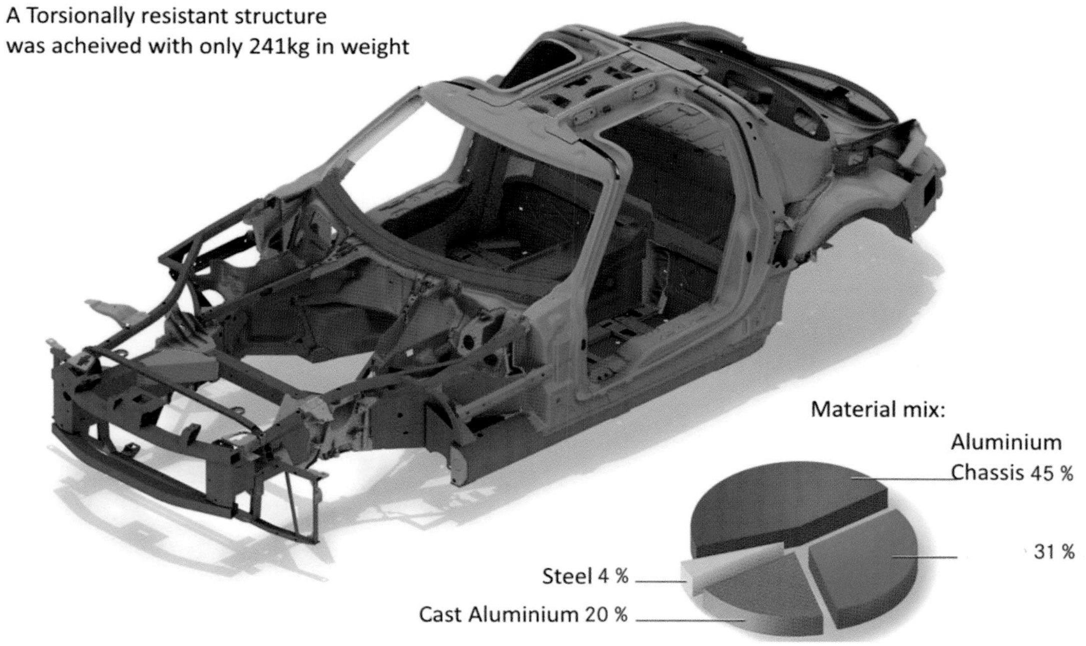

By mixing construction materials it was possible to keep weight to a minimum.

Transaxle plus dry sump lubrication:
Low centre of gravity and ideal weight distribution for perfect driving dynamics

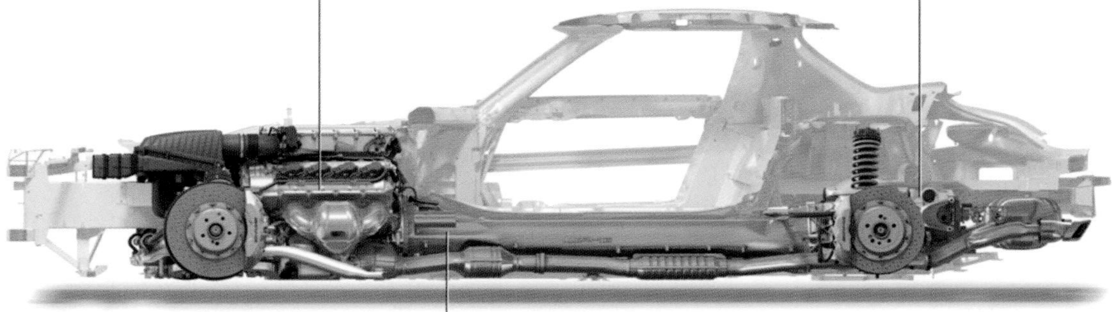

Almost perfect weight distribution was achieved.

BELOW RIGHT:
The interior was well appointed, providing both a touch of luxury as well as sportiness.

the ultra-high-tensile, hot-rolled steel passenger safety cell) and body were constructed from high strength aluminium. Not only did this achieve significant weight savings compared with the traditional steel construction, but the high strength, lightweight design added to its excellent handling dynamics. The complete shell contributed a miniscule 241kg (531lb) to the overall kerb weight of 1,620kg (3,572lb).

The aluminium space frame amounted to 45 per cent aluminium profiles, 31 per cent aluminium panelling, 20 per cent cast aluminium and 4 per cent steel.

The suspension was conventional, with dual 'A-arm' control arms all around constructed from forged aluminium, as were the steering knuckles and hub carriers. At anything above 120km/h (75mph), the rear spoiler springs into action to maintain the front-to-rear balance; go below 80km/h (50mph), and it recedes. According to Volker Mornhinweg: 'Using the spoiler as an airbrake was entirely unnecessary' – unlike that of the SLR.

The AMG high-performance brake system with composite brake discs on the front axle ensures short braking distances. An even better braking performance system was offered by the optional ceramic-composite brake system.

Two types of aluminium, weight-optimized, AMG light alloy wheels were standard, with optional five double spokes or seven spokes (9.5 × 19in at the front, and 11.0 × 20in at the rear), and were fitted with 265/35 R19 tyres up front and 295/30 R20 tyres.

The Interior

The interior might be described as luxurious with sporting accoutrements; the side panels and headlining were covered in Alcantara juxtaposed with brushed aluminium and carbon-fibre trimmings. The large 'transaxle tube' meant that the occupants were separated by a large centre console, and the all-electric sport seats sat a mere 360mm (14in) off the ground, perhaps as a solution to the slight difficulty of getting into and out of the car without hitting one's head on the gullwing door.

The dash and controls were equal in standard to most high-end Mercedes.

The SLS was supplied with air conditioning, a three-spoke multi-function steering wheel, a colour audio-GPS unit, and only two large analogue dash dials; however, the standard on-board technological equipment was quite impressive: a 7in colour Command GPS, Bluetooth, Linguatronic voice control, keyless start ('Keyless Go'), door remote control for the garage, and telephone pre-equipment.

Prior to the 2009 SLS there were three different Mercedes cars with gullwing doors, but only one of them, the 300SL, made it into production.

Design Awards

Since 2009 the Mark Fetherstone-designed SLS AMG has won a number of design awards, including the 2010 red dot 'Best of the Best' award, the iF (International Forum Design GmbH) product design award 2010 for the 'Transportation Design' category, and the Auto Bild Design Award 2010 as 'Europe's most attractive car'. It is also the only automobile to have won the gold Design Award of the Federal Republic of Germany.

SOME OF THE MAIN OPTIONS FOR THE SLS

- AMG ceramic composite high-performance braking system
- AMG performance suspension with a stiffer set-up for optimum lateral dynamics
- AMG light-alloy wheels in a five twin-spoke design, size 9.5 × 19in (front) and 11.0 × 20in (rear), tyre sizes 265/35 R19 (front) and 295/30 R20 (rear)
- AMG forged wheels in a ten-spoke design, size 9.5 × 19in (front) and 11.0 × 20in (rear), with tyre sizes 265/35 R19 (front) and 295/30 R20 (rear)
- AMG performance steering wheel in leather/Alcantara
- AMG sports bucket seats
- AMG carbon-fibre engine compartment cover
- AMG Alu-beam silver paint finish
- AMG Monza grey Magno paint finish
- AMG carbon-fibre trim (front stowage tray and rear stowage compartment including lid, AMG Drive Unit surround, surrounds for the centre console, shift gate and rear, trim strips for centre console and door armrests)
- AMG interior carbon package (carbon-fibre trim, trim on seat backrests and sides, door sill panels)
- Leather Napa exclusive single-/two-tone
- Memory package with electric seat and steering column adjustment, as well as four-way lumbar support
- Six-disc DVD changer and Bang & Olufsen Beo-Sound AMG surround sound system

MODELS AVAILABLE OF THE SLS AMG COUPÉ (2009)

SLS AMG 'AMG Desert Gold' (2010)

Unveiled at the 2010 Dubai International Motor Show, this variant offered further customization options for the SLS AMG, including body colour finished in 'shining chrome' or 'Silver Shadow', and a matte gold body colour dubbed 'Desert Gold'. It had black-painted AMG light-alloy wheels in sizes 9.5 × 19 at the front and 11.0 × 20 at the rear, with a golden ring on the rim flange.

SLS AMG 'Blackbird' (2010)

Ordered for the Australian International Motor Show, the Blackbird was a one-off variant of the 2010 Mercedes-Benz SLS AMG Coupé with 'Designo Magno Night' black body colour with red highlights.

SLS AMG E-Cell Prototype (2011)

This model was powered by four electric motors providing a combined power output of 392kW (533PS; 526bhp) and 880Nm (649lb ft). The battery was a 400-volt lithium unit with a capacity of 48kW. Other features include pushrod damper struts, and 402 × 39mm (front) and 360 × 32mm (rear) carbon ceramic brake discs; also full LED headlamps, AMG ten-spoke light-alloy wheels with smooth-surfaced design, 265/35 R19 (front) and 295/30 R20 (rear) tyres, the AMG Drive Unit angled towards the driver, sports seats made of quality Napa leather in a black/white colour combination, a performance leather/Alcantara steering wheel and door linings, and a centre tunnel.

E-Cell prototype.

Desert Gold.

SLS AMG GT3 (2011–2014)

The official introduction of the SLS AMG GT3 took place at the 2010 New York International Auto Show, and later at Puebla in Mexico and the 2010 Pebble Beach Concours d'Élégance. It was developed in accordance with the GT3 regulations of the FIA (Fédération Internationale de l'Automobile).

Noteworthy changes included the following: sequential six-speed racing transmission with shift paddles, multi-disc locking differential and traction control, adjustment facilities for the springs and shock absorbers, the suspension height, the stabilizers, the track width and camber. Also rack-and-pinion steering with a more direct ratio and servo assistance, AMG 18in light-alloy wheels, a steel racing braking system with racing ABS, a seat shell that was individually foam-

GT3 version.

padded, featuring the 'HANS' ('head and neck support') system located in a high-strength carbon-fibre (CFRP) safety cell, a six-point racing harness, an optimized fire-extinguisher system, and the central display positioned within the driver's field of vision.

SLS AMG Matte Black Edition (2011–2013)

As a limited version of the SLS AMG Coupé for the Japanese market, this model commemorated the first year of Mercedes-Benz SLS AMG. It included Designo Magno Night Black body colour with red highlights at the three-pointed star, grille fin, bonnet fin, SLS/AMG rear emblems, and a fuel lid (from the Blackbird car); also matte black exhaust tip, high gloss black interior trim, leather upholstery in classic red/black, AMG Ride Control sports suspension, AMG red brake calliper, 19in front and 20in rear AMG ten-spoke alloy wheels in matte black, and an AMG performance steering wheel in leather/Alcantara.

SLS AMG GT (2012)

Available in both Coupé and Roadster body styles, the SLS AMG GT had an increased engine power output to 591PS

BELOW LEFT: **Matte Black edition.**

BELOW RIGHT: **GT version.**

(435kW; 583bhp) at 6,800rpm and 650Nm (479lb ft) of torque at 4,750rpm, which resulted in a slight decrease in the 0–100km/h (60mph) acceleration time, to 3.4sec.

Other notable additions were AMG Ride Control selectable performance mode suspension; three further AMG light-alloy wheel options; Alcantara black interior upholstery, red seat belts, contrasting stitching on the AMG sports seats and the centre console, and the door panel lining in red; floor mats in red edging; high-gloss black AMG trim on the centre console and door panel; high-gloss black edging on the adjustable cross-shaped air vents and the high-gloss real metal insert on the AMG performance steering wheel with Alcantara grip; also the AMG instrument cluster with black faceplate, AMG Designo Exclusive Style leather option (a diamond design with contrasting stitching); Designo leather finish for the entire dashboard, the beltlines and door armrests, and the hand-rest on the centre console; AMG floor mats in black with porcelain leather edging, roof lining in 'porcelain' Alcantara; and the parcel shelf in three colour combinations – mocha brown/porcelain, titanium grey pearl/porcelain, mystic red/porcelain.

Other options include AMG carbon-fibre exterior mirrors, AMG carbon-fibre engine compartment cover, AMG interior carbon-fibre package (carbon-fibre trim, trim on seat backrest and side, door sill panels), AMG ceramic high-performance composite braking system, AMG Performance Media, AMG ten-spoke forged wheels in various colours, AMG carbon-fibre exterior package, and a Bang & Olufsen Beo-Sound AMG surround sound system.

SLS AMG Black Series (2013)

Unveiled at the 2012 LA Auto Show, the Black Series is 70kg (154lb) lighter than the standard model, accomplished by increased use of carbon fibre in the body panels, mechanical components and the space frame. Further, a switch from steel to titanium for the exhaust system reduces weight by 13kg (29lb). The use of lithium-ion batteries reduces weight by 8kg (18lb).

Notable changes over the SLS AMG include increased engine power to 631PS (464kW; 622bhp) at 7,400rpm, and decreased torque to 635Nm (468lb ft) at 5,500rpm along with increased engine redline of 8,000rpm; fully revised high-speed valvetrain with modified camshafts, adapted cam geometry, and optimized bucket tappets having a special coating, which is otherwise exclusive to racing cars; modification of the intake air ducts (de-restriction and adaptation to the new maximum engine speed); adaptation of the engine application, and increase in peak pressure. This results in an acceleration time from 0–97km/h (60mph) in 3.2sec and a top speed of 196mph (315km/h).

SLS AMG Electric Drive (2013)

Following the introduction of the SLS AMG E-Cell prototype, the production of the SLS AMG E-Cell was originally announced at the 2011 North American International Auto Show. The SLS AMG Electric Drive was a collaboration between Mercedes-AMG and Mercedes AMG High Performance Powertrains Ltd and included a liquid-cooled 400V lithium-ion battery rated to 60kWh that had a range of 250km (160 miles) under the combined 'New European Driving Cycle'.

Original SLS AMG Specifications 2010–2015

Model	C 197
Production	2010–2015
Units produced	150
Wheelbase	2,680mm (106in)
Length	4,638mm (183in)
Width	1,939mm (76in)
Height	1,252mm (49in)
Vehicle weight	1,619kg (3,570lb)
Engine type	M159 dohc V8
Displacement	6208cc
Maximum speed	317km/h (197mph)
Acceleration	0–100km/h (60mph) in 3.6sec
Maximum output	563bhp @ 6,800rpm

CHAPTER SIX

EPILOGUE

The Coupé was, and remains, an exclusive body design. This was true even in the days of the horse-drawn carriage, and every Coupé from Mercedes-Benz has always been the embodiment of elegance on four wheels, and every one of them has become a legend of the eras in which they were built.

Throughout its history Mercedes-Benz has endeavoured to offer a Coupé in a variety of designs, from the 10bhp Benz Mylord Coupé of 1901, which still bore a close resemblance to the horse-drawn carriage from which it was derived, with a seat for the driver open to the elements, or the Daim-

The Dos-à-Dos Mylord Benz Coupé body from 1901.

The Mercedes-Daimler Simplex 28HP Coupé.

ler Mercedes Simplex 28HP with its Coupé rear seat and separate driving cubicle – all the way to the first production sports car version with the new-style grille: the W198.

Among early automobiles the Coupé retained a strong focus, essentially on two persons travelling in style. By the 1950s, however, it was commonplace for a Coupé to have a place for four people. What has stood the test of time, though, is that the body incorporates several basic features that persist to this day: thus a Coupé generally has exceptionally low, flowing lines that create a stretched silhouette. It often dispenses with the B pillar altogether, leaving frameless side-windows, and the C pillar slopes gently into the tail, so the roof is generally shorter than in the case of a saloon, and curved at the rear.

The term 'Coupé' has evolved and grown over the decades with every manufacturer, Mercedes-Benz included; however, what has remained is the fact that nowadays, owning a Coupé and enjoying utility value are no longer mutually exclusive aspirations, although many Coupé enthusiasts would contest the fact; even in a Coupé, a spacious trunk, folding rear seat bench and ski bag are popular equipment features. After all, the body does not need to reveal outwardly all the other things that need transportation in addition to the passengers. Ultimately it has become more than just an incidental automobile for high days and holidays that is used to show off in: it has become an individual choice.

A COUPÉ IN EVERY CLASS

Although this book has dealt predominantly with the early 'high end' S-versions and their history and development, Mercedes-Benz have carried the same attention to detail through to every classified model, whether it be a C-Class C203, an E-Class Coupé from the C207 series, or the

CL-Class from the C216 S-Class series, all to the further enhancement of the product portfolio of Mercedes-Benz. What this means in reality is that there really is no hard and fast rule of what makes a Coupé, and Mercedes-Benz has proved this over and again.

Recent proof of this could be the revolutionary four-door coupé that was presented at the IAA Frankfurt Motor Show in 2003 as the 'Vision CLS'. It caused an immediate sensation, and gave the motoring public a fore-taste of what was to come in the shape of the Mercedes-Benz W219 CLS, the following year. This car combined the best of two worlds, offering the spaciousness of a four-door saloon, while at the same time exhibiting its clear coupé roots with a skilfully designed body shape. It quickly quietened its naysayers, and established itself as a modern automotive icon; it created an entirely new market segment, and other car makers with four-door coupés followed in its wake.

The type of person who buys a Coupé enjoys a discreetly impressive appearance with a discrete amount of power, and since the 1950s, Mercedes-Benz has been offering an uninterrupted line of exclusive Coupés, and each and every one addresses a clientèle with a reassured taste, people who select this type of car quite consciously.

The sales brochure for the C126 summed up the Coupé to a T:

> This vehicle concept has always embodied a felicitous combination of perfect engineering and out-of-the-ordinary aesthetic styling. It is the role model for a refined sporty automobile because it additionally boasts all the other characteristics that distinguish a Mercedes.

This book is in effect Volume One of the Coupé story. It will be followed by Volume Two, which will give you an insight into the history of the Saloon Coupé.

INDEX